WHERE VALUE HIDES

WHERE VALUE HIDES

A New Way to Uncover Profitable Growth for Your Business

STUART E. JACKSON

John Wiley & Sons, Inc.

Published by John Wiley & Sons, Inc., Hoboken, New Jersey
Published simultaneously in Canada

For general information on our other products and services or for technical
support, please contact our Customer Care Department within the United States at
(800) 762-2974, outside the United States at (317) 572-3993 or fax (317) 572-4002.

Designations used by companies to distinguish their products are often claimed by
trademarks. In all instances where the author or publisher is aware of a claim, the
product names appear in Initial Capital letters. Readers, however, should contact the
appropriate companies for more complete information regarding trademarks and
registration.

Wiley also publishes its books in a variety of electronic formats. Some content that
appears in print may not be available in electronic books. For more information
about Wiley products, visit our web site at www.wiley.com.

ISBN-13: 978-0-470-00920-8
ISBN-10: 0-470-00920-9

Printed in the United States of America

10 9 8 7 6 5 4 3 2 1

CONTENTS

ACKNOWLEDGMENTS   vii

INTRODUCTION: WHERE VALUE HIDES
AND WHY IT MATTERS   1

I
WHY PROFITABLE GROWTH IS SO HARD TO FIND

1   WHERE YOU SHOULD COMPETE   11

2   BIGGER MAY BE WORSE   35

3   UNCOVERING WHERE VALUE HIDES   55

II
HOW TO USE STRATEGIC MARKET POSITION TO CHART YOUR BUSINESS STRATEGY

4   CAPTURING VALUE   79

5   DOING THE DETECTIVE WORK   105

6   APPLYING SMP TO SALES AND MARKETING   139

CONTENTS

III

KEY APPLICATIONS OF STRATEGIC MARKET POSITION

7 USING SMP TO FIND NEW MARKETS   165

8 SMP STRATEGIES FOR LOW-GROWTH
OR LOW-MARGIN BUSINESSES   191

9 WHEN DO ACQUISITIONS MAKE SENSE?   217

APPENDIX: GUIDE TO INFORMATION SOURCES
FOR COMPETITIVE AND MARKET INTELLIGENCE   249

NOTES   261

INDEX   273

ACKNOWLEDGMENTS

THIS BOOK IS the result of efforts by a team of people without whom the project would never have been completed. In chronological order, I would like to thank Iain Evans for his leadership in creating the firm that enabled me to develop these ideas. Thanks to Leon Schor and Marc Kozin for encouraging me to begin this initiative. Thanks also to Greg Austin, Lorin Rees of the Helen Rees Literary Agency, and Jeff Cruikshank of the Cruikshank Company, who were all instrumental in helping to turn the idea into a proposal. I am also grateful to Richard Narramore of John Wiley & Sons, Inc. for seeing the book's potential and helping to shape the content.

I am grateful to Jeff Cruikshank, Sharell Sandvoss, Adnan Azam, Richard Przekop, and Larah Kent for their editorial and research support. I also wish to thank those who helped with case examples on their companies, particularly Scott Petty and Janelle Sykes of C.H. Guenther, Donna Williams of Baxter International, and Marcello Bottoli of Samsonite.

Finally, thank you to all those who provided feedback on the manuscript and to you, the readers.

Introduction

WHERE VALUE HIDES
AND WHY IT MATTERS

WHERE DOES VALUE hide—and why does that matter?
Take the second half of the question first. Competing successfully in the business world means creating value. Yes, there is a whole
host of things that successful managers must do beyond simply adding
to the bottom line. But without strong performance on that bottom
line, many of the other tasks of management simply won't matter.

But as most businesspeople have learned from firsthand experience, creating value is far from easy. All too often, it seems to be a hit-
or-miss proposition. Some seemingly great value-adding ideas turn
bad, while some seeming long shots turn in an outstanding performance. Some acquisitions turn into boat anchors, dragging down your
corporate performance; others put wind in your sails—although not
necessarily for the reasons you thought they would.

Sometimes value-creation seems random, but in fact it isn't. You
and your company can get better at spotting and capturing value by
adopting value-creating strategies. In *Where Value Hides*, I provide

you with the tools to make strategic value-creation in your company more systematic, and more predictable.

This brings us back to the first half of my opening question: *Where does value hide?*

If you were to study the shareholder returns for the top 1,000 U.S. companies over the past five years, you would discover something very interesting. Look at Figure I.1. This is derived from the annual *Wall Street Journal* "Shareholder Scoreboard." It reports on shareholder returns for 1,000 of the leading companies listed on U.S. exchanges. In Figure I.1 we show for a range of sectors both the average return for the sector (the shaded bar) and the return for the best and worst company in the sector (the two ends of the I-beam). There is some variation across sectors, but not nearly as much as the variation in company performance *within* each sector. In fact, in almost every sector, the top-performing company is not 5 or 10 percent better than the worst performer; it's more like 200, 300, or even *1,000 percent* better! So if you accept my premise that value is "hiding" somewhere out there on the competitive landscape—waiting to be discovered and appropriated by the skilled manager—then you either have to make the case that some companies are simply much luckier than others (up to 1,000 percent luckier), or you have to agree with me that those top performers are far better than their competitors at sniffing out value.

Let me make that same point again in slightly different words. As I do so, keep in mind that I'm not comparing companies in a hot sector with companies in a cool one. I'm comparing apples to apples, mining companies to mining companies, and computer companies to computer companies. *Within each industry, there's an enormous range of performance over a five-year period.* Some companies turn in stellar performances. Others go bankrupt.

In *Where Value Hides* I tell you an important reason why. Here it is in a nutshell: The high-performing companies have learned the discipline

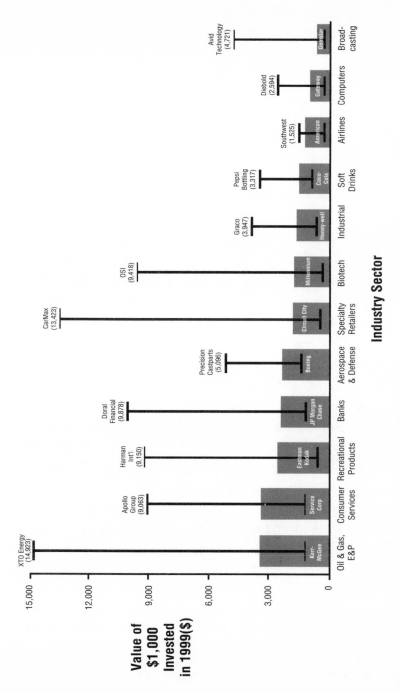

FIGURE I.1 Variations in Performance for U.S. Top 1,000 Companies and Sectors (1999–2004)

Data Source: Wall Street Journal.

of what I call "Strategic Market Position," or SMP. They have learned how to tie together the principles of customer preference, producer economics, and corporate finance so that they understand where and how expanded operations and increased market share pay off—and *don't* pay off—for their business. They have learned how to find strategic value and capture it.

For instance:

- Not so long ago, Circuit City was one of the strongest and most admired performers in the specialty retail sector. Then it spun off its used-car division, CarMax. CarMax has since gone on to be the highest performer in the sector. In the same five-year time frame, Circuit City came dead last among its peer group of large-scale specialty retail companies. A $1,000 investment in CarMax at the beginning of this period was worth $13,427 five years later. The same $1,000 invested in Circuit City lost almost half its value, declining to $535. The difference in shareholder returns between the hot spin-off and the parent that spun it off? A startling *1,289 percent!*
- In the food products sector, Oakland-based Dreyers Ice Cream topped the list by delivering $4,842 for every $1,000 invested. Campbell Soup came in dead last, destroying $113 to yield only $887. The difference: 396 percent.
- Among food retailers, Austin-based Whole Foods Market delivered $4,143 on a $1,000 investment, while Safeway returned $552, $448 less than the original $1,000.

Remember: *These are all top 1,000 companies*, run by some of the United States' smartest and most skilled managers. So what explains these huge differences in performance?

Certainly not a lack of information. Executives today are positively bombarded by statistics, data, analyses, and opinions. In fact, most of the senior executives I work with tell me they get *too much* information.

No, a big part of the difference comes from companies' respective choices about where and how to grow. It comes from their respective capacities to *build* and *improve* their Strategic Market Position (SMP).[1]

Where Value Hides explains the discipline of strategic market positioning—a discipline that will help you better understand how your customers' preferences, your production costs, and your corporate functions affect your profitability. My goal is to help you build a "value map" for your company's industry sector. It shows where and how increased scale and market share can reduce your costs, increase the demand for your products or services, and improve shareholder returns.

Finding the path to profitable growth is neither easy nor obvious. But having worked with dozens of leading companies over the past 20 years, I know, *for a fact*, that companies can master the discipline of SMP. They can use this powerful tool to *improve their overall performance dramatically*.

What's the evidence? Here's one good data point: Ninety percent of the clients I work with to implement SMP are repeat buyers—people who want to apply it to new business units in their corporation or former clients who invite me in to new corporations that they have either joined or founded. I've helped dozens of companies understand SMP, and—as a result—create billions of dollars in value through targeted growth. This means that *SMP works*. If your goal is to learn "where value hides" and transfer it to your bottom line, you need to understand and embrace SMP.

THE ORIGINS OF STRATEGIC MARKET POSITION

I began developing and testing SMP as a tool for creating strategic growth in the course of my work with L.E.K. Consulting, one of the premier global management consulting companies. (I'm a senior partner with L.E.K. and for the past 11 years, I've headed L.E.K.'s Chicago office, and two years ago helped establish the firm's first office in Japan.) Over the years, my clients have included a large number of Fortune 500 companies—including Baxter, General Mills, and General Electric (G.E.), among many others—as well as many high-growth emerging companies and leading private equity investors. These clients have enjoyed higher growth, increased their profit margins in existing businesses, added scores of new services and products, and made more than 100 mergers and acquisitions (M&A) transactions—all based, in part, on the concept of SMP.

In addition to helping companies implement SMP in specific business units, I've also developed growth strategy training programs for leading companies such as Shell, Cargill, and Eaton. I've been a guest lecturer at Northwestern University's Kellogg School of Management and I've published articles on strategy-related issues.

Practicing managers, especially at the senior level, have responded very positively to SMP. In fact, it was the strong positive response on the part of these executives that convinced me that there is a need for this book.

They believe, and I believe, that SMP *works*.

What You Can Find in *Where Value Hides*

I'm presenting the ideas in this book in three parts. Part I (Why Profitable Growth Is So Hard to Find) explains why growth and profitability are largely based on *how a company defines its markets*. (The wrong definition is often the root cause of a misguided growth strategy.) It explains why most definitions of "market share" are irrelevant or applied inappropriately. It distinguishes between "market segmentation"—a concept that most people in business are familiar with—

and the more complex and much more powerful concept of Strategic Market Position (SMP). It explains why an SMP-based growth strategy is in most cases a prerequisite for profitable growth, and why your market share *in your strategic markets* is an important contributor to your success (or lack thereof).

Throughout the book I include numerous real-world examples of companies getting it right, and also of companies getting it wrong. In many cases, I reinterpret familiar business stories through the lens of SMP.

This raises an important introductory point: You may think that much of the analysis and many of the prescriptions in *Where Value Hides* sound vaguely familiar. If so, I encourage you to read a little more closely—especially if your company resembles one of those underperformers I spotlighted earlier. SMP is *not* about marketing (although it draws on key marketing principles). It is *not* a pure financial strategy (although it draws on the fundamentals of finance). It is *not* about portfolio analysis because, at least in my opinion, companies that simply invest in and manage a portfolio lack a growth strategy. I believe that a clearly articulated growth strategy is critically important; in fact, it's second only to operational excellence, in terms of determining a company's prospects for success. So strategic thinking in this book doesn't apply just to large, diversified corporations; it applies to any company that works consciously and actively to pursue a growth strategy based on SMP.

Part II (How to Use Strategic Market Position to Chart Your Business Strategy) explains how to implement SMP. After all, a tool isn't useful unless it can be applied profitably. So who exactly should use SMP and when should they use it? How do you gather the market data and competitive insights needed to determine SMP for your company? How do you allocate your resources in ways that will make future sales easier and at the same time improve your long-term profitability?

In Part III (Key Applications of Strategic Market Position), I dig deeper into the specific ways that SMP can be used to help your business. How can SMP help to uncover value in new and profitable—but hidden—markets? How can SMP help to improve low-growth and low-margin businesses? I also look at the critical issue of acquisitions and explain how the SMP lens can sometimes be used to pour cold water on acquisition fever and, conversely, to justify what to many people might appear to be an exorbitant acquisition premium. (Simply put, it's not a "premium" if you're getting great value for your money.)

WHY YOU AND YOUR COMPANY SHOULD INVEST IN SMP

As a businessperson your ultimate task is to create value that will generate above-average returns for your shareholders. SMP is a powerful tool designed to help you do this. *Where Value Hides* presents a broad and coherent way of thinking—a *strategic* perspective, which will change the way that you and your company think about where to invest resources.

I

WHY PROFITABLE GROWTH IS SO HARD TO FIND

1

WHERE YOU SHOULD COMPETE

L ET'S IMAGINE THAT it's Friday night, and you and your family are sitting down to a friendly game of Monopoly.

Monopoly is a real estate game. As you'll probably recall, players go around the board buying properties with an eye toward assembling one or more monopolies. As such, it captures many of the basic principles contained in this book. Like Monopoly, business is about investing resources in the right things and not wasting money, people, and time going after low-growth/low-profit opportunities. Business is about finding out where value hides.

Companies buy properties, too—either by creating new products, investing in new markets, or buying other companies. *Ideally these decisions about where to invest are based on a clear and compelling strategy.* But not always.

At the bottom of the value heap in Monopoly are the purple properties: Baltic and Mediterranean. At the other end of the spectrum are the blue-chip properties: Boardwalk and Park Place, dressed in royal blue.

Real-life properties—the kinds that corporations buy—also have value to potential purchasers. *But the value of a specific property grows out of the specifics of the competitive circumstance.* The value of that property also varies from one potential acquirer to another (even if they don't know it).

Let's assume that it's you, your spouse, your son, and your daughter who are sitting down to play Monopoly. Your daughter is smart, honest, and old enough to count, so she is made the banker. As she doles out the opening-round money, each member of the family plans his or her buying strategy. Let's review the respective game plans, beginning with your own.

You are a firm believer in buying properties in as many neighborhoods as possible. This, you figure, spreads your risk. It also blocks other players from assembling monopolies and gives you bargaining chips.

Portfolio diversification makes sense for individual investors. Most of the time, though, it makes less sense—much less sense—for companies.

Your spouse, by contrast, is really interested only in Park Place and Boardwalk. Yes, these properties are very expensive to buy and build on and, of course, you also have to overcome long odds to land on both of them first or pay a very high premium to acquire them from someone else, but the simple fact is your spouse wants only to deal in high-end properties. There's a *prestige* factor at work here.

Your daughter is focused on acquiring all the properties in a neighborhood (all the yellows, all the greens, all the browns, etc.). Unlike your spouse, though, your daughter doesn't much care *which* neighborhood. She wants to put her monopoly together and start building houses and hotels as quickly as possible. She is focused on *return*.

What do executives really care about? Profits, and more specifically, return on investment (ROI). But profits vary wildly. In fact, among the top 1,000 U.S. companies over the past five years, in almost every sector, the top-performing company is not 5 or 10 percent better than the worst performer; it's more like 200, 300, or even 1,000 percent better! *Do some players know something about finding value that the others don't?*

Your son summarizes his strategy as follows: "Buy the cheap ones that nobody else wants, so that my cash goes further, and I can scoop up the most properties of *anyone*!" So your son buys railroads, utilities, and anything else he lands on, as long as he has the cash on hand.

And the winner is . . .

How do you think the game is going to turn out? Assuming that the luck factor is pretty well divided among your family members, who's going to win?

If you picked your daughter, you're right. Her strategy of maximizing investment in a given neighborhood is the winner, statistically speaking. Figure 1.1 shows how it looks in graphic form.

This figure shows the rental rate of return for different levels of investment in a neighborhood (calculated as rent for one player landing on property, divided by total investment-base property plus houses or

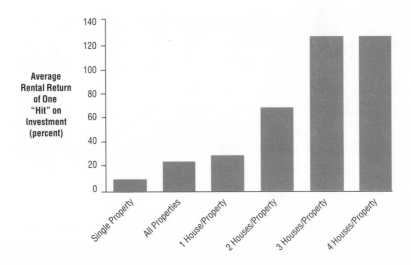

FIGURE 1.1   ROI in Monopoly Neighborhoods

hotels). As you can see—and as you can probably remember from your own experience at the Monopoly table—owning a single property isn't worth very much, in terms of how much rent you collect when someone lands on that property. The rental return doubles when you own all the properties, and increases a little bit when you build your first house.

But look what happens when you build those second and third houses. Now the return on investment is more than *10 times* what it was for owning a single property. Not for nothing is your daughter known as the smartest girl in the fifth grade.

What about your spouse's blue-chip strategy? Well, to the extent that this represents monopolistic thinking, your spouse is on the same track as your daughter (that is, the *right* track). But to the extent that your spouse is drawn to Boardwalk and Park Place because he or she is anticipating much higher returns from those properties, he or she is going down the wrong track. Look at Figure 1.2.

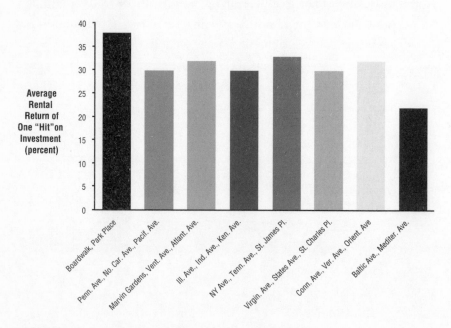

FIGURE 1.2   Rental Returns in Monopoly Neighborhoods

Yes, it *is* gratifying to own those high-end blue properties and to watch the mounting fear in people's eyes as they approach your built-up Boardwalk or Park Place. But the truth is that the real "rate of return" in Monopoly—rent charged, divided by investment in property and houses—*varies very little among different neighborhoods*.[1] If you let monopolies in other neighborhoods slip out of your grasp while you hold out for the Big Blues, you make a serious strategic mistake, because the Monopoly race goes to the swiftest monopoly builder.

STRATEGIC MARKET SEGMENTS ARE MORE IMPORTANT THAN MARKET SHARE

So what does all this have to do with real business? There are several important points that your daughter should carry forward into her successful business career.

First, in many cases, achieving increased market share along one or more dimensions can lead to substantial improvements in the rate of return (profit divided by investment). This principle works for several reasons: (1) economies of scale, (2) greater customer appeal by offering a broader product range or a more complete solution, (3) better attention from distributors, (4) more efficient logistics, or (5) other benefits of scale. However, many companies try to exploit this principle by pursuing growth in markets that place new demands on them without unlocking benefits of scale or scope, and the result is that their profitability plummets. The fact is that market share, as most companies use it, is a misleading and dangerous measure.

The trick lies in identifying the right market segments in which to improve one's share. How do you do that? And according to which definition of "market share"? The answer is Strategic Market Position (SMP).

15

Throughout this book I use the following definitions:

Strategic Segment   This is a defined competitive arena (similar to a Monopoly neighborhood) within which greater scale or market share for a competitor will, other things being equal, always create the opportunity for higher profitability and competitive advantage. I apply the term *market segment* to a market or sector that may be useful for some types of business decisions but does not represent a single strategic segment.

Strategic Market Position (SMP)   For a business or product line that competes in only one strategic segment, SMP is simply the market share of the business in its strategic market segment. For a company competing in multiple strategic segments, its overall SMP is the average of its SMPs in each strategic segment, weighted by the business's sales or investment in each strategic segment. I also use the term SMP to describe the *process* of identifying strategic segments and positioning your company to achieve higher overall SMP and increased profitability and growth.

Companies use SMP to find where value hides and ultimately enhance shareholder wealth. They break down their industry into strategic market segments in such a way that pursuing higher market share *selectively*—that is, in some market segments but not others—generates higher returns. This requires a much more sophisticated analysis of market share than most companies currently use.

One difference between the game of Monopoly and the real world of business is that in Monopoly there are clearly spelled-out rules defining the relationship between market *share* (of available investment opportunities in a neighborhood) and *profitability* (rental rates). In the real world, of course, these relationships are fuzzier; value is hidden. Higher market share often means lower profits and lower return.

A second major difference is that in Monopoly the different property colors show clearly where one strategic segment (neighborhood) ends and another begins. In the real world, the relationships between different dimensions of market share and profitability are often obscured, as are the boundaries between market segments.

But to succeed in today's competitive landscape—to find where value hides—you have to find the strategic segments where you can achieve strong SMP. If you don't, you're likely to get into trouble. SMP is a powerful tool for showing your business where to find growth *and* profitability.

You may be saying to yourself that SMP is obvious; everyone *knows* that higher market share companies do better, on average. Well, if so, how come so many companies get it wrong by growing in the wrong places and leaving profits behind? How come more than 70 percent of the business unit strategic plans that I review claim to be "number one in market share for their selected markets," when in any market there can only be one market leader and the rest followers?

The answer is that understanding SMP is *not* obvious. Nor is its implementation. (In fact, there are organizational factors that I describe later that often work in direct opposition to the principles of SMP.) This means that those who get it right will put their companies at a real advantage in finding where value hides and delivering superior returns to their shareholders.

That is what this book is all about.

Let's look at a few case studies to get a feel for how companies win and lose, based on the Strategic Market Position they pursue. In this chapter, we examine three company pairs:

- Wal-Mart versus Kmart
- Southwest versus America West
- Nintendo versus Sega

I contend that the first company in each of these pairs understood where to find value and engaged in its own application of Strategic Market Position. The second ones, unfortunately, did not.

Wal-Mart versus Kmart

Although these two retailers' starting points were eerily similar, their endpoints (as of this writing) could not be more different. Both opened their first discount store in 1962. Since that time, they have pursued growth at a different pace, with different financial means and different strategies. Now, 40-plus years later, Wal-Mart is one of the fastest-growing retailers in the United States—and, by some measures, the biggest corporation in the world.

Kmart, in stark contrast, filed for bankruptcy protection in January 2002, laying off thousands of workers and closing hundreds of stores. It merged with Sears in 2005 and by most accounts is still struggling.

Where did the two retailers' paths first diverge? Kmart grew faster initially, opening its new stores in major cities. By 1980, as a result of this strategy, nearly 80 percent of the U.S. population had convenient access to a Kmart store.[2] Wal-Mart, by contrast, focused its growth on rural areas. It progressed more slowly, remaining number 2 behind Kmart until around 1990, when it finally matched Kmart's sales.[3]

Around this time the two companies' differing strategies began to have an impact on their share of a defined market and share of profits. By concentrating on the rural population, Wal-Mart became the dominant discount retailer for this marketplace, with 52 percent share of the rural market, where the majority of its stores were located. Kmart—with the same level of sales in 1991—was a similarly sized discount player, but concentrated on the major metropolitan areas. But because these markets were so much larger and there was so much more competition in the large cities, Kmart commanded only a 12 percent share of its preferred market: the urban/suburban market.

Wal-Mart's rural locations had lower-cost properties and lower wages, combined with little competition from other large-scale discounters. By and large, its stores were new builds with their own parking lots, easy access to interstates, and streamlined delivery processes.

Kmart stores, by contrast, were in higher-cost locations and faced much more competition from discounters and other mass merchandisers, including Sears.

These differences, combined with Wal-Mart's superior supply-chain management processes, created operating margins that were consistently two to four percentage points above Kmart's. See Figure 1.3. Between 1987 and 1997, Wal-Mart's operating margins averaged 5.7 percent, while Kmart's equivalent number was 2.4 percent.[4]

By choosing to compete where the strong competitors were not playing, Wal-Mart was able to build a higher-profit, more sustainable business model. Kmart, meanwhile, made the mistake of focusing on national market share and scale, which led it to emphasize urban markets

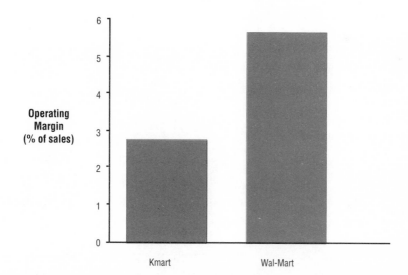

FIGURE 1.3 Kmart versus Wal-Mart: Average Profitability (1987–1997)
Data Source: Bloomberg.

with their greater concentrations of customers. A secondary effect was that Kmart's lower margins led it to underinvest in its stores and look for new sources of growth beyond the discount retail format. The Kmart shopper, previously enticed by blue-light specials, became disenchanted with the dowdy, shabby appearance of Kmart stores, especially when compared to the new inviting superstore format of Wal-Mart.

From 1987 to 2003, sales revenue for Wal-Mart grew at a compound annual growth rate of 20 percent, versus 2 percent for Kmart. Wal-Mart's net income and operating income grew at 18 percent, while Kmart's net income fell at 6 percent, and operating income fell from $1.0 billion in 1987 to negative $2.0 billion in 2003—in the process, driving Kmart into bankruptcy.[5]

This situation is summarized in Figures 1.4, 1.5, and 1.6.

Figure 1.4 shows that, *according to traditional definitions of market*

**U.S. General Merchandise Retailing
(1991)**

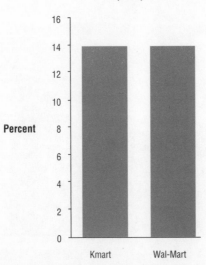

FIGURE 1.4   Kmart versus Wal-Mart: Market Shares
Data Source: Bloomberg, Census Bureau, Economic Census.

share, both companies were similarly positioned as of 1991. Each had around 14 percent of the U.S. market for general merchandise retailing.

Now look at Figure 1.5, which depicts the two companies' Strategic Market Positions—and where value was hiding. This figure shows that Wal-Mart's high market share in rural markets was much more valuable than Kmart's lower market share in urban markets. Although retailers at this scale—that is, enormous—obviously achieve some national economies of scale, their true competitive advantages emerge on a city-by-city basis, because there is a limit to how far customers will drive to go to a different store. In each city, customer convenience (measured by distance to the nearest store), customer choice (measured by size of store), and advertising effectiveness are all correlated with market share within a city. The urban markets that accounted for the

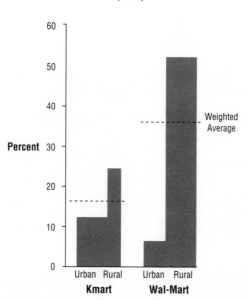

FIGURE 1.5   Kmart versus Wal-Mart: Strategic Market Position
Data Source: Bloomberg, Census Bureau, Economic Census.

bulk of Kmart's sales were much larger than places like Bentonville, Arkansas—Wal-Mart's home—and Kmart's city–market shares therefore were much smaller than was the case for Wal-Mart.

In Figure 1.5, the width of each bar is proportional to each company's sales in the two types of market. We could have plotted each company's market share for each of the hundreds of cities where they competed. To simplify the picture, we have split the country into rural and urban markets, with each company's average market share in each market type. The dotted line represents each company's overall Strategic Market Position, calculated as its weighted average position across the two market types. (In other words, it is the average height of the bars for each company, adjusted for their width.)

Finally, in Figure 1.6, we show how each company's overall Strategic Market Position is correlated with the value it delivered to shareholders over the ensuing years.

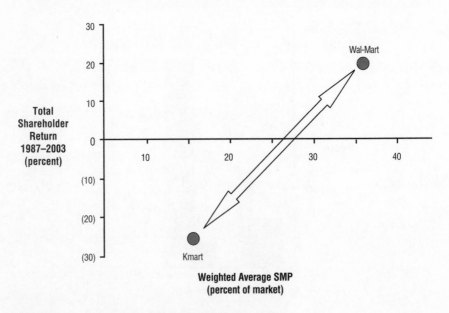

FIGURE 1.6 Kmart versus Wal-Mart: Value Creation
Data Source: Bloomberg.

The lesson from our first company pair? Wal-Mart discovered a highly profitable market segment—rural consumers with few other good retail options—and focused almost all of its time, energy, and treasure on expanding and exploiting that segment. (Even today, despite a massive expansion effort in recent years, only a relatively small percentage of Wal-Mart stores are to be found in areas like the Northeast.) Kmart lacked a similarly profitable focus, and paid the price. Looking at the two companies' Strategic Market Positions, it is clear that *Wal-Mart's choices about where to compete positioned it much better to create value for shareholders.*

Would Wal-Mart have been successful if it had first concentrated on metropolitan markets, as Kmart did? Possibly. Certainly, Wal-Mart has shown itself to be a very tightly run company with excellent supply-chain systems. But without the benefits of low costs and more limited competition in rural locations, Wal-Mart would have found it much more difficult to achieve the margins and cash flow needed to fund its aggressive growth.

The differences in the two companies' Strategic Market Positions were increased further by their strikingly different acquisition strategies. Wal-Mart never strayed far from its rural discount retailer marketplace. Although it made more than a dozen acquisitions, all were in the variety or general merchandise retail sector, and all were aimed at strengthening the company's position in this market.[6] Kmart, by contrast, drifted away from its focus on general merchandise discount retailing and moved into specialty retailing (Builders Square, Sports Authority, Waldenbooks, PayLess Drugs, and OfficeMax), and made ill-advised investments in restaurant chains.[7] While this acquisition strategy allowed Kmart to gain share in retailing *overall*, its discount retailing continued to suffer. This is a theme we return to throughout this book: the right definition of "market share" is critical. *Building up the wrong share can be fatal.*

Southwest versus America West

Our second company pair contrasts two airlines: Southwest and America West. Once again, we see two companies that started in roughly the same place and wound up in very different places.

In the late 1980s, America West and Southwest were both profitable, low-cost regional airlines with flexible, nonunion labor and around $1 billion in sales. America West's growth plan emphasized a hub-and-spoke network, which called for international routes, which in turn called for a heterogeneous (and expensive to maintain) fleet. Southwest focused on a single aircraft type with high-frequency, point-to-point routes. Pursuing these different strategic market positions, Southwest generated consistently high growth and profitability and created billions of dollars of value for shareholders while America West declined into losses and bankruptcy.

America West's expansion has been described by William Franke, the company's president and CEO, as "random and based on market expectation, rather than real demand." This underlying lack of a strategy—the weak Strategic Market Positions—contributed significantly to the company's downfall.[8] America West filed for financial reorganization under Chapter 11 in June 1991.[9]

Since 1990, Southwest's growth and performance have been phenomenal. Revenue and seat miles have grown at a compound annual growth rate of 13 and 12 percent, respectively, with operating profit margins increasing from 6.9 percent to 8.5 percent. America West, meanwhile, plagued with slow growth throughout its bankruptcy, has generated revenue and seat-mile growth of just over 4 percent annually. As of this writing, the airline continues to be unprofitable, with an average five-year operating profit margin (2000–2004) of –4.2 percent.[10] The picture looks the same in terms of comparative stock performance.

America West neglected the basic tenet of Strategic Market Position: *build the right kind of market share.*

The situation is summarized in Figures 1.7, 1.8, and 1.9.

I do not talk our way through these figures in the same detail as the Wal-Mart versus Kmart example introduced earlier, because it follows the same general structure. (In fact, I use these figures to contrast companies throughout *Where Value Hides.*) But we start in the same place: with overall market share. This is the "market share" measure that's most often reported, and sometimes even earnestly dissected, in the business press. The problem is, *it's not a meaningful measure.* Although America West and Southwest had

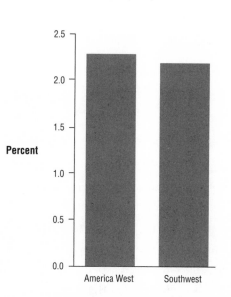

**U.S. Airline Market Share
(1990)**

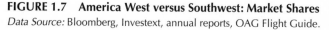

FIGURE 1.7   America West versus Southwest: Market Shares
Data Source: Bloomberg, Investext, annual reports, OAG Flight Guide.

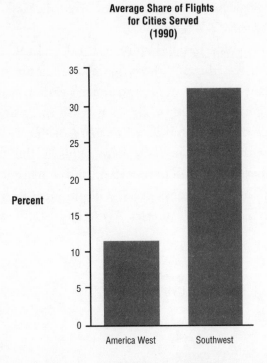

Average Share of Flights
for Cities Served
(1990)

FIGURE 1.8 America West versus Southwest: Strategic Market Position
Data Source: Bloomberg, Investext, annual reports, OAG Flight Guide.

similar U.S. market shares in 1990, this measure obscures their relative competitive strength. In the airline business, pricing power and
operating costs are much more driven by share of flights between
states—or even more precisely by *share of flights between specific city
pairs*. At the same time, travelers prefer to fly an airline that has
many daily flights between two points, because it gives them more
flexibility in case of a missed or delayed flight.

Southwest Airlines recognized this all-important fact and was
careful to enter new markets only when it felt it could offer a good

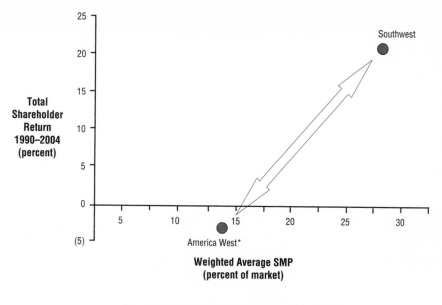

FIGURE 1.9   America West versus Southwest: Value Creation
Data Source: Bloomberg.

share of the flights in a proposed market. America West completely missed the point. Its leaders assumed that, by going after larger and increasingly international markets, the company was strengthening its overall position in the airline market. In fact, it was neglecting its core franchise and at the same time was spending treasure to enter new market segments where it had little to offer against strong competitors.

It is a little bit like your daughter suddenly deciding to splurge and buy Park Place, instead of building houses on the yellow monopoly she already controls. As the history of Southwest and America West amply demonstrates, you ignore the lessons of SMP at your peril.

Nintendo versus Sega

> . . . The name of the game is the games . . .
> —Hiroshi Yamauchi, President, Nintendo Co., Ltd.

Our third company pair involves Nintendo and Sega, two leaders in electronic games and interactive entertainment. (And, as we will see, this example eventually involves Sony and Microsoft.) The two gaming companies engaged in a pitched battle for the better part of two decades, dueling on two fronts simultaneously.

Nintendo and Sega began their modern-day gaming operations in the coin-operated arcade game market.[11] In the early to mid 1980s, after the release of Atari's 7800 home game system, Nintendo and Sega both released an 8-bit alternative home game system. Nintendo became the number 1 selling toy in the United States and the leading game system worldwide. To prevent low-quality software production, Nintendo put an early emphasis on strict policies for game developers, including exclusivity, royalty payments, and approval of all game designs.

Sega focused its attention on next-generation design and in 1989 released its 16-bit console, Sega Genesis, in the United States. It promoted the aggressive slogan, "Genesis does what Nintendon't." By means of its novel mascot, Sonic the Hedgehog, and in-your-face marketing campaigns, Sega developed a "cool" image among teens.[12] In 1991, Sega sold more than 1 million Genesis consoles.

Nintendo, notably, did not panic. Instead of rushing to release its 16-bit system, Nintendo continued to milk its 8-bit system, and concentrated on introducing a new market definition to the gaming industry: *gaming anywhere*. With the release of Game Boy—the first handheld and portable gaming system with exchangeable game cartridges—Nintendo retained its focus on its games, which were becoming more and more popular.

Two years later, Sega released its handheld gaming system, Game

Gear. Nintendo countered the Genesis system by releasing Super Nintendo, a 16-bit home console. Meanwhile, though, Game Boy had emerged as the most popular handheld gaming device by far. Between 1991 and 1993, its unit sales were about four times as large as Sega's Game Gear.[13] This kept Nintendo visible in the market and kept its game titles alive.

By the early 1990s, the situation was as shown in Figures 1.10, 1.11, and 1.12.

What's going on here? According to Figure 1.10, Sega was ahead of Nintendo in home consoles, but Nintendo had the lead in the new portable devices. On balance, you might think that the two

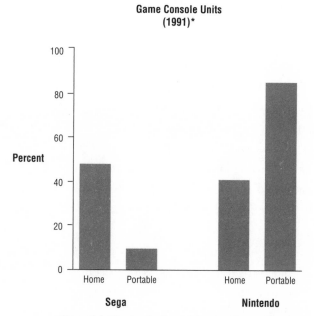

Game Console Units (1991)*

Notes: *Calculations based on the cumulative sales of 8-bit and 16-bit models.

FIGURE 1.10   Sega versus Nintendo: Market Shares
Data Source: Informa Media Group, Apex Group, Icon Group, Euromonitor.

companies were similarly positioned for success. In fact, Nintendo had a far superior SMP.

Why? Keep in mind that the electronic game industry is something of a razor-and-blade business. Companies try to break even (or even make a little money) on the consoles, but the really fat profits come from the follow-on sales of game cartridges. *The real driver of value is not console sales, but future sales of games.* Well, it turns out that the market opportunity for portable consoles and games became much larger than home consoles. Have you watched a gang of ten-year-old boys playing electronic games recently? If they play on a home console with multiple controllers, they need only one console and one copy of the game. But if they want to compete using (portable) Game Boys, each needs his own console with its own copy of the software cartridge. If you don't believe me, ask any parent with several kids how many Game Boy cartridges they have in the house versus home console games.

This SMP story is a little more complicated than the two that preceded it in this chapter. It is important for an electronic gaming company to play in both portable *and* home console markets, because that way it can leverage development spending across both platforms and negotiate better deals from software partners. For this reason, Figure 1.11 shows home and portable markets as one strategic segment with home and portable units added together. But *the need for individual software and hardware for the portable units makes them far more important in terms of generating future profits.* That is why (as shown in Figure 1.11) Nintendo is able to generate so much of its Strategic Market Position from its sales of portable units. When we combine the two companies' market shares applying a higher weighting to the portable units, it becomes clear how much stronger Nintendo really was vis-à-vis Sega.

Figure 1.12 shows the widely different shareholder returns for the two companies. Here's a telling statistic: Between 1992 and 2001,

**Game Console Units
(1991)**

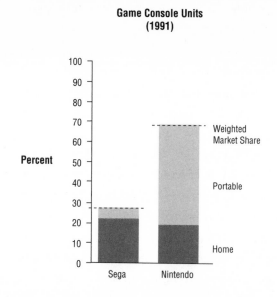

FIGURE 1.11   Sega versus Nintendo: Strategic Market Position
Data Source: Informa Media Group, Apex Group, Icon Group, Euromonitor.

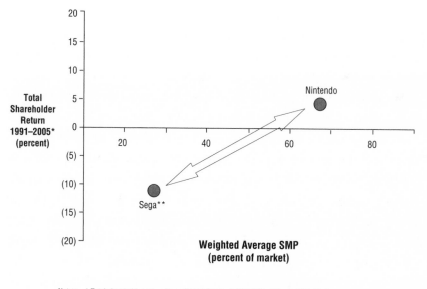

Notes: * Total shareholder return from 12/31/1991 to 12/31/2005 relative to Nikkei Index.
          ** In 2003, one share of Sega stock was exchanged for 0.28 shares of Sega Sammy stock.

FIGURE 1.12   Sega versus Nintendo: Value Creation
Data Source: Bloomberg.

Nintendo's sales revenues were, on average, 184 percent greater than Sega's. In the same time period, its net income was, on average, *935 percent greater*. And here's one direct outgrowth: Between 1991 and 2005, Nintendo's stock price grew at a CAGR of 1.5 percent, while Sega's stock price declined at a CAGR of –13.3 percent.[14] During the same period, the Nikkei Index declined at a CAGR of –2.1 percent.[15] A $1,000 investment in Sega in 1991 would be worth only $135 today, whereas the same investment in Nintendo would have yielded $1,240. Since a $1,000 investment in the Nikkei Index would be worth $747 today, the return from the investment in Nintendo would be worth $492 more than the return from the market, while the return from the investment in Sega would be worth $612 less than the return from the market.[16]

Enter the 800-pound gorilla. Sony's arrival in the gaming market in 2000, with its PlayStation entry, completely disrupted the competitive duopoly that Nintendo and Sega had enjoyed up to that point. Due to Nintendo's strength in the handheld market (more than 100 million Game Boy units had already been sold), and also thanks to the staying power of its games, Nintendo was able to hold the number 2 position behind Sony. Meanwhile, Sega exited the console market altogether in 2001. In short, Nintendo was rescued by its Game Boy line—the world's greatest selling game system of all time—which protected and expanded the company's Strategic Market Position in the gaming market.

In the meantime, I should point out, Nintendo is not neglecting its position in home consoles. Despite the fact that it's now playing catch-up not only to Sony and to the equally scary Microsoft—now the number 2 player in the game console market—Nintendo still plans on releasing its newest console-based system, Revolution, in 2006. I argue that this is the right thing to do, because—for the reasons stated previously—it spreads costs across a bigger base of sales, and reinforces Nintendo's overall SMP in gaming.

Broader Application of SMP

In the first quarter of every year, my company—L.E.K. Consulting—crunches a lot of numbers and puts together an analysis that is then printed as a special section in the *Wall Street Journal*. The analysis is called the "Shareholder Scoreboard" and (as the name implies) it shows how the top 1,000 companies in the United States performed for their shareholders in the preceding year.[17]

If you study the "Shareholder Scoreboard," you quickly start to see two interesting things. The first is captured in a box called "How Industry Groups Fared." When you eliminate the wild outliers on each end of the industry performance spectrum—things like home construction on the high end, and fixed-line telecommunications on the low end—you find that these industries' performances over a 10-year period tend to cluster in the 5 to 15 percent range with amazing consistency. This is one of the lessons that I hope you took away from the story of the color groups in the Monopoly game: Across a broad range of industries, from the technology-driven world of computer services (12.1 percent) to the fashion-conscious world of footwear (12.5 percent), returns are pretty comparable. In terms of return on dollars invested by shareholders, lowly Baltic is just as good as lofty Boardwalk.

The second thing you start to see, which I've already alluded to, is that there are spectacular differences across companies *within industries.* The big winners win huge, and the losers look awful. In Mining & Metals, for example, NuCor goes up 89.1 percent (in a year when the industry average is 11.9 percent), while Alcoa goes *down* 15.8 percent. In Software—up 15.6 percent, overall—Autodesk goes up 209.6 percent, while Novell goes down 35.9 percent.

Of course, all kinds of things go into those extreme numbers, and it's safe to predict that they will bounce around from year to year. (No one returns 209.6 percent for long.) But based on my experience of looking at literally hundreds of major companies in depth, *the long-term consistent winners are the ones that embrace the principles of SMP*, and build their competitive positions accordingly.

I settled on two of the three company pairs in this chapter (Wal-Mart/Kmart; Southwest/America West) not because they were the rare companies that proved my point, but because I liked the fact that (1) they had similar starting points, and (2) they had similar-sounding names, which made their contrasting fortunes that much more interesting. (I included the dissimilar-sounding Nintendo/Sega pair to begin to make the point that SMP applies not just in the United States but also internationally.)

You may be thinking that the three examples I have given do not prove that Strategic Market Position is a primary driver of each company's differential performance, and that other factors fully explain the growth and profitability differences. If so, I hope you will keep an open mind as I describe dozens more examples in different industries throughout this book.

2

BIGGER MAY BE WORSE

WHEN IT COMES to operating a successful business—as the common wisdom goes—bigger is better.

Bigger means you have more purchasing power. Bigger means that your fixed costs are spread over a larger base, which—as a rule—helps your profitability. Bigger means that it's scarier to compete against you, and maybe fewer competitors will venture into your market space. In many cases, bigger means that you've successfully acquired or otherwise vanquished many of your competitors, which gives you the opportunity to raise your prices with relative impunity, which means you can spend more on research and development (R&D) and on marketing your product, which means that you've created a virtuous circle.

Much of the thinking coming out of universities and consulting firms in the past half century follows these general lines. For the most part, the scholars and consultants have argued that big companies have big advantages vis-à-vis their smaller competitors. Or, conversely, they argue that the little fish must eventually be forced out of the pond.

So bigger is better, right?

Not necessarily. In this chapter, I argue that in many cases bigger is worse. I'm not just talking about conglomerates that compete in multiple industries. I show that even within a specific industry, bigger is not always better. More specifically, I argue that the *right* definition of "market share" is far more helpful than the *wrong* definition of market share—even if your resulting market share is smaller as a result.

To help make this point, I briefly review some of the strategy theories and models that got us to where we are today—those that mainly convinced us that bigger is better. You'll probably recognize several of these theories and models, which—in part through their interpretations of market share—have had enormous impact on the practice of business.

And lest you think that this is only of historical or academic interest, I devote the second half of the chapter to a story that is still unfolding and that has been heavily influenced by the champions of "bigger is better." In 1998, explicitly in the name of getting bigger, automakers Daimler-Benz and Chrysler undertook the largest industrial merger in history. The enterprise that resulted from that merger, DaimlerChrysler, is certainly bigger—but it definitely does not look better.

Meanwhile, Daimler's traditional rival on the luxury end of the spectrum, BMW, chose not to pursue size for its own sake. It chose to define market share in a highly focused—and more profitable—way.

LIFE ON THE EXPERIENCE CURVE

The notion of "strategy"—which can be defined informally as doing things in a systematic way to achieve a desired end—dates back at least to the ancient Greeks, who coined the word. ("Strategia" referred to both the chief civil leader and the top general in the army.) But strategy remained mostly a military concept until the twentieth century, when corporations got large enough to shape their industries and affect the fortunes of their competitors.[1] Henry Ford was a prestrategic thinker, in a sense; he just focused on making cars cheap enough for his workers to afford. Alfred Sloan, by contrast, was a strategic thinker; he realized that he could make life difficult for Ford by reshaping the auto industry to the advantage of his own General Motors.

World War II brought advances in strategic thinking that appeared to have implications for the business world. The devastation caused by that war delayed the commercial implementation of that strategic thinking, but by the 1960s, the business world was primed for some new strategic approaches. The business schools made their contribution, including the SWOT analysis model (strengths, weaknesses, opportunities, and threats) that emerged from Harvard. Large corporations, too, looked for more systematic approaches to strategy. General Electric, for example, came up with a Profit Optimization Model, or PROM, which attempted to explain the variability of returns across the huge GE empire.

But the real center of strategic gravity from the mid 1960s through the 1970s was the consulting arena—and in particular, Bruce Henderson's Boston Consulting Group (BCG). In 1965 BCG introduced a model that it called the "experience curve." It wasn't completely new, of course—something called a "learning curve" had been talked about in the aircraft industry since the 1920s[2]—but it promised great things to companies that were trying to figure out how and where to make their most important investments.

In its essence, the experience-curve model argued that the more you did something—made a product, offered a service—the better you'd get at it, and the less you'd have to charge for that product or service, and the more market share you would command, and so on. It was a virtuous circle that, when charted, resulted in Figure 2.1.

"The experience curve is the means of measuring probable cost differentials," BCG wrote in 1973. "A difference (i.e., a ratio) in market share of 2 to 1 should produce about 20 percent or more differential in pretax cost on value added."[3] In other words, if you command twice as much market share as your nearest competitor, your pretax cost of doing business ought to be 20 percent lower than that competitor's. This model led, in turn, to another "powerful oversimplification" (Henderson's term) from the offices of BCG: the "Growth-Share Matrix." This was simply a two-by-two box that plotted growth along one axis and share along the other, and assigned memorably salty names to the enterprises that fell into the resulting boxes. See Figure 2.2.

As a CEO, you'd use this matrix to perform "portfolio analysis." After analyzing your portfolio, you'd invest in your stars, milk your cows, unload your dogs, and keep your eye on your question marks. It's important to note how much weight is being given to something called *market share* in this analysis. In this framework, it is a relative measure: If you make 1 million widgets out of the 100 million widgets

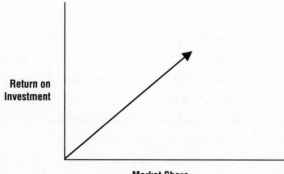

FIGURE 2.1   Benefits of Market Share

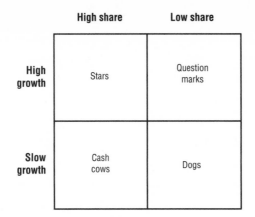

FIGURE 2.2   The Growth-Share Matrix

produced every year, you have a 1 percent market share. If your largest competitor makes only 500,000 widgets, you have a relative market share of two times, and you should have a 20 percent cost advantage over that competitor.

Or you would have up until about 1978. In that year, BCG revised downward the power of the experience curve: from 20 percent to 10 percent.[4] Presumably, this came as an unpleasant surprise to those CEOs who, in the previous decade, had been using the Growth-Share Matrix to make some of their most important decisions. But most likely, it did *not* come as a surprise to those managers of highly profitable companies who somehow managed to make big returns despite their relatively small market share.

STUCK IN THE MIDDLE: THE PORTER VIEW

One of the prominent critics of the experience curve was Michael Porter, who in 1979 wrote a column in the *Wall Street Journal* outlining the perils of using the experience curve to develop corporate strategies.[5]

Now that Peter Drucker is gone, Porter is, arguably, the world's most influential business scholar. His *Competitive Strategy*, first published in 1980, has been through more than 50 editions, and has been translated into more than 20 languages worldwide.[6] *Competitive Strategy* introduced the celebrated and enduring "five forces" framework, which focused on industry competitors, suppliers and buyers, and new entrants and substitutes. It was this broad focus—beyond the established players in a market, to include the players in an "extended competition"—that made Porter's analysis relevant and useful to managers.[7]

Porter explicitly took aim at the direct correlation between market share and ROI that was described by BCG's experience curve. While acknowledging that this correlation existed in some industries, Porter argued that in others, both small players *and* large players could make good money. Where you didn't want to be, Porter asserted, was "stuck in the middle." In Figure 2.3, Porter's alternative to the experience-curve chart took the form of a U-shaped curve.

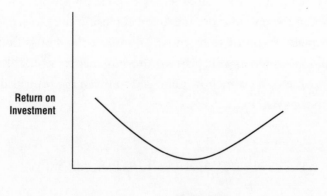

FIGURE 2.3   U-Shaped Curve

As an example of an industry whose players tended to get "stuck in the middle," Porter cited the auto industry. And as an example of an auto company that had escaped the "stuck in the middle" trap and had figured out a way to make good money with low market share, Porter cited Daimler-Benz, a company that we return to shortly.[8]

By escaping from the straight-line worldview of the experience curve, Porter was moving in the right direction. But he was still defining "share" as a business unit's sales in relation to a broadly defined industry. He was focusing largely on how well a given company's capabilities fit with an existing competitive structure, and advocating the adoption of one of three "generic strategies" (cost leadership, differentiation, or focus) to avoid being pulled in contradictory directions—a sensible caution, but still too broad-gauge to be actionable.[9] And finally, he appeared to assign some degree of inherent value to "being small." As one pair of critics observed:

> By suggesting that small-share businesses typically earn high rates of return, he implies that this performance is *caused* by having a small share. In fact, the examples he cites illustrate how successful product differentiation can *offset* the disadvantages of a low share.[10]

Bigger may be worse. At the same time, there's nothing inherently good about being small. What matters is *determining a sustainable strategic market segment*, based on both customer preferences and producer economics.

PIMS: A Promising Dead End

Now turn to our third and final model. I've already mentioned GE's PROM model, which attempted to interpret returns from the scores of operating units across GE's sprawling industrial empire. This basic strategic planning model was broadened in the early 1970s to include data from multiple companies. By the late 1980s, the model included data from more than 3,000 strategic business units in more than 450 companies. This database was dubbed "PIMS": profit impact of marketing strategy, and, in an ambitious way, it attempted to link strategy to performance.

Of the three models described in this chapter, PIMS comes closest to SMP. Consider the following passage from *The PIMS Principles*, which summarizes how the researchers behind PIMS looked at market share.

> All of our market-share figures are measured in relation to each business unit's *served market*. The served market is defined as that part or segment of an industry (in terms of products, kinds of customers, and geographic areas) in which a business actually competes. For most businesses, the market defined in this way is considerably smaller than the overall industry in which it participates. For example, one of the successful small-share competitors cited by Porter is Mercedes-Benz. This highly profitable firm has a very small share of total worldwide automobile sales. But, applying our concept of its relevant served market, Mercedes-Benz has a *large* share of the luxury car market.[11]

So far, so good. But the problem with the PIMS database was that it was all self-reported. And the problem with self-reporting is that you can *think* you have a strong market share in a particular "served market," but if what you're defining as a served market isn't really clearly separate, then you're at risk. It's like owning only one of the orange properties in Monopoly, and failing to understand that without the other two orange properties, your orange served market isn't worth much.

Or, to cite a real-world example, think back to the example of Sega, as described in Chapter 1. Suppose you're Sega, and you're saying, "We're going to focus all our efforts on making the world's most advanced home console machines. We're not going to worry about the games market, or the portable market." With that strategy, you might, *for a time*, be able to command a strong share of your served market, and you might fool yourself into believing that you're in a very strong strategic position. If Sega's strategists had turned in the relevant Sega data to the PIMS researchers in that time period, they would have reported that they had a high market share of their served market.

But by so doing, they would have missed two points. First, a lot of the console economics are shared with the portable machines. So a company that has *both* the portable and the home platform—like Nintendo and unlike Sega—is in a much better position to leverage its economics.

Second, as we've seen, the *real* profits are in the games, rather than the machines themselves. Sega completely missed that point. They didn't recognize that the portable units actually generated a lot more game sales than the home ones, and so they didn't capture those revenue streams.

This leads us to the punch line of the PIMS discussion. *You don't get to define your own strategic segments.* What actually defines a strategic segment are (1) customer preferences and (2) producer economics. You don't get to make up the rules; you only get to uncover them, segment by segment. If you say, "My niche is shirts for kids; I'm not going to compete in other shirt niches," you may be in for an unpleasant surprise. What if shirt economics are the same for both kid shirts and adult shirts? In *that* case, your real market share (of "shirts with the same economics") is actually dangerously *low*, rather than comfortably high. The Nintendo of the shirt industry may be sitting out there, waiting to pounce on your bad economics.

DAIMLERCHRYSLER VERSUS BMW: IS BIGGER BETTER?

Perhaps you're wondering why we've made this detour through ancient history—PIMS researchers doing battle with Michael Porter, and so on. Let's update the oft-cited Mercedes-Benz story, and contrast it with the BMW story.

Today, BMW is one of the most profitable car manufacturers in the world, with an operating margin of more than 8 percent.[12] By comparison, DaimlerChrysler—the current incarnation of Daimler-Benz—is yielding operating margins of around 3 percent.[13] Yes, BMW has been a strong operator in recent years. (As noted in earlier chapters, strong operating fundamentals are at least as important as SMP in defining success.) But Daimler also has a long reputation for operating excellence. To a significant degree, BMW has done better because it has been run in a way that's consistent with the principles of SMP, whereas DaimlerChrysler has not.

As recently as 1994, these two luxury car manufacturers—represented primarily by BMW and Mercedes luxury cars—were at a roughly similar starting point, although the then Daimler-Benz was (and still is) much bigger than BMW. See Figure 2.4.

	1994 Revenue (Billions of Euros)	1994 Average Gross Profit (%)	1994 Average Operating Profit (%)
BMW	21.6	13%*	2.1%
Daimler-Benz (Mercedes)	53.2	13%	1.8%

Note: *Estimated.

FIGURE 2.4 BMW versus Daimler-Benz (1994)
Data Source: Bloomberg.

Since that time, the two companies have pursued very different growth strategies. In the balance of this chapter, we contrast those two strategies, in light of Strategic Market Position.

BMW: Looking to the Long Run

BMW traces its roots back to 1913, when a Bavarian engineer formed the Rapp Motoren Werke in a suburb outside Munich. Three years later, the company renamed itself Bayerische Motoren Werke (the Bavarian Motor Works, or BMW). BMW originally specialized in aircraft engines—its current logo is a stylized aircraft propeller, reflecting those early origins—but it branched out into motorcycles in 1923, and cars in 1928.

For most of its history, BMW could boast of advanced design and engineering skills, but it enjoyed only small markets and had notoriously thin capitalization. As recently as 1959, the company's management seriously considered selling out to its older and larger rival, Daimler-Benz. At that point, the Quandt family—which then owned about 30 percent of BMW (as well as 10 percent of Daimler)—purchased a substantially bigger share in BMW, thereby stabilizing its finances. Today, the Quandt family still owns a controlling interest in the business, and—in their rare public statements—simply say that they are seeking value-creation in the long run.[14] Their half-century-long investment certainly substantiates this claim.

BMW has grown by strengthening its position in a narrow marketplace: the high-end performance car market. (It entered the domestic U.S. market in 1974, with the creation of BMW of North America.) Through expert engineering, it has consistently released high-performance cars and has gained share within the luxury market: the Z series, the X series, and more recently the 6 series. To further solidify its position at the high end of the market, the company purchased (in 1998) the rights to the Rolls-Royce name. As the company's web site explains:

> With the three brands, BMW, MINI and Rolls-Royce Motor Cars, the BMW Group has its sights set firmly on the premium sector of the international automobile market. To achieve its aims, the company knows how to deploy its strengths with an efficiency that is unmatched in the automotive industry. . . . The company's phenomenal success is proof of this strategy's correctness. (*Corporate Strategy*, BMW Group web site, December 2005)

BMW has certainly made its share of mistakes. One came in 1994, when the company acquired the Rover Group PLC. After sustaining heavy losses from its United Kingdom operations, BMW sold the Land Rover division to Ford, while holding on to its MINI brand. Overall, however, the company has stuck to a well-defined Strategic Market Position.

Trouble at Daimler

Daimler and Benz were rival German carmakers who joined forces in 1926. Along with Horch—the company that would later be known as Audi—Daimler-Benz defined and captured the German luxury car market in the 1930s. World War II sidetracked the company, and few Germans were buying luxury cars in the immediate postwar years. But in the 1960s and 1970s, Daimler-Benz gradually emerged as the world's leading luxury car manufacturer, displacing British and U.S. brands.

When Jürgen Schrempp took over as chairman of Daimler-Benz in 1995, he reversed the conglomerate-building ways of his predecessor. He focused on creating shareholder value, explicitly adopting a

12 percent return on capital as the company's overriding goal. The overall number of businesses was cut from 35 to 23, and—despite the powerful resistance of German labor unions—the company's work force was reduced by 10 percent.

Concurrently, Schrempp pursued a policy of expansion, mainly through diversification and globalization. Despite its global reputation, the company sold only 600,000 Mercedes luxury cars in 1995, making it only the fifteenth largest carmaker in the world. Most specialty brands—Jaguar, Saab, Volvo, Alfa Romeo, Ferrari, and many others—had already been merged into broad-line auto manufacturers. The high-end brands of Toyota, Honda, and Nissan had made huge inroads into the luxury market. Along with BMW and Porsche, Daimler-Benz was one of only three independent producers of high-end cars left in the world. The handwriting seemed to be on the wall: *Grow or die*. Bigger is better. To survive, as Schrempp saw it, Daimler-Benz would have to learn how to make smaller and cheaper cars. And the easiest way to get there was to buy a company that already knew how to do that.

In May 1998, at a press conference in London, Daimler-Benz and Chrysler Corporation announced a "merger of equals made in heaven," and valued at some $36 billion. The resulting combination, DaimlerChrysler, would have revenues of $132 billion, with more than 421,000 employees worldwide.[15]

Secrecy had been well maintained, so the business press in attendance that day were surprised by the proposed merger. (It later emerged that it was less a merger of equals, and more an acquisition of Chrysler by Daimler.) They listened carefully to Schrempp's rationale for the merger, which even then seemed like an unlikely marriage. DaimlerChrysler, Schrempp explained, sought synergies across its supply chain and production portfolio through the sharing of parts, pooling purchasing costs, merging R&D budgets, and other cost-saving measures. In a press release, Schrempp emphasized "value," "strategy," and other key buzzwords:

> The two companies are a perfect fit of two leaders in their respective markets. Both companies have dedicated and skilled workforces and successful products, but in different markets and different parts of the world. By combining and utilizing each other's strengths, we will have a pre-eminent strategic position in the global marketplace for the benefit of our customers. We will be able to exploit new markets, and we will improve return and value for our shareholders. This is a historic merger that will change the face of the automotive industry. (Jürgen Schrempp, Chairman, Daimler-Benz AG, press release, May 7, 1988)

In that last opinion, as it turned out, Schrempp had it right.

The Verdict

Since 1994, therefore, BMW and Daimler-Benz/DaimlerChrysler have pursued markedly different strategies. While the dust is still settling, and probably will be for some years to come, it's not too early to ask which company has fared better.

Simply put, BMW has outperformed DaimlerChrysler along every measurable dimension. BMW's sales have more than doubled, and its operating profits have risen from 2.1 percent to more than 8 percent.

Mercedes, meanwhile, has nearly tripled its sales, but—despite Schrempp's prognostications to the contrary—growth has come at the expense of margins and shareholder value. Just after the Chrysler acquisition in 1998, Daimler's operating margins were at an all-time high of 6 percent. Since then, they have plummeted to 3.2 percent. See Figure 2.5.

	2004 Revenue (Billions of Euros)	2000–2004 Average Gross Profit (%)	2000–2004 Average Operating Profit (%)
BMW	44.3	23%	7.8%
DaimlerChrysler (Mercedes)	142.0	18%	2.5%

FIGURE 2.5 BMW versus DaimlerChrysler (2004)
Data Source: Bloomberg.

The recent stock performance of these two companies highlights how important growth strategies are for shareholder value. Between December 1998 and the end of 2005, BMW's stock appreciated by more than 38 percent.[16] In stark contrast, DaimlerChrysler's stock peaked at €95.35 a share shortly after the merger, and by year-end 2005 was worth less than half that amount.[17]

MARKET SHARE AND VALUE CREATION AT BMW AND DAIMLERCHRYSLER

Look at market share and value creation at our two subject companies, using the same three-chart sequence that we used for Wal-Mart/Kmart and our other company pairs in Chapter 1, beginning with Figure 2.6.

Here you have the unsegmented market-share picture of Daimler-Chrysler on the left and BMW on the right. At something just under 2 percent market share in the United States, BMW appears to be hanging on by its fingernails. But now look at Figure 2.7.

This figure reveals, in graphic terms, how BMW is able to achieve a superior Strategic Market Position despite selling only a fraction of the vehicles DaimlerChrysler does. The figure represents the U.S. market, although you would get a similar picture if you looked at other regions

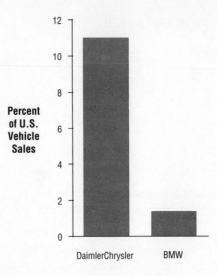

FIGURE 2.6   BMW versus DaimlerChrysler: U.S. Auto Sales (2005)
Data Source: Ward's.

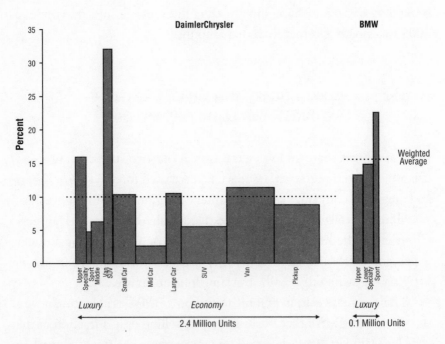

FIGURE 2.7   Average U.S. Market Share by Platform and Class
Data Source: Ward's.

of the world. I have first broken the market down into luxury versus economy brands to reflect the fact that it is hard to share components and manufacturing between these two categories because of the different volumes and specifications involved. (Even today, there is very little sharing between the Daimler and Chrysler divisions of the same company). For similar reasons, I have further broken the market into broad classes: small cars, large cars, SUVs, pickup trucks, vans, and so on.

We could debate exactly how to draw these class distinctions, but it would not change the answer very much. What really drives the difference in SMP is measuring market share in terms of *average share per model platform*, rather than aggregate market share for the class. This is because manufacturing and development are much more efficient if you have a single model class (e.g., BMW 3 series), versus a range of different platforms within the same class (e.g., Dodge, Chrysler, Plymouth). Even within Mercedes, we now have a proliferation of model platforms, including E, C, S, CLK, CLS, CL, SLK, SL, R, M, and G-class vehicles.

In Figure 2.7, each bar represents a class of vehicle, organized into the two larger segments of luxury or economy. The height of any given bar measures the percent U.S. market share the company holds per model platform within each class (two brands that share the same body are counted as one platform). The width of a bar represents the unit sales within that class, adjusted for higher prices of luxury brands.[18]

The point? DaimlerChrysler's strategy in recent years has been to spread out comprehensively over a broad range of price and class segments with multiple overlapping platforms in each, while BMW focuses its production in just a few isolated luxury segments with a more limited range of model platforms. As a result, the *weighted average market share* (the dashed line) is higher for BMW. So even though BMW is smaller in size, and commands a much smaller share of the market than DaimlerChrysler, BMW employs SMP to focus

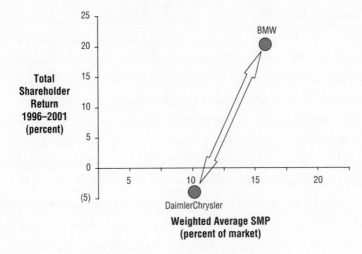

FIGURE 2.8   BMW versus DaimlerChrysler: Value Creation
Data Source: Ward's, Bloomberg.

its efforts, and thus is more successful in achieving profits for its shareholders. This is shown in Figure 2.8.

Once again, we see the power of SMP in action. Between 1996 and 2001, BMW's shareholders enjoyed a better than 20 percent return on their investment, while DaimlerChrysler's stock wound up slightly below water.

It would be wrong to conclude that BMW's strategy was simply to target a profitable niche and benefit from the higher returns from the left side of Porter's U-shaped curve. Many other specialty carmakers tried that and are now history. On the contrary, BMW has sought to aggressively seek out market share. It has become a global car company with plants in 12 countries on 4 continents. But it has done this by sticking to its strategy of *pursuing only the specific market share that drives value and profitability* and steadfastly avoiding all else.

LESSONS IN SMP: BIGGER MAY BE WORSE

Early in his tenure as CEO of General Electric, Jack Welch promulgated a hard-nosed policy for his company's divisional managers: *Either get to be number 1 or number 2 in your markets*, he warned them, *or expect to be dumped by the Mother Ship*. And Welch delivered on his threat: He unloaded 117 businesses—or 1 in every 5 GE businesses— valued at $9 billion. When the heads of those number 3 and number 4 industry players protested, pointing out that (in many cases) they were highly profitable, Welch shrugged off the objections. "When you're number four or five in a market," he explained, "when number one sneezes, you get pneumonia. When you're number one, you control your destiny."[19]

Now, I'd be the first to admit that Welch had some housecleaning to do when he first took the helm at GE. Nevertheless, there is one thing wrong with this *sneeze = pneumonia* approach. It assumes that someone in the organization can define "market share" in a meaningful (i.e., "profitable") way. As the BMW/DaimlerChrysler example amply illustrates, fuzzy thinking about market share can infiltrate the corner offices of some of the world's smartest corporations.

Insisting on being number 1 or number 2 in your market—without first having a very clear understanding of what definition of market share really drives profitability—can take some very interesting opportunities off the table. Howard Stevenson, an expert in entrepreneurship at Harvard Business School, jokingly used to thank Jack Welch for creating so many good opportunities for "the rest of us." As mighty GE packed its bags, unfurled its sails, and sailed out of the harbor, smaller competitors were quite happy to move in on the abandoned territory.[20]

In the next chapter, we dig deeper into the concept of "good" market share and techniques for uncovering where value hides.

3

UNCOVERING
WHERE VALUE HIDES

B Y NOW YOU probably have at least a rough sense of what Strategic Market Position (SMP) is. Now we need to start figuring out how to find it—the central theme of this book.

In this chapter, we look at another industry, the world of fractional horsepower motors. This may seem very different from the industries we have looked at so far—autos, discount retailing, airlines, and electronic games—but as you'll see, the smart players in all these industries uncover value in *very similar ways*. Obviously, selling electric motors is hugely different from selling cars, toys, or travel. But if you dig down into the strategies of leading companies in these industries, you'll find some very interesting similarities—all in the realm of SMP.

In this chapter I once again use my value creation chart to depict the fundamentals of those strategies in SMP terms. I also introduce a new tool—which I call the "value map"—to further explore the process of uncovering value by understanding Strategic Market Position.

A Tale of Two Motor Makers

The first of our two case studies involves two motor makers with similar-sounding names: Magnetek and Ametek. I first encountered these companies back in the 1990s, when my company was doing some consulting work for another player in the fractional horsepower (FHP) electric motor industry.[1] It was our close examination of the companies in this industry, in fact—including our close look at Magnetek and Ametek—that helped bring into focus the application of Strategic Market Position to this industry.[2]

At that time, FHP was about a $5 billion industry in the United States. It was (and still is) a largely invisible industry, since its products almost always wind up inside someone else's product. The compressor motor in your refrigerator, the motors that power your garage door opener and make your car windows go up and down, the motors that drive all those various fans and blowers in your office: All are FHP motors, manufactured for an original equipment manufacturer, or OEM. Konosuke Matsushita, the founder of Matsushita Electric, prompted skepticism when he predicted, way back in the 1930s, that people's homes would one day have dozens of small motors in them, but history proved him right. The FHP market soon grew far beyond even the visionary Matsushita's wildest dreams.

The FHP industry was (and still is) highly competitive. Although in 1992 two giants—Emerson Electric and General Electric—together commanded almost one-quarter of the total market for FHP motors, more than two dozen companies fought over the remaining three-quarters of that market—a substantial $3.75 billion prize. The strategic question for each of those companies was *how* and *where* should they fight?

Our two subject companies, Magnetek and Ametek, were the number 4 and number 8 players, respectively, in 1992, battling for their share of that $3.75 billion. Those market positions translated into overall market shares of about six and four percent, respectively. See Figure 3.1.

As you can probably anticipate, the SMP question I pose goes as follows: Does this picture of total FHP market shares represent the true competitive positions of the various companies, or is there a different strategic market segmentation that better represents the true competitive arenas that each firm competes in?

If the answer to the first part of the question is yes, then neither Ametek nor Magnetek are in a good position to prevail against the much greater scale of GE and Emerson.

One way we can begin to answer this question is to look at the relative profitability of companies of different sizes. Figure 3.2 shows that there is no direct relationship between operating margin and total FHP sales.

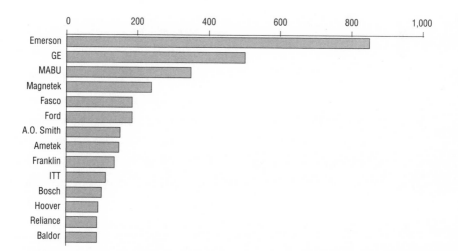

1992 U.S. FHP Motor Sales ($M)

FIGURE 3.1   Sales of Leading Competitors
Source: L.E.K. analysis of company financial data.

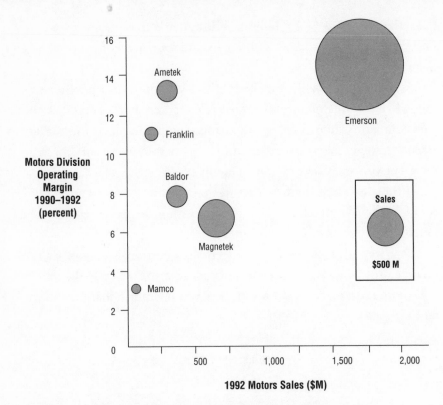

FIGURE 3.2   Relationship between Operating Margin and Total Sales

As you can see, Emerson is the largest player overall, and—as is typical for the blue-chip St. Louis-based manufacturer—it also makes strong margins. But there are also mid-sized and small players, Ametek and Franklin, which also earn good returns. At the same time, Magnetek, one of the larger players, is lagging behind in terms of operating margin. Maybe you're hypothesizing that the lack of correlation to scale is because some companies have not configured their plants to realize the scale efficiencies that are available to them. There may be some truth in this, but an analysis of operating margins and plant scale also shows no direct relationship.

This suggests that we should look for some other explanation. Is there some kind of industry segmentation that defines the different strategic markets in which the various competitors operate? As it turns out, the answer is yes. There are many possible ways to break down the FHP motor industry:

- By geography (e.g., global share, including international or share by country).
- By type of electric power (DC, AC, or Universal).
- By size or power rating.
- By end-user market (consumer, industrial, etc.).

A breakdown of the industry by end-user market, and the shares of competitors within each, are shown in Figure 3.3.

According to this segmentation, Emerson and GE dominate most segments of the market. Magnetek appears to have a good position in industrial motors as the number two behind Emerson. Ametek and

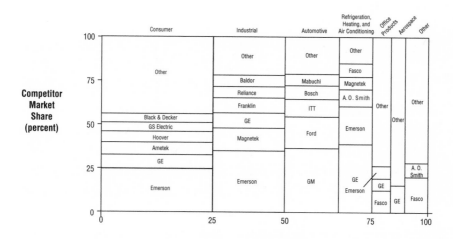

FIGURE 3.3   FHP Market Shares by End-User Market
Source: L.E.K. analysis of company financial data.

Franklin both look as though they are in difficult positions—that is, well behind Emerson in Consumer and Industrial motors, respectively. But we have already seen that these companies are doing well in terms of profitability. Perhaps we also need to consider some of the other possible segmentation criteria. The question then becomes, "Which ones?" If we break down the industry by all of the possible criteria, we will end up with dozens of tiny market segments, and that may not be the right answer, either.

Introducing the Value Map

The key to uncovering the true Strategic Market Position in an industry lies in assessing *which dimensions of scale or market share contribute to increased profitability and value*. Let's look at a tool for uncovering these profitability and value relationships: the Value Map.

Look at Figure 3.4.

This is a little less complicated than it may at first appear. The concentric circles represent increasing economic or customer benefits of scale or share. If only the inner circle sector is shaded, it means that there is little benefit from increasing share or scale on that dimension. An outer shaded circle sector suggests that a company possessing this attribute should enjoy significantly lower costs or a more attractive product offering than a company without this attribute, assuming that the two companies are equivalent on all other dimensions.

The circle sectors or pie slices in Figure 3.4 lay out a number of possible dimensions of scale or scope that may lead to competitive advantage. If you were a motor manufacturer, you could think of these as choices that you might explore as you considered where to target your sales efforts or where to invest in expanded operations or new product development.

I lay them out going clockwise from the top in roughly the order

Economic and Customer Benefits of Scale or Share

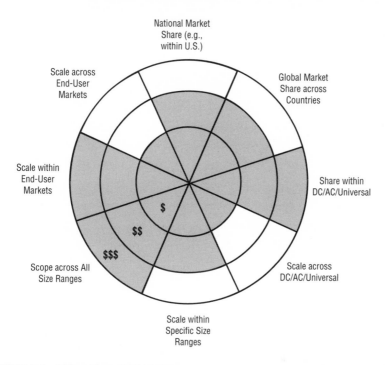

FIGURE 3.4   Value Map: FHP Motors

that they tend to occur to people—that is, geographic scale or scope coming first, technological scale/scope coming next, size ranges next, and market scale/scope coming somewhere behind them. In other words, if you asked a reasonably bright person to guess how a company should invest to achieve scale that would earn a relatively high return, the first thing that person would be likely to say is, "Invest in such a way as to achieve high market share as defined by geography." I take that one step further to include several kinds of geography, including "global" and "national."

So now go around the different dimensions of scale and scope.

National/Global Market Share

Start from a national perspective. As noted, most motors are not an end product; they are used in someone else's product. Since the manufacturers of those end products—ranging from cars to washing machines—have plants all over the United States, it's important for you as a motor supplier to serve your customers wherever they are. All other things being equal, if you have greater sales across the country you should be in a better position to understand and respond to your customers' needs and deliver cost-effective product to them. For this reason, I score national market share as fairly important in achieving economic or customer benefits of scale.

But even by the 1990s—and certainly to a much greater extent today—manufacturing of many electric-powered products was becoming a global, rather than a national, industry. With many OEMs locating operations in China, Eastern Europe, or wherever else the economics are most favorable, motor manufacturers have to serve them cost effectively wherever they are in the world. This means that global scale across countries is at least as important as national market share within a country. It also means that the optimal production location will often be in a low labor cost country. The exception, of course, is protected industries, such as defense-related products. U.S. policymakers are generally comfortable letting a Chinese motor go into a hair dryer; they're generally less comfortable using a Chinese motor in a torpedo. (The sentiment, presumably, runs both ways.) On balance, I score global market share as being as important as national market share in achieving benefits from scale, although the answer varies, depending on whether it's a standardized motor or a premium motor for defense applications.

In Chapter 5, I discuss a more rigorous approach to determining the economic and customer benefits of scale or scope.

DC/AC/Universal

This is my shorthand for economies of scale on the manufacturing line for different motor types. FHP electric motors are basically wires wrapped around a frame, with the right contacts stuck in the right places. The winding technology is pretty much the same for all DC motors, so the same lines can be used to turn out various shapes of DC motors. But you have to use a different winding technology for AC, and still another technology for Universal motors. So while you can do well by specializing in one of these three types, there's almost no benefit to scale across different motor technologies.

This is represented by the third and fourth sectors on the Value Map. A company manufacturing large volumes *within* any one of the DC, AC, or Universal motor types will be able to realize substantial economies of scale in production. They will also benefit from being able to spread their R&D over higher volumes. But there are few benefits to be realized from scale *across* motor types, as indicated by the lower rating on the Value Map. This doesn't mean that a large company offering multiple types of motors can't be well positioned competitively. It just means that if there are two companies making 1 million DC motors per year and one of them also makes 300,000 AC motors, then this company will not realize significant additional scale economies from the combined output.

Size and Power Rating

Unlike motors using different winding technologies, different sizes or power ratings of the same FHP motor can mostly be made on the same production line. So on the Value Map, we show that there are benefits to scale both *within* specific size ranges and *across* size ranges for the same winding technology. (Remember: When we score each dimension of scale, we are assuming that all the other attributes are the same for the added scale or market share we are considering.) Most customers expect their motor suppliers to offer a range of motor sizes and power ratings, so there are additional benefits to having scale across sizes.

End-User Industries

Other things being equal, scale or market share within an end-user industry is a good thing. It enables more efficient sales and marketing to a targeted customer group and allows for products that are well suited to a particular industry.

Scale across end-user industries tends to yield low benefits, because different industries have such different requirements. At one end of the spectrum, military applications are incredibly demanding, requiring high reliability in the face of adverse temperatures, massive shocks, lots of downtime punctuated by periodic intensive usage, and so on. *Reliability* is key, and the design life of a military motor may be measured in the thousands of hours. Price is usually not the main determinant, and production runs are usually small to very small.

Consumer applications, at the other end of the spectrum, are dramatically different. Many end products are used only a few times, and their motors aren't particularly stressed. Design life may be 100 hours or less. What's key in most consumer applications is *cost*. The factory that's appropriate for making a low-cost, short-lived motor is not appropriate for making a high-cost, indestructible motor, and vice versa.

Industrial markets tend to fall somewhere in between. There, you don't need the ultimate reliability of military applications, but you *do* want a product that will work and work and work. A motor that will be used in a factory, for example, is probably going to be used one, two, or three shifts a day, day in, day out, month in, month out. So you want a motor with a very long design life that will last for thousands of hours, or maybe even tens of thousands of hours. It doesn't have to withstand the abuse of a military motor, but it has to be easy to maintain, moderately priced, and superreliable.

Note the sectors pointing west and northwest in the FHP Value Map. You can find great value in achieving scale *within* end-user industries. On the other hand, there is almost no value to be found in trying to satisfy the very different needs of multiple end-user industries. (The factories and processes are simply too different.)

Now let's apply what we have learned from the Value Map to determine the strategic market segments in the FHP motors industry. The low scores for scale across DC/AC/Universal and for scale across end-user industries mean that segments that are different on either of these dimensions are *best thought of as separate markets*, when one is determining Strategic Market Position. Cutting the industry along these two dimensions creates the information shown in Figure 3.5.

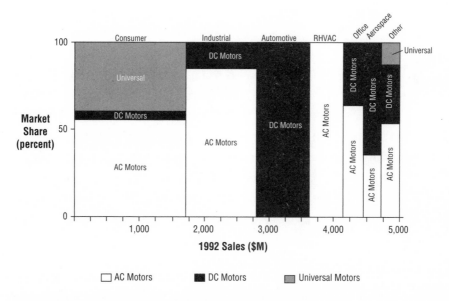

FIGURE 3.5   U.S. FHP Motors: Strategic Market Segments
Source: L.E.K. analysis.

This breaks the $5 billion U.S. market into 14 strategic market segments. Along the bottom axis, we show how much of the market is attributable to each end-user industry. For example, consumer products account for almost $1.8 billion in motor sales. The vertical axis shows how each industry's motor usage breaks down by motor type. Using this display, the area of each segment in the figure is proportional to its total motor sales. This figure is what we use to evaluate the Strategic Market Position of the leading players, although the fact that there are substantial scale benefits from global scale across countries means that we also need to be thinking about global market shares and about competition from companies with low labor cost overseas.

Using our new understanding of strategic market segments, we look at Magnetek and Ametek and consider where they positioned themselves in terms of the dimensions on our Value Map. With this insight, you will see why Magnetek did so poorly and Ametek did so well. In 1992—and apparently in subsequent years—Ametek was making these SMP decisions correctly, while Magnetek was making them incorrectly. Look at Figure 3.6.

You'll recognize Figure 3.6 as the first of the three figures in the larger value creation figures introduced in Chapter 1, which compared the SMPs of several company pairs, such as Wal-Mart and Kmart. Once again, this market-share figure tells you less than you might think it does. Based on this figure alone, if you had to bet on one player or the other as the winner in the cutthroat FHP business, you'd probably bet on Magnetek, which in 1992 had a 50 percent greater market share than Ametek. If so, you'd be making a bad bet. Consider Figure 3.7.

You'll recognize Figure 3.7 as the second component part of our value creation figures from Chapter 1. This figure presents the various product lines of our two subject companies in terms of their market shares *in strategic market segments*, as laid out in Figure 3.5. Each

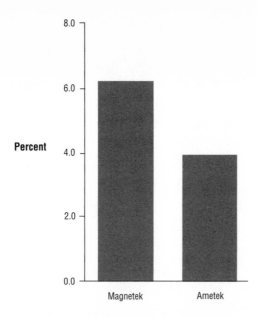

FIGURE 3.6   U.S. FHP Motors: Market Shares (1992)

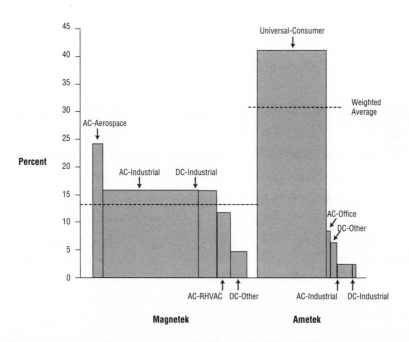

FIGURE 3.7   U.S. FHP Motors: Strategic Market Position (1992)
Source: L.E.K. analysis.

bar represents a different strategic market segment with the width proportional to each company's sales in the different segments. Note that the bulk of Magnetek's sales come in the AC-Industrial segment, where it has a 15 percent share. Ametek, meanwhile, does almost *three times* as well in its biggest market (Universal-Consumer).

The contrast in the performance of the two companies illustrates the point that the market within an industry shouldn't be defined so broadly as to encompass all segments of that industry (as is implied by Figure 3.6). Magnetek defined its market more broadly than Ametek did, and thus decided to diversify its product range across various segments. Ametek, by contrast, realized that the best segmentation strategy was to consider the strategic segments separately and to focus on segments with two key characteristics:

1. The absence of industry giants like Emerson and GE from that niche.
2. The feasibility of erecting higher barriers to entry (whether technological, distribution-channel related, or otherwise).

Following this strategy, Ametek established itself as a successful player in the FHP motor industry, securing a greater weighted market share than some other competitors—including Magnetek—that had a greater share in the overall market. That weighted average is shown by the dashed horizontal lines in Figure 3.7.

This logic is at the heart of SMP. There are endless ways to segment a market, but only one of those ways is the strategically *best* way. It's not good enough to have a small slice of lots of pies, which is the position of Magnetek in Figure 3.7. In the long run, it's also not good enough to have a commanding share of a relatively tiny market (e.g., DC-Industrial). You need to find, seize, and hold a significant market segment. For example: Providing 40 percent of the vacuum cleaner motors purchased in the United States in 1992—which is what that big fat Ametek bar in Figure 3.7 represents—is a very powerful SMP.

THE LAST WORD ON MOTORS

Traditional strategic thinking argues that *bigger is better*. A greater market share—no matter what you have to pay to get it—is the way to go, right?

Wrong.

The evidence? We saw in Figure 3.2 that there was no clear relationship between profitability and overall sales or market share. But if we plot average Strategic Market Position against profitability where this is available, we see that there is a correlation. See Figure 3.8.

In 1992, Magnetek—a reasonably large player in the FHP

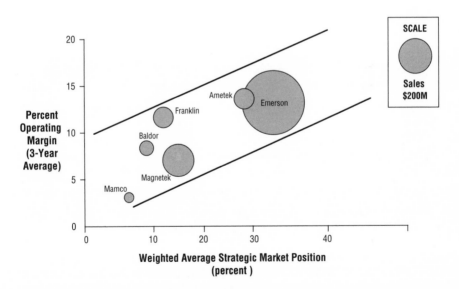

FIGURE 3.8 Market Share of Appropriately Defined FHP Segments Correlated to Overall Returns

industry—earned roughly a 7 percent return on its approximately $240 million in sales. But in the same year, Ametek—a significantly smaller player—earned 13 percent return on approximately $150 million in sales.

Wait a minute: The company that's *half as big* makes *twice as much?* How can that be? You've already heard the answer: The smaller, more profitable company avoids going head-to-head with the likes of mighty Emerson and GE. It steers most of its investments into segments where (among other things) the giants don't play. It *segments its industry strategically*, and puts more eggs into fewer, carefully chosen baskets. As a result, it has a much higher market share *in its chosen segments*. So yes, market share is good, but only when you get there strategically.

These differing approaches partly account for the variation in the two companies' shareholder returns from 1992 to 2005, as summarized in Figure 3.9.

It's worth noting that in 1999, Magnetek waved the white flag, ex-

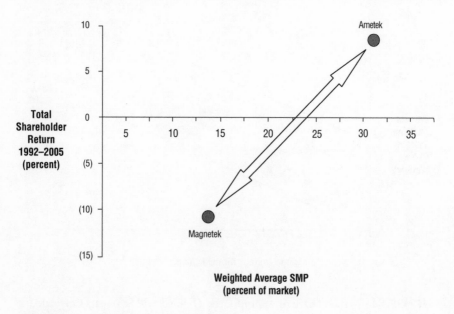

FIGURE 3.9 Ametek versus Magnetek

iting the FHP business entirely. (The divestiture, Magnetek explained in a recent annual report, was one of several designed to "tighten [our] business focus, strengthen [our] financial position, and improve [our] competitiveness."[3]) Meanwhile, Ametek has continued to compete successfully in the FHP business, although it has had to adapt to a more global market for many types of motors, with the corresponding need to shift some manufacturing overseas. The company has also expanded into other segments, such as aerospace and defense, where it has the ability to acquire or build strong differentiated positions that are more insulated from mass market global competitors.

Now that we have the concept of the Value Map on the table, look at Value Maps for several of the industries we visited in Chapter 1, starting with general merchandise retailing. Look at Figure 3.10.

This Value Map depicts the arena in which Wal-Mart and Kmart

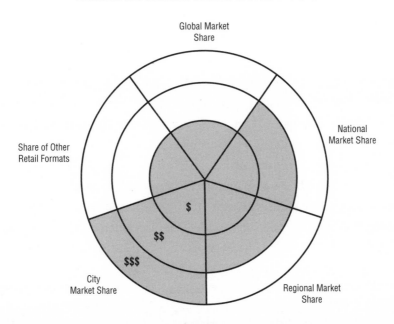

Economic and Customer Benefits of Scale or Share

FIGURE 3.10   Value Map: General Merchandising Retailing

slug it out. Note that I've assigned the most value to City Market Share, and that other kinds of geographic scale or share decline in importance as you get away from that location-specific measure. In other words, general merchandise and many other retailing sectors in the United States (and most other countries) can be thought of as the combination of dozens or scores of city markets; national market share is largely meaningless in determining the ability of a company to succeed and earn higher returns. This explains the existence of strong players—such as ABT Electronics in Chicago—that exist in only one or two city markets.

Share of Other Retail Formats is also mainly irrelevant to creating value in general merchandise retailing. According to this interpretation, therefore, all of Kmart's adventures into restaurant chains and specialty retailing—Builders Square, Sports Authority, Walden Books, PayLess Drug, and OfficeMax—were always going to be of dubious potential in terms of value creation.

While we're on the subject of the Great Retailing Wars, we should take a sideways look at Target, which has emerged as the second-biggest U.S. discounter in recent years. Target opened its first store in 1962—the same year as Wal-Mart and Kmart, curiously enough—and now operates nearly 1,400 Target and Supertarget stores in 47 U.S. states. I mention Target here because the upstart chain (almost anything is an "upstart" compared to Wal-Mart) has been very successful, particularly in urban locations where Wal-Mart is not as strong. The company offers more upscale, fashion-forward merchandise, relying on private-label offerings from big-name designers.[4] When people deliberately mispronounce the company name—"tar-*zhay*," rather than "*tar*-get"—they are in fact pointing toward this increasingly important differentiator.

The point? Just because you are up against a company with strong SMP doesn't mean that there aren't ways to challenge that company, especially in a business with disparate geographic segments as in retailing.

Target's emphasis on *style* hit a vulnerable spot for Wal-Mart, because of its relentless pursuit of low cost. Wal-Mart is now trying to develop more stylish and fashionable offerings, but it is a long way behind.

There is some indication that Target is also rethinking its store-location strategy. Although most of its stores today are still standalone, Big Box outlets along the Wal-Mart model, the company appears to be aiming toward a greater presence in enclosed malls. "The same people that shop at Neiman-Marcus shop at Target," explained one commercial real estate portfolio manager. "There's no reason why they shouldn't be in malls."[5] Will Target's strengths translate into mall retailing, or is this a separate strategic segment that could prove a distraction? It will be interesting to see how this strategy evolves. . . .

In Chapter 1, we also compared two airlines: Southwest and America West. Figure 3.11 is a Value Map for that industry context.

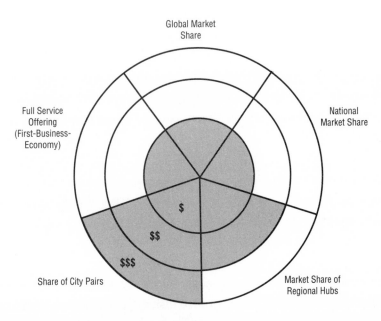

Economic and Customer Benefits of Scale or Share

FIGURE 3.11   Value Map: Airlines

You'll remember from our discussion of the relative fates of Southwest and America West that pursuing national market share—the traditional objective of the major legacy carriers, dating back to the days of tight government regulation of the industry—proved to be a poor strategy. National market share simply doesn't matter much. What *does* matter is *share of city pairs*—that is, the number of daily flights that you offer between two cities where travelers want to go.

Beyond the geographic dimensions, something else you will notice in the Value Map is relatively low benefits from a combined offering of premium and economy services. If this is true, it suggests that premium and economy services are separate strategic segments, and it should be possible to compete effectively in one without offering the other. Southwest took advantage of this with its single-cabin economy offering. At the other end of the spectrum, it is interesting to note that the past few years have seen the launch of several new single-cabin premium airlines targeting the transatlantic market.

Eos Airlines, founded in March 2003, is a privately held carrier that focuses exclusively on the transatlantic business traveler. Basically by taking 172 seats out of a 220-person-capacity Boeing 757, Eos has found a way to offer a relatively huge amount of space (21 square feet) to each of its 48 passengers—40 percent more space than is available in typical business-class cabins. Each seat on the modified plane offers podlike privacy to the traveler, and fully reclines into a private, six-foot-six-inch bed. The round-trip fare of $6,500, while not cheap, is certainly competitive. Before the Concorde was grounded, it was commanding just over $10,000 per seat, and the typical corporate business-class fare today runs around $6,000.[6]

According to Bonnie Reitz, Eos's president:

Eos will take the stress and hassle out of flying, and return to the "Concorde-like" experience of exclusivity and community that is missing from today's airline marketplace. All of our employees are passionate about serving today's discerning traveler, and doing so with a sophisticated, perceptive, confident, and human personality.[7]

Starting up a new airline in today's environment is a challenging (some might say heroic) task. It will be interesting to see how Eos and other premium-only airlines succeed in the years ahead.

Our last example of a Value Map—Figure 3.12—is based on the case study from Chapter 1 that focused on the game console industry. You'll recall that in this arena, Nintendo and Sega used to battle it out—at least until Sony and Microsoft dropped into the competition, and Sega dropped out.

Again, we see a value map with several important dimensions.

Economic and Customer Benefits of Scale or Share

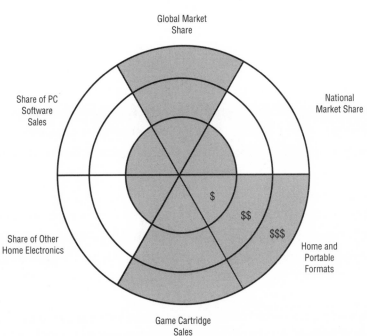

FIGURE 3.12 Value Map: Game Console Systems

Global market share is key; national market share is far less important. Having both home and portable formats is critically important, in part because it leverages your game-development costs over multiple platforms. Most important of all—as Nintendo was happy to discover—was being able to sell tons and tons of game cartridges through portable systems. If four 10-year-olds are playing your game in someone's media room, you want each of those kids to have his own copy of the game.

For the moment, don't worry too much about how to come up with the different dimensions or how to assess their relative importance. (We look at that in later chapters.) For now, I simply want you to start getting into the habit of thinking along the lines implied by the Value Map—a device I return to later in this chapter and throughout this book. Your ability to achieve SMP depends on your ability to determine the right Value Map for your own circumstances.

What, Why, How, Who, and When

Obviously, there are many ways to present a business framework like SMP with broad implications to strategy and operations. In the first part of this book, I choose to lay out this story in terms of *what* SMP is and *why* it is important (Chapters 1 and 2), and *how* to determine SMP (this chapter).

In Part II of this book, you find more detail on how to use this framework to improve many different aspects of decision making in your business. I also explain how organizational pressures often push companies and managers into making decisions contrary to the principles of SMP if there is not a clearly defined strategy for where and how to create value.

I begin Chapter 4 by explaining *who* should use SMP, and *when* they should use it.

II

How to Use Strategic Market Position to Chart Your Business Strategy

4

CAPTURING VALUE

THE BEST TOOL is useful only if two preconditions are met:
The right person is using it, and it's the right tool for the job
at hand.

We've seen that SMP can be a very useful tool. So who should
use SMP, and under what circumstances should they use it?

In discussing SMP with corporate audiences, I find that something interesting tends to happen. People tend to break the phrase
"strategic market position" into its component parts, and then conclude that SMP must belong to either the strategists or the marketers
within the organization. But this isn't true. Yes, SMP draws on concepts from both the strategy and marketing areas (as well as from finance, production, and other areas). But it doesn't belong to any
particular group. Ideally, SMP is used by a broad range of people
within the organization. It serves as a common language and as a
shared tool for decision making. In this chapter, I explore how that
ideal situation might be brought about in your company.

What about *when* to use SMP? This is the second question addressed in this chapter. Stated simply, there are two large categories of circumstances under which you should consider using SMP:

1. When your company is allocating limited resources to pursue growth opportunities in established lines of business.
2. When your company is considering entry into a new line of business, either through an internal product launch or through acquisition.

Who Should Use SMP?

SMP ≠ Market Segmentation

First, let's deal with a definitional issue that sometimes arises in preliminary discussions of SMP: the difference between "market segmentation" and "strategic market position." I raise it here because market segmentation is clearly a tool for the marketing and sales organization, whereas SMP—as noted previously—can have a much broader base of potential users across the organization for different types of decisions.

Look at Figure 4.1, which contrasts market segmentation and SMP.

The left-hand side of Figure 4.1 depicts a market that is divided into groups of customers (groups A, B, and C) who respond in similar ways to a specific marketing mix. So if the circle in Figure 4.1 represents the U.S. domestic beer market, for example, then group A responds to one kind of beer marketed in a certain way (premium ingredients, low-calorie, etc.), and group B responds to another kind of beer marketed in another kind of way.

It's worth noting, in passing, that market segmentation involves

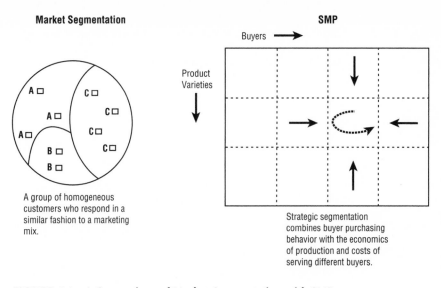

Market Segmentation

A group of homogeneous customers who respond in a similar fashion to a marketing mix.

SMP

Buyers →

Product Varieties

Strategic segmentation combines buyer purchasing behavior with the economics of production and costs of serving different buyers.

FIGURE 4.1   A Comparison of Market Segmentation with SMP

two seemingly contradictory processes. In its simplest sense, market segmentation means breaking down a market into subgroups that have similar interests or needs. This is *disaggregation*—a dividing action—whereby you try to get down to a level where you have a more or less homogeneous group of consumers, to whom you can speak in a single compelling marketing language.

But in practical terms, market segmentation also argues for *aggregation*. Advertising is expensive, both to produce and disseminate. This means that you need to assemble the largest possible group that will still respond homogeneously, and positively, to your marketing pitch. To return to the beer-drinkers' market: The disaggregation aspect of market segmentation means carving up the beer-drinking population into its component parts and making sure that you have a product for each of them: light, dark, low-carb, more/less/no alcohol, bottles/cans, 7-12-16-ounce servings, and so on. The aggregation part involves marketing in such a way that you pull together as many beer-drinking segments as possible behind your product lines (and your line extensions).

Corporate marketers charged with figuring this stuff out look for ways to reposition existing products to appeal to larger or faster-growing market segments and demographic groups. The General Motors campaign to refurbish the Oldsmobile marque—*not your father's Oldsmobile*—comes to mind: How can we persuade young people to plunk down their money for a century-old brand with a dowdy image? Anheuser-Busch has worked hard, over the years, at using advertising to defend existing market segments and to call forth new ones. Does our research tell us that young adults are drifting away from our beer in favor of more sophisticated (and less fattening) beverages? Okay; let's use cartoony frogs, dancing ants, and whatever else we can think of to make Bud Light their drink of choice.

These kinds of efforts—dancing ants, and so on—have a playful face. But in fact, using market segmentation to define and direct your market communications is deadly serious business. The consumer-products companies that are good at it tend to win, over the long run, and the companies that are bad at it tend to lose. And although I'm not in the business of creative marketing communications myself, I have a lot of respect for those people who earn a living doing this. But *market segmentation is a fundamentally different discipline from SMP*.

SMP, as the right-hand side of Figure 4.1 indicates, is a very different kind of tool. It combines buyer purchasing behavior—which is at the heart of market segmentation—with the economics of production and the costs of serving different buyers. It, too, may involve some kinds of disaggregation and reaggregation: What are the component parts of our strategic market segment, and how might they be reconciled to our competitive advantage?

Think back to the Sega/Nintendo example introduced in Chapter 1. The strategic market segment was electronic game consoles, and its building blocks were home consoles and handheld units. Within each of those submarkets, market segmentation undoubtedly occurred: For example, shaping products and campaigns aimed at the preteen home gaming aficionado, and shaping other products and campaigns aimed at adult gamers, and so on.

To that extent, at least, market segmentation can be seen as an activity that makes an important contribution to a strong SMP *after* the fundamental question of the SMP itself has been straightened out.

The Cast of Characters

So who is responsible for this straightening-out process? As I've already suggested, key players *across the organization* can and should take responsibility for SMP. Or, stated somewhat differently, key players across the organization will find it easier to do their jobs successfully if they understand and draw upon the basic principles of SMP.

One way to think about the cast of characters involved in SMP is to ask, *Where do your organization's ideas come from?* And more specifically, *What kinds of ideas come from which directions?* And even more specifically, *Where do good ideas come from?*

Look at Figure 4.2, which presents a spectrum of corporate players and their roles.

On the left-hand side of Figure 4.2, you see the sales management side of the organization. This is the group that is charged with maximizing the sales of your existing products and services. They worry about things like market segmentation, as described previously. They figure out how to deploy marketing resources—dollars and bodies—in the ways that are most likely to generate top-line revenues. Their focus is on new ways to sell the heck out of our existing bag of goods. If they are doing their jobs, the result is increased sales while still staying within the bounds of business as usual.

So they think about demographic segmentations. They think about channel segmentations. They think about geographic

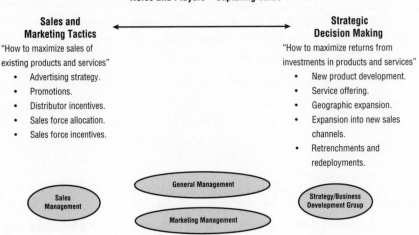

FIGURE 4.2   Roles and Players—Capturing Value

segmentations. The point of all this thinking is to answer the question, Are there places where we're simply overlooking sales? Are there gaps in our go-to-market strategy? If so, let's fill them. Are there places where we could be selling more if we had a better message or a better offering to the customer? If so, let's plug the hole and increase our overall sales.

The best salespeople tend to be highly aligned with the customer. So you can imagine the kinds of ideas that tend to emerge from this end of the spectrum. If the customer says, "You're only selling me blue ones, but I want red ones as well as blue ones," the salesperson comes back to Corporate with what he or she takes to be a compelling message from the marketplace: *We need to add red ones!* But where do we draw the line between a minor product variation and a new strategic segment? That's the job of the group on the right-hand side of Figure 4.2.

Here, you see something called the Strategy/Business Development Group, which is my catchall phrase for those individuals and groups who worry about *departures* from business as usual. Picture a small group of strategists ensconced in a suite of offices, pondering the mandate that has recently come down from the CEO's office: *Develop a plan to achieve and maintain a 15 percent average annual growth rate over the next 5 years* (which happens to be well above existing product sales, growing at 5 percent per year).

In response to this kind of pressure, the group asks questions like, How can we maximize returns on investments in new product or service lines, new geographic areas, or new channels? What new products should we be developing? Should we be entering new geographic markets? If we're already in the eastern United States, should we be going to the Midwest and the West? Should we be expanding overseas? Should we provide some service offerings to complement our products? Should we be expanding into new kinds of sales channels? So if we've historically been selling direct, should we think about some distribution partners? Should we think about redeploying, or retrenching in certain areas? Are there certain products that aren't working and which we should abandon in order to better focus our efforts on remaining products and new products? Rather than looking for incremental product-line variations, in other words, these planners are looking for when it makes sense to go beyond existing product lines.

Note the top-line overlap with their counterparts on the other end of the spectrum. One is a bottom-up source of ideas; the other (the strategists) is more top-down. Both tend to be revenue-driven. Either can be disconnected from the kinds of systematic thinking that informs SMP.

So far, we haven't talked much about the third group depicted in Figure 4.2. Sitting between the two ends of the spectrum—sometimes comfortably, sometimes not—are the marketing manager and general manager. They are sometimes mediators, sometimes interpreters, and sometimes the bearers of good or bad tidings from one end of the spectrum to the other. The marketing manager, who tends to be rewarded more on the basis of sales and less on the basis of profitability and value, shades toward the sales management end of the spectrum. The general manager, to whom the various functional areas report, may be more squarely in the middle of the spectrum. He or she is presumed to see the big picture, in part because his or her compensation generally includes a hefty bottom-line component. The general manager is the person on the receiving end of all the ideas—good and bad—that flow in from across the organization.

So that's the cast of characters. The opening question in this section was, In this mix, who should use SMP? The shortest answer is that—as the *S* in SMP implies—the strategy group should definitely use SMP. In a sense, SMP is a strategic decision-making tool, which helps answer the kinds of questions that are raised on the right-hand end of the spectrum. Conversely, SMP is *not* a tool that should be applied to day-to-day changes in advertising strategy or adjustments in distributor incentives—although as we show in Chapter 6, it should help prioritize where to invest advertising and incentive spending.

This brings us to a longer answer. I argue that SMP can be equally useful to people on the left-hand end of the spectrum. There are many, many situations in which a company's strategy is actually set through a series of incremental marketing and sales tactical decisions, rather than an explicit strategic direction. Why? Because most companies start out as intensely sales-driven and operationally inclined, and many simply stay in that mindset, even when a strategic component gets subsequently overlaid on the organization. So rather than try to swim against that strong tide, I argue that *the sales and marketing end of the spectrum should learn to think in SMP terms.*

Consider the case of one of my clients, a leading producer of machines and equipment for processing donated blood for transfusions. The division had a very successful product in the United States, and since the parent company had a global structure with operations in more than 30 countries, it was natural to start selling the blood machines overseas. The international sales started coming in, but so did a series of requests to the global organization: "We need a French language version of the operating manual." "We need new software in German." "We need a different connection point for the Italian market."

Each request seemed reasonable, but the problem was, they just kept coming: "We need a stronger service operation in Belgium." "We need to place machines in China on different terms from those in the United States." "Products for Japan need tighter manufacturing tolerances to satisfy the country's rigorous inspection process."

Before long, almost all the effort of the R&D group was being spent on product variations to meet global demands. When R&D prioritized its spending initiatives, the minor fixes always came to the top, because each country was always one fix away from unlocking its full sales potential. But it meant that there was nothing left to support more fundamental product development for the U.S. market.

Some years later, when all the spending on specific country requirements was taken into account, half the countries were found to be losing money. The United States accounted for the vast majority of the division's profits but was losing share as a result of underinvestment. If the company had taken a more strategic perspective, it would have realized that for a product this complex, with different clinical practices around the world, different countries were best thought of as separate strategic segments. It would have been much better to have a clear strategy targeting a strong SMP in a few countries, rather than spreading efforts across dozens of countries through hundreds of incremental decisions.

In other words, the right answer is not for the marketing organization to think in an SMP vacuum. (*We need to add red ones!*) Nor should the marketing people, whose ears tend to be closer to the ground than those of the "pure planners," delegate all the key decisions to the strategy and business development group. Instead, the right answer is for the marketing and general management organizations—and even, to some extent, the sales organization—to really grasp some of these fundamentals about strategic decision making, so that they can be on the lookout for when decisions should be thought about from a strategic perspective, as well as from a day-to-day sales and marketing perspective.

So where do ideas come from? They come from everywhere, all across the spectrum. Where do *good* ideas come from? They tend to come from people who think in terms of SMP.

A CASE IN POINT: EASY AIRLINES

Assume that you're a busy and practical-minded person and that you find all this talk about spectrums and idea-generation a little too general for your purposes. With that in mind, let's bring this discussion down to earth by means of a concrete example.

Say that you're the manager of route operations for Easy Airlines. (This is an imaginary carrier, but we get to a real-world version shortly.) You have the goal of maintaining profitability, but you also have a clear directive to achieve growth in the business. (Maybe you got one of those 15 percent annual growth guidelines from the corner office.) Easy has a strong market share in the two cities it currently serves: Springfield and Lincoln. On a regular basis, you're hearing from some of your key corporate accounts that Easy needs to offer service in additional cities. In addition, your modest sales force is delivering a more specific version of the same message: *We need to start offering service to Bay City.*

Well, is this a good idea? Does it conform to SMP principles?

You've read in previous chapters that the particular definition of "market share" that you embrace is critically important. In the airline industry, should you be looking at national market share, global market share, share of departures from a particular city, or some other definition?

Once again, this is important because a particular growth initiative may cause a company's average market share to move in different directions, depending on the definitions used. Yes, a decision to add new daily flights to serve Bay City (where you currently have no market share) might cause your national market share to increase. At the same time, however, the *weighted* city-by-city average market share could easily decrease at the same time. Table 4.1 shows a simplified example of how this can occur.

National market share is calculated as total Easy flights divided by total flights for all markets (100 ÷ 5,000, for the current position). Weighted average city share is calculated by multiplying Easy's market share by the number of Easy flights in each city, and then dividing by the total Easy flights in all cities. For the current position, this is 50 percent × 50 for Springfield plus 50 percent × 50 for Lincoln, all divided by 100, which yields a 50 percent weighted average city share.

Now look at the result of the proposed growth strategy. Although it will certainly increase your national market share, adding flights to serve Bay City will reduce Easy Airlines' competitive strength and profitability. Why? Because a higher proportion of your sales are now coming from low market-share cities, which, as you discover when you dig a little deeper into airline economics, are also much less profitable.

Does that mean that Easy should just resign itself to staying where it is and not growing? Almost certainly, the answer is no. (For one thing, that mandate for 15 percent annual growth hasn't gone

TABLE 4.1 Easy Airlines Example

Current Position

	Number of Easy Airlines Flights	Total Number of Flights	Easy Airlines Shares
Springfield	50	100	50%
Lincoln	50	100	50%
Bay City		1,000	0%
Other		3,800	0%
Total	100	5,000	
National Market Share		2%	
Weighted Average City Share			50%

Proposed Growth Strategy

	Number of Easy Airlines Flights	Total Number of Flights	Easy Airlines Shares
Springfield	50	100	50%
Lincoln	50	100	50%
Bay City	100	1,000	10%
Other		3,800	0%
Total	200	5,000	
National Market Share		4%	
Weighted Average City Share			30%

away.) The key is to think about strategic options in SMP terms. For Easy, these could include:

- Adding even more flights from Springfield and Lincoln to increase share even more.
- Entering other second-tier markets where Easy has the potential to achieve strong share.
- Partnering with an airline that is strong in Bay City so that Easy can compete effectively even with a low share of flights.

Obviously, this is a much-simplified example, constructed to make a point. But it grows out of analyses that my firm has conducted for a number of U.S. domestic and international airlines.

Figure 4.3 helps make the point that the same SMP principles

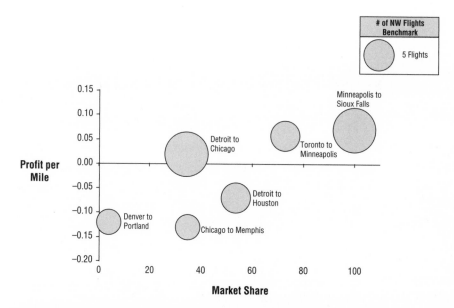

FIGURE 4.3 Northwest Share versus Profit on Select Routes
Data Source: Official Airline Guide, company financials, interviews with flight agents.

that underlie the Easy example also are at work in the real world. It shows a rough approximation of Northwest Airlines' market share versus profit on a number of city-pair routes that Northwest serves.[1]

What's going on here? Well, you can see that these city pairs pretty much follow the principles illustrated in the Easy Airlines example. The higher your market share in a given city pair, the more profitable your traffic between those two cities is likely to be.

WHEN SHOULD YOU USE SMP?

The Easy Airlines example actually straddles the two questions with which I opened this chapter:

1. Who should use SMP?
2. Under what circumstances should they use it?

Obviously, the manager of route operations needs to be thinking in SMP terms, and so should anyone else who has influence over Easy's growth strategy. More broadly, the SMP screen should be called upon whenever someone proposes a significant new avenue for growth.

As noted earlier, this can mean either substantial commitments of time, money, and energy to existing product or service lines, or it can mean the sort of stair-step departure that a merger or acquisition tends to represent. In the balance of this chapter, we look at one example from each of these domains.

Allocating Resources for Growth

For our first example, let's look at an industry that's been in the news a lot recently: the energy industry. How would you apply the logic of

SMP in the context of oil and gas exploration and production? Backing up a step further: *Would* you?

Conceivably, some people would argue that you would not. They would argue that the main growth driver in the oil and gas exploration and production industry is your success rate in avoiding dry holes (through luck or otherwise) and that the discipline of SMP therefore does not apply.

Alternatively, they might argue that global scale and a strong balance sheet are the most important contributors to success. The investments needed to compete in oil and gas exploration and production are huge and the uncertainties and challenges that exist in this business are equally enormous. As a result—the argument might go—it's extremely important for a company in this industry to be large enough to be able to absorb capital expenditures on the order of billions of dollars. In addition, since most of the reserves in locations that are easy to work have already started to dry up, companies now have to go to geographically and geopolitically difficult places from which to extract oil and natural gas. Given the risky and challenging nature of this business, investors might conclude, the ability to be able to leverage global scale is the key driver of success.

This might be the conventional wisdom and, if so, it would not be totally wrong. Global scale *is* important. But when the industry is seen through the lens of SMP, global scale turns out not to be the most important value driver. In fact, economies of production—and therefore profitability and shareholder value—are driven by a much more local factor: *scale within a drilling basin*. Why? To state it simply, the company that has a large-scale operation within a specific region will develop greater expertise in understanding the geology of the region, be able to develop better, more cost-effective local infrastructure, and be in a position to gain a competitive advantage in delivering the product once it has been taken out of the ground.

That being said, vertical integration is no longer an important factor in the industry. (These factors do change over time.) There was a time when all of the major oil and gas companies were completely integrated—from exploration and production all the way through to refining, distribution, and retailing. But it has become increasingly obvious that with efficient trading operations and the efficient market for transfer of product between one part of the value chain and another, producers don't need to be fully integrated in order to be highly successful. Conversely, if you *are* still fully integrated, that isn't going to create a big advantage for you versus companies that are focused on one part of the value chain or another.

The relative weight of these different factors is captured in Figure 4.4, which is a Value Map for the energy industry.

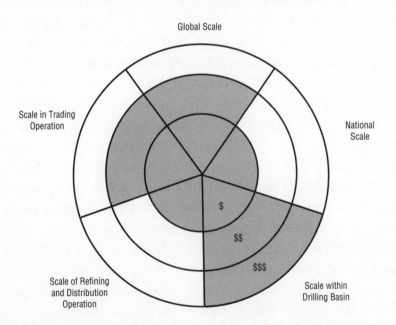

Economic and Customer Benefits of Scale or Share

FIGURE 4.4   Value Map: Oil and Gas Exploration and Production

To ground this general analysis in specifics, we can compare two real-life companies: Anadarko Petroleum Corporation and Phillips Petroleum Company.

First, a quick snapshot of the two companies. Founded in 1959 and headquartered in Houston, Anadarko is one of the world's largest independent oil and gas exploration and production companies, with about 80 percent of its reserves located in the United States in 1996 (primarily midcontinent in Kansas, Oklahoma, and Texas). Beginning in the mid 1990s, Anadarko undertook significant exploration of some strategic international locations, and particularly in Algeria's Sahara. The company began international production in May 1998.

Phillips Petroleum Company—older, bigger, and better known—was founded in 1917 with headquarters in Oklahoma. Its main production areas are more widely dispersed across the globe than Anadarko's: in the United States, United Kingdom, Norway, Canada, Nigeria, and off the coast of China. In 1996—the year of our comparison—only about 30 percent of Phillips' crude oil was produced in the United States.

Phillips production in 1996 was 234,000 barrels per day of oil/natural gas liquids (NGL) and 1,527 million cubic feet per day of natural gas. Anadarko, meanwhile, averaged only about 28,000 barrels per day of oil and NGL and 451 million cubic feet per day of natural gas. As you can see in Figure 4.5, Phillips is substantially larger and much stronger than Anadarko in terms of market share in their relevant global markets.[2] In production, Phillips has about 1.1 percent of global market share (in the markets where they play), where Anadarko has less than 0.2 percent.

Based on similar analyses in earlier chapters, you can probably anticipate that I describe the information in Figure 4.5 as relatively worthless. To understand SMP, we need to consider a different definition of "market share": the one previously highlighted in our energy-industry Value Map, which is *the scale of the two companies' operations in*

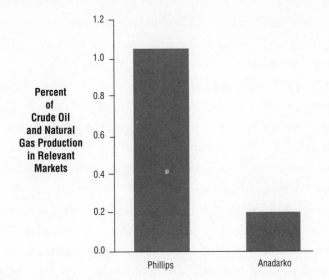

FIGURE 4.5   Phillips Petroleum versus Anadarko Petroleum: Market Shares (1996)
Data Source: Company financials, EIA.

their respective drilling basins. As can be seen in Figure 4.6, while Phillips has concentrated its operations in some regions, they have not focused their resources on any particular basin. As a result, the company is pretty well spread out over a number of geographic markets and has a low market share in each of them.

In contrast, Anadarko has focused its efforts in Kansas and Oklahoma and has established a very strong market position in those regions. Its concentration in Kansas has given it an advantage in terms of better information, larger operational scale, and stronger position in negotiating with suppliers. Therefore, Anadarko's overall strategic market position (weighted average of the market shares in each of the geographic regions) is actually stronger than that of Phillips.

This stronger market position is evident in shareholder returns from investing in Phillips versus investing in Anadarko. If we look

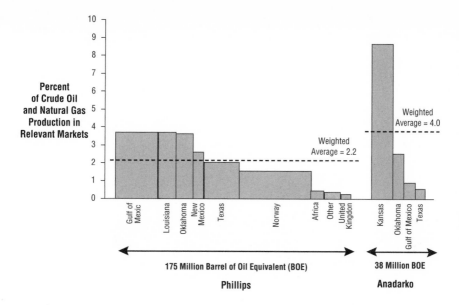

FIGURE 4.6 Phillips Petroleum versus Anadarko Petroleum: Strategic Market Position (1996)
Data Source: Company financials, EIA.

at performance over the 1996–2001 period, we can see in Figure 4.7 that total shareholder returns on investing in Anadarko were approximately 5 percent higher than investing in the S&P 500 Oil and Gas index, whereas the returns from investing in Phillips were actually about 6 percent lower than if one were to invest in the S&P index.

Again, you can see how "thinking SMP" increases your chances of success in a highly competitive context. For the most part, oil and gas exploration companies have to bid on drilling rights. How do they determine those bids? Well, one approach—which appears to be the one favored by Phillips and other industry giants—is simply to assign a net present value (NPV) to anticipated reserves in the ground, and bid based on that NPV assumption. Under this approach, you bid for

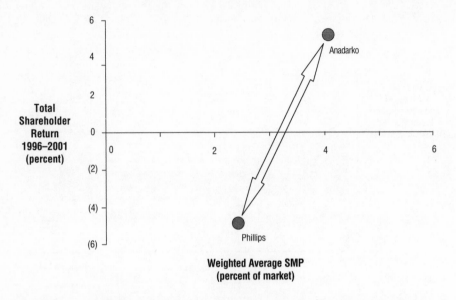

FIGURE 4.7   Phillips Petroleum versus Anadarko Petroleum: Value Creation
Data Source: Bloomberg.

drilling rights in auctions all over the world and hope to win your fair share of them. The alternative—which appears to be the approach employed by Anadarko—is *to bid more aggressively in basins where you already have a dominant position*, and less aggressively (if at all) outside of those basins.

The point of this quick tour through a complex industry is, once again, to make the point that SMP can be a very valuable tool for figuring out how and when to make key investments in ongoing lines of business. And my ulterior motive in picking the oil and gas industry is to make the point, once again, that the logic of SMP can be—and should be—applied almost everywhere.

Thinking Through Complementary Acquisitions

To continue in this vein of finding SMP at work in unexpected places, look at an acquisition in an entirely different industry: the acquisition of Mail Boxes Etc. (MBE) by United Parcel Service (UPS).

Again, start with some industry background. At the outset of the twenty-first century, heavyweights Federal Express (FedEx) and United Parcel Service shared nearly 70 percent of the package-shipping market and competed head-to-head in the business to business (B2B) segment. In this segment, both companies offered a full range of services to their business customers, not only picking up boxes at the point of shipment, but also providing boxes, labels, and even software for automating labeling and tracking on the customers' own PCs.

At this same time, the package-shipping market was going through some important new developments, mainly driven by the explosive growth in e-commerce. Online consumer sales in the United States were expected to rise from $5 billion in 1998 to $35 billion in 2002, and as a result, home delivery was an increasingly important link in the value chain. Internet retailers relied (and continue to rely) upon third-party package delivery services, particularly UPS and FedEx.

But out of this changing landscape was emerging an unmet need. Suppose a given shipment was in error, or an online customer simply decided to take advantage of the retailer's return policy. How was he or she supposed to *return* the unwanted package? Neither UPS nor FedEx was very interested in making individual pickups at residences—a service that would never pay its own way. Of course, the residential customer could go down to the local post office, but the U.S. Postal Service was not particularly service-oriented, and post office hours didn't always coincide with residential customer schedules. As an alternative, the residential customer could try to make his or her way out to a UPS or FedEx depot, but these were almost always located in some out-of-the-way industrial park and by definition weren't particularly consumer-oriented.

So UPS and FedEx faced an interesting strategic challenge. Comfortable and successful in their established SMPs—the business package-shipping market—they now had to decide whether it made sense to define that SMP more broadly to include consumer services. If they did choose to expand in that direction, *how* would they do it? Although they could certainly ship residential customers' packages at competitive rates, setting up a nationwide network of storefronts to compete with the local post offices would be prohibitively expensive. And—as FedEx had realized in its founding era—a partial network wouldn't fit the bill. The only way to get residential customers to use *your* service was to be (just about) everywhere.

On March 2, 2001, UPS revealed its solution to this dilemma: the acquisition of Mail Boxes Etc. for $191 million. San Diego-based MBE (a division of U.S. Office Products) was a franchised operation that then consisted of some 4,300 retail locations, including nearly 900 centers overseas. At root, the MBE storefront—first introduced in 1980 as an alternative to the local post office—was a convenient drop-off point for the occasional shipper.[3] MBE accepted a shipper's package on behalf of UPS, FedEx, or some other shipping company and marked up the price of the shipping. At the same time, however, MBE had developed a range of ancillary services—providing packing and shipping materials, for example—which not only made for happier customers, but also pushed up MBE's margins.

By acquiring MBE, therefore, UPS was gaining a distribution network that would more than pay its own way and, of course, would pump new volumes of packages into the existing UPS infrastructure. (Not surprisingly, UPS henceforth would be the preferred shipper at your local MBE outlet.) "This is a strategic fit that complements UPS's existing access channels and underscores the common vision MBE and its franchisees share with UPS to meet the changing needs of customers," said UPS chairman and chief executive Jim Kelly at the time. "The alignment of our brands and the retail expertise MBE and its franchisees bring to UPS will open doors of opportunity for us to better serve small businesses and consumers around the world."[4]

Kelly further explained that the transaction would strengthen the important physical link UPS has to a growing segment of retail customers, such as Internet consumers, small-office and home-office owners in an increasingly mobile, technology-connected society. Finally, Kelly said, the acquisition would allow UPS to develop new opportunities in such areas as small business services, e-commerce, and financial services.

In retrospect, it's clear that the acquisition redefined the customer segments UPS served and—by extension—broadened and strengthened UPS's SMP. UPS now owns more than 23 percent of the consumer market and expects that market to grow more rapidly than other parts of the business in the future.

In fact, in the half-decade since the acquisition, UPS has enjoyed growth in excess of 7 percent in a market that has been growing at roughly 5 percent annually. And, since the acquisition, UPS stock—which had been trending down—has jumped from about $55 per share to more than $70 per share.

Sometimes imitation is the sincerest form of validation. Seeing UPS's successes growing out of its retail presence, FedEx followed suit in February 2004 with the acquisition of Kinko's Inc. A key goal of the acquisition, according to FedEx, was to achieve a "broader reach to customers of all sizes."[5] The result of this acquisition—combined with the earlier acquisition by UPS—has been a substantial increase in the biggest shippers' combined share of a growing market. See Figure 4.8.

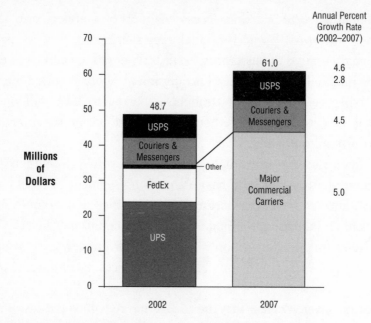

FIGURE 4.8   Priority, Overnight, and Package Mail Market Share
Data Source: Business Communications Company (BCC).

In 2003, UPS management issued a statement about the success of the SMP-broadening effort (to use my terminology):

> The [2003] rebranding of about 3,000 Mail Boxes Etc. centers into The UPS Store—the largest such rebranding in franchising history—has increased UPS volume through the stores by more than 100 percent and also more than doubled franchise applications. The UPS Store is one part of an increased focus on improving retail access points and offers an effective vehicle for pursuing the retail shipping segment now controlled by the U.S. Postal Service.[6]

How much value did UPS uncover through its acquisition of Mail Boxes Etc.? Since the deal closed in 2001, UPS's total return to shareholders has averaged 10 percent per year, while the overall S&P has delivered a negative 3 percent annual return. That excess return translates into $9.7 billion of value created for shareholders. If you were to allocate just half of this to the faster growth achieved through MBE, that equates to $4.8 billion, or 24 times UPS's cost for the acquisition.

LOOKING AHEAD

This brings us to the end of our who and when discussion. Obviously, I'm advocating the broadest possible base of SMP thinking, across the organization. Most companies don't lack for ideas, but lots of companies have trouble separating the good ideas from the bad ones. Embracing SMP across your company will increase the percentage of good ideas in the overall idea stream. And putting this improved idea stream through a formal SMP review process can only improve your odds still further.

Assume that you now have a feel for SMP and its whos and whens. If so, you're probably wondering about the hows. That is the subject of our next chapter.

5

DOING THE DETECTIVE WORK

W E'VE TALKED ABOUT who should use SMP and when. Now, as we continue to investigate how to use SMP to chart your business strategy, let's look at how you gather the necessary market data and develop the competitive insights to determine your business's SMP. It is critical to get this step right. As we show later in this chapter, drawing the wrong conclusions about the Value Map and Strategic Market Position can lead to very different outcomes for company performance.

Determining SMP involves art as well as science and is different for each business. You've seen that in the Value Maps we have looked at so far there are different dimensions for which we consider the benefits of scale or scope. The reason is that different attributes create advantages in costs or customer preferences for different businesses. This makes it harder for you to figure out your SMP, but it also makes it harder for competitors, too. If your business is able to figure out your SMP, it's likely that you will have a real advantage against competitors who don't have this understanding.

Every effort to do the detective work for an SMP implementation is necessarily different and relies heavily on information collected on costs, customers, and competitors. In this chapter, I focus on how to use this research to develop insights on SMP. At the back of the book, I also include an Appendix, which provides some of the detail on data sources you are likely to want to use in gathering the information needed to make sure that your SMP insights are built on facts and hard evidence rather than just guesses and intuition. This is important, because often the greatest wins in SMP come through developing insights on the market that differ from the conventional wisdom held by the rest of the industry. I suggest that you read the summary treatment that's contained in the following pages and then—when the time comes to do the real detective work—make your way through the denser material in the Appendix.

At the same time, I also include toward the end of this chapter a detailed case study, which will give you the benefit of the details referred to previously. The industry is the health-club business. So I open the chapter with a hypothetical take on the industry, and then—in the second half of the chapter—get down to real-life specifics. In that second round, we look at a well-known national player—Bally Total Fitness—and a lesser-known regional player, Town Sports International Holdings (TSI). One of these players understands SMP and the other doesn't.

IN THE CONFERENCE ROOM

In Chapter 4, we talked about how the decision-makers within a company often face no shortage of ideas and opportunities for growth and improvement. In many cases, the challenge is not to find something interesting to pursue, but rather to choose among alternatives that seem to be equally promising.

Place yourself in the conference room of an imaginary company—American Fitness—where a planning session is well underway. At this point in the discussion, most people in the room have agreed that their company is on a pretty good strategic track. In advance of the meeting, they've scoped out the competition and they're convinced that they've hit upon the right mix of services, which the company is continuing to fine-tune. (For example, their centers emphasize Pilates classes and aerobic classes and equipment, but downplay weight training. The tanning facilities at most of their centers recently have been expanded, with positive results.) American's marketing seems to be connecting very well with its target audience: mainly singles in their twenties and thirties with disposable income. By concentrating its facilities in several major cities in the Northeast, American has leveraged its resources (financial and managerial) very effectively, to the extent that the company has money in the bank and enjoys one of the strongest balance sheets in the industry.

In short, a successful strategy, well executed, has made American into a regional powerhouse. Everyone around the table is committed to a strategy of continuing growth. (There's talk of an IPO several years down the road, and continued growth will be critical to a successful public offering.) What has emerged at the table, though, is a disagreement over the *geographic* strategy that American should pursue.

One group believes that the time has come for American to make the leap to a national presence. This group argues that the economies of scale that have helped make American a strong regional player will provide even greater benefits on a national scale. A faster national rollout, they argue, will reinforce the American brand and increase the odds that existing members who move to a new city can stay in the fold.

To pull off this fast rollout, this group argues, American has to establish toeholds in selected new markets around the country. It's time to invest some of that war chest in the next phase of the company's existence. Yes, they admit, this may hurt the bottom line in the short-term, but it's the only way to sustain American's tradition of robust revenue growth. They talk in compelling terms about first-mover advantage—being the first big player into city markets that are currently underserved—and also about increased economies of scale. *Everything we've learned on the regional level*, they argue, *can only help us on the national level.*

If the group had stopped to draw a Value Map of the health-club industry, it would have looked something like Figure 5.1. According to this Value Map, the country is best thought of as a single strategic

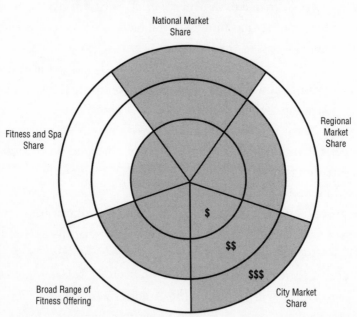

Economic and Customer Benefits of Scale or Share

FIGURE 5.1   Value Map: Health Clubs (a)

market, with cost economies and customer benefits driven by national market share.

But there's another point of view. The other group at the table is arguing for a significantly different geographic strategy. Rather than scattering relatively isolated centers across the country, they contend, American should stick with the strategy that has made it successful to date. True, there might be some marginal economies of scale to be gained by going national, but they would be overwhelmed by the costs of the leap to a national presence.

American, this group contends, should continue to consolidate its regional position in the Northeast, which appears to be nowhere close to saturation. To the extent that American needs to expand its geographic footprint, the company should build out from the edges of its existing regional base. It should pursue opportunities only where it has the ability to build scale quickly

This group's Value Map looks something like Figure 5.2.

For American, the good news is that the two SMPs represented by these two Value Maps are different only along one dimension: the geographic dimension. The bad news is that this debate can't be resolved on the basis of instinct alone. Both camps at the table are making valid points. Yes, there are real risks inherent in departing from the tried-and-true patterns of the past. But there are also real risks inherent in refusing to look forward, and—as a result—failing to invent new ways of doing business.

So whose view of the industry is right? What is needed to answer this question is some good old-fashioned detective work. As I take you through the process for determining SMP, think about two things: (1) How it applies to your own business and (2) how it applies to the health-club example I have laid out here. Once I have taken you through the general framework, we return to the specifics of the health-club industry, and you will see if your instincts were right.

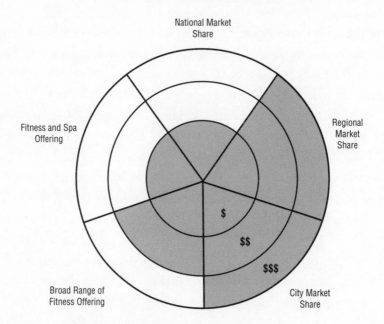

Economic and Customer Benefits of Scale or Share

National Market Share

Regional Market Share

Fitness and Spa Offering

$

$$

$$$

Broad Range of Fitness Offering

City Market Share

FIGURE 5.2   Value Map: Health Clubs (b)

The Five Steps for Determining SMP

How do you do the detective work for determining SMP? I break the process down into five basic steps:

1. Define the possible strategic segmentation dimensions (that is, the compass points of the Value Map that you've seen in earlier chapters.)
2. Score those dimensions according to their relative values.
3. Define the relevant strategic segments based on the Value Map scores.
4. Plot your company's and your competitors' SMPs.
5. Test your conclusions and refine if needed.

As you read through the descriptions of these five steps in the following pages, think realistically about your company's capabilities and capacities. Some companies are quite capable of doing the detective work on their own; others may need to get help from the outside. You will make that call based on the specifics of (1) your company and (2) your competitive context.

Step One: Define the Possible Strategic Segmentation Dimensions

The compass points of the Value Map include a number of dimensions that are important to competitors in a given market. (The concentric circles, discussed in the next section, gives you a way to assign relative importance to those various dimensions.)

The default assumption—on the table at American Fitness's planning session, and at lots of similar sessions that I've sat in on—is that *bigger is better*. But as we've already seen in Chapter 2, bigger is sometimes worse. So we have to come up with a more useful strategic framework. Exactly *how* and *where* do economies of scale, or benefits to customers resulting from scale, arise in this industry? The list of plausible answers to this question are the dimensions that you will include on the Value Map.

At this point, these dimensions are only hypotheses. As a result, it's better to err on the side of comprehensiveness. What we're looking for here are the dimensions along which products and buyers differ, in ways that carry important structural or value-chain implications. Typically, there are four major classes of possible candidates for inclusion as Value Map dimensions (which might be termed "segmentation variables"):

1. Product variety
2. Buyer type
3. Channel
4. Geographic buyer location

Table 5.1 summarizes a range of possible segmentation attributes that come under these four classes.

As you review these different categories in your specific circumstances, ask yourself whether scale across these categories creates the potential for higher profitability. Take Product Variety, for example. Is it important for you to be able to offer one-stop shopping to your customers, or is that simply irrelevant in your situation? In the same product-variety category, how does manufacturing scale come into play? In Chapter 3, we talked about the fractional horsepower (FHP) motor industry, which is characterized by (among other things) a wide variety of products across a range of signifi-

TABLE 5.1   Segmentation Attributes

Product Variety	Buyer type	Channel	Buyer Geographic Location
Physical size	*Industrial*	Direct vs. distributed	Local/Regional
Price level	Buyer's industry	Direct mail/retail	Climate zones
Features	Buyer's strategy	Distributors/Brokers	Development
Technology/Design	Technical ability	Types of distributor	
Inputs used	OEM vs. user	Exclusivity	
Packaging	Vertical integration		
Performance	Decision maker		
New vs. After-market	Size		
Product vs. Service	Ownership		
Bundled/Unbundled	Financial strength		
	Consumer		
	Demographics		
	Lifestyle		
	Language		
	Decision maker		
	Purchase process		
	Purchase occasion		

cantly different technologies. You might decide that it would be advantageous to offer one-stop shopping—and maybe your sales force is telling you that—but the test is not whether additional product varieties would be nice to have. The real test is whether having the additional product offerings would create a significant competitive differential between two companies that are similar in every other respect. As we discussed in Chapter 3, AC, DC, and Universal motor technologies have different manufacturing requirements and most OEM motor customers do not purchase multiple motor types. There are therefore very few economies of scale to be derived from the combined offering.

Buyer Type and Channel speak to these same sorts of issues. What buyer types and channels hold the most potential for delivering profits to you if you scale up in their direction? If you already specialize in supplying hermetically sealed motors to OEMs that manufacture refrigerators, for example, should you step sideways into selling sealed motors to the Department of Defense? Are they in the same segment, or—for whatever reason—do they appear to be in different segments?

And finally, look at Geographic Buyer Location. Who's where, wanting what? In the previous chapter, we looked at the critical importance of city pairs to profitability in the airline industry. Is there a natural constituency of buyers who want to fly from Portland (Maine) to Portland (Oregon)? Will increasing the number of flights on that route mean greater convenience to customers and lower operating costs for the airline (assuming it can keep the extra flights full)?

Remember: You do not have to have answers to all the questions we have discussed in this section at this stage of the game. All we are doing is identifying segmentation dimensions that are potentially important in your industry. For now, these dimensions are just a set of hypotheses that need to be tested.

Step Two: Assign Relative Values to the Strategic
Segmentation Dimensions

So far, we've been talking about only the skeleton of your emerging Value Map. Now we have to complete it, by assigning scale-and-scope values to each of the dimensions that you've identified as seemingly relevant to your particular industry dynamics.

There are two categories of value that we can consider in assigning value benefits to the different dimensions. The first category includes *economic* benefits of scale or scope. If you do more of something or grab a larger market share, do you get better at it? Do you buy your inputs cheaper? Do you manufacture it more cost effectively? Is making a whole lot of AC/FHP motors much better than making fewer? (In this case, yes.) Economies of scale make things less costly to supply and therefore more appealing—and/or more profitable. This is Economics 101, but it's more applicable to some circumstances than to others. Figure 5.3 lays out some of the

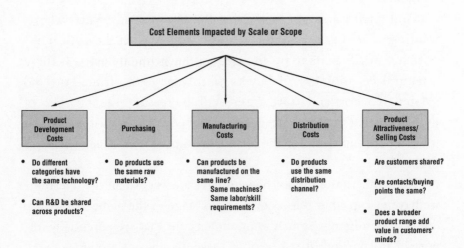

FIGURE 5.3   Cost Elements Impacted by Scale or Scope

typical cost elements for a company's operations to help in considering how these are impacted by scale or scope.

The second category includes *customer* benefits of scale or scope. Again, if you do more of something or grab a larger market share, do you make your customers happier as a result? If you do, you can (1) count on their loyalty and (2) charge them more than would otherwise be the case.

One way of thinking about rating the dimensions is to ask the question: *If two companies are the same along every other dimension, is adding scale along this particular dimension likely to be an advantage?* If the answer is yes, the outer circle sector is shaded for that dimension.

Look at the FHP Value Map in Figure 5.4, which we first saw in Chapter 3.

I've already explained the scoring on the concentric circles in Chapter 3, but to summarize: The outer circle is shaded for scale *within* a particular motor type, and only the inner circle is shaded for scale *across* motor types. Say that Company A has a 20 percent share of *all* the different DC motor types from 1 volt to 20 volts, and Company B has a 20 percent share only of DC motors up to 12 volts. Does Company A have an advantage? Certainly, because DC motors of all different voltages and sizes can be made on the same manufacturing line. R&D is leveraged, investments in manufacturing are leveraged, and—most likely—distribution networks are exploited more effectively.

Now assume that both Companies A and B have a 20 percent share of the DC motor market. Further assume that Company B also has a 20 percent share of the AC motor market. Does that give it a significant advantage over Company A? Not necessarily. The R&D is too different; the technologies (and therefore the manufacturing processes) are too different. There may be some leveraging of general overhead costs, but this is not enough to provide a significant competitive advantage.

Look at the west and northwest dimensions of Figure 5.4. As explained in Chapter 3, scale and scope *within an end-user market* are important. (If you supply some of the AC motors to a toy maker, you want to supply *all* of those motors, because the requirements in terms of quality and rated life are likely to be very similar.) But note the low score for the northwest dimension: Scale and scope across different end-user markets—consumer motors plus industrial motors—don't get you much, because the requirements are too different. On the face of it, these appear to be different strategic market segments.

If this were easy, people would get it right all the time (and there'd be no need for a book about how to get it right). So what if

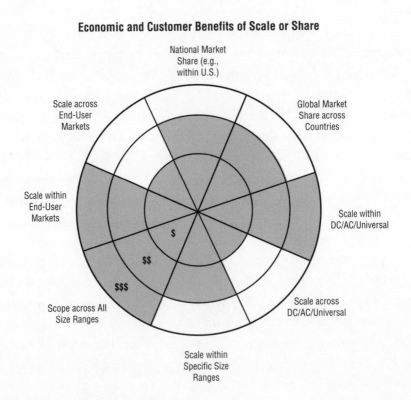

Economic and Customer Benefits of Scale or Share

FIGURE 5.4   Value Map: FHP Motors

you're not *sure* whether adding a new product line to your existing operation makes sense? How do you decide whether the new products lie in the same strategic market segment or lie outside where we risk being a weak player against larger-scale competitors? Here's where a tool that I call the "50 percent rule" may prove useful. Simply stated, *if more than 50 percent of the value-added in two product lines are shared, then they are best thought of as being in the same strategic market segment* (in other words, they'd earn a high score on the Value Map for adding scale across the two categories). If the value-added is less than 50 percent, the two product lines would score low on the Value Map and would be best thought of as two separate strategic market segments.

Look at Table 5.2, which illustrates how you might determine

TABLE 5.2 Cost Sharing Example: Automotive versus Industrial Clutches

Cost Categories	A. Percent of Total Value-Added (%)	B. Percent of Cost Sharing (%)	A × B (%)	Comment
Direct labor	50	30	15	Different volumes, different production lines.
Manufacturing overhead	20	40	8	Could be produced in same factory, but would need to be separate group.
Research/ Engineering	10	50	5	Some sharing of engineering.
Sales	10	0	0	Different customers.
General and administrative	10	80	8	Some sharing of general overloads.
Total	100		36	

whether the kinds of clutches used in industrial applications are in the same strategic market segment as automobile clutches.

Obviously, there's a false precision to that 36 percent figure at the bottom of the table. Every entry in the table involves a certain amount of informed guesswork. Nevertheless, since the 50 percent rule has not been met, Figure 5.2 should give you pause about branching out from automotive clutches into industrial clutches. They don't appear to be in the same strategic market segment.

It's conceivable that your sales force will argue that in the case of a close call—say, if the bottom line in this example were closer to 45 percent—the benefits to the customer are great enough to bump automotive clutches and industrial clutches into the same strategic market segment. Sales may argue that the company that offers both types of clutches has an advantage over the company that offers only one type.

Well, it is true that in some cases the benefits to customers may be enough to make two different product or service offerings best thought of as a single strategic market segment, even if there are only limited operating cost savings. So you might decide to test this argument. There are lots of ways to do so. Salespeople can be a useful source of information, but be careful of relying on them too much when you are considering a proposed new offering. Salespeople may not get unbiased answers when talking to customers about any new offering. A better approach is to see if any competitor has tried anything like this before and determine whether it worked. (There is not a lot under the sun that is brand-new.) Is the company with the expanded product line gaining market share? If their numbers are public, how do those numbers look? Can you call a few of their biggest customers and ask whether they're happier as a result of the expanded product line?

If the evidence from competitors is mixed, then the final approach is to survey your customers and potential customers in a systematic way, either using your own company's research organization or external resources if you do not have internal capabilities.

My firm was retained by a direct-mail fulfillment company to help them figure out whether to acquire an advertising agency in order to have a full-service offering to clients. (Fulfillment companies are the ones who actually print, fold, stuff, and mail those things that fill up your mailbox; advertising agencies are "upstream," writing the copy and designing the pieces that the fulfillment companies work with.) We surveyed current and potential customers and found that those customers would, indeed, prefer to deal with an integrated "direct mail advertising agency," mainly because they were tired of all the finger-pointing that tended to go on when something went wrong. With a single soup-to-nuts vendor, they told us, there would be one vendor (and hopefully, one point of contact) responsible for the whole process.

As you can see, there is a lot of judgment and research that may be required to define the Value Map for your company. And it is made more difficult because the final considerations will be different for each business. But if you do the detective work I have described, you will be well on your way to uncovering new value for your business.

Step Three: Define and Quantify the Relevant Strategic Segments

If you have defined the Value Maps correctly, then Step 3 is relatively straightforward. Quite simply, any breakdowns of the market that differ only a dimension that scores highly on the Value Map (i.e., have high benefits to scale or scope between the sectors) are best thought of as a single strategic segment. Any market sectors that are distinguished by an attribute scoring low on the Value Map are best thought of as separate strategic segments.

In the FHP motors example, the attributes on the Value Map with low scale benefits are scale across different motor types (DC,

AC, Universal) and scale across end-user markets. This means that the $5 billion motors business could in theory be broken down into 21 strategic segments (3 motor types × 7 end-user markets). In practice, when we quantify the dollar purchases along these breakdowns, we find that not all end-user markets use all three motor types in significant quantities (cars, for example, use 12 volt DC motors almost exclusively), so we end up with 14 strategic market segments. See Figure 5.5.

Creating a two-dimensional chart of your industry is an important step. It is most helpful if you scale each strategic segment such that its area is proportional to the sales or value-added in that segment. This is done by first breaking down the industry into bars, with the width of each bar proportional to the sales breakdown for one segmentation criterion (in this case, by end-user industry segment), and then segmenting the height of each bar according to the second criterion. If you have more than two segmentation criteria, you will

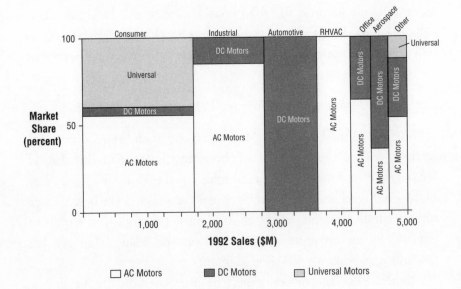

FIGURE 5.5   FHP Strategic Market Segments

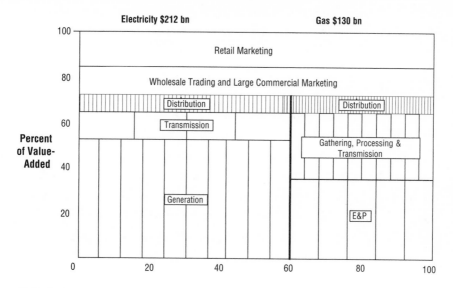

FIGURE 5.6   U.S. Energy Industry: Deregulated Scenario

need to break down the slices of each bar even further. As an example, Figure 5.6 shows a strategic segmentation breakdown for the U.S. energy industry in the event of further deregulation.

The benefits of creating this "strategic chessboard," as I call it, are threefold:

1. It provides an easy way to review and challenge your segmentation hypotheses. Does this look right? Are any of the implications counterintuitive? Are there any assumptions we should revisit?

2. It provides a sense of the scale of different strategic segments, so that you can easily see what is important (if you are a large company) or where you can find a defensible niche (if you have more limited resources).

3. If you draw the figure so that segments that are more similar are closer to each other, it provides a way to think about making moves into new strategic segments.

Step Four: Plot SMPs for Yourself and Your Competitors

Now comes the hard part: You have to locate yourself and selected key competitors within this framework, by breaking down their sales into the relevant strategic segments.

So where do these numbers come from? Publicly held companies are required to report their overall sales, but in many cases they guard very closely information about the *breakdown* of their sales by product line, and their market share. Privately held companies, of course, generally reveal far less than their publicly held counterparts. Again, you have to do the detective work.

Look again at the FHP motors market (Table 5.3). Suppose Magnetek has $232 million in sales, in an overall market of $3.7 billion. Well, we know that Magnetek has a 6 percent market share, but as explained in earlier chapters, this is a pretty useless number. We need to understand how those $232 million in sales are spread across the relevant SMPs.

The best place to start is the web sites and annual reports of individual companies, where available. (See Appendix for details.) Also helpful, again, are trade journals and analysts' reports. Working with the best available sources, you engage in a process of triangulation— filling in the blanks a little bit like you fill in the boxes in a crossword puzzle. Exactly which segments are those companies competing in? How do they talk about those segments in their public pronouncements? Is there any pattern to their recent acquisitions or divestitures? Can we learn anything about Magnetek from its suppliers' or customers' web sites?

TABLE 5.3 **Strategic Segmentation of FHP Motors Market**

Company	Public Information	
	Annual Sales ($M)	Market Share (%)
Magnetek	232	6%
Ametek	145	4%
Other	3,317	90%
Total	3,694	100%

	Strategic Segments		
	Magnetek Sales ($M)	Ametek Sales ($M)	Total Sales ($M)
AC Motor Segment			
Aerospace	15	0	36
Automotive	0	0	—
Office	0	5	25
Consumer	0	0	623
RHVAC	25	0	530
Industrial	148	21	954
Other	0	0	56
DC Motor Segment			
Aerospace	0	0	14
Automotive	0	0	785
Office	0	0	55
Consumer	0	0	76
RHVAC	0	0	—
Industrial	25	4	159
Other	19	10	44
Universal Motor Segment			
Consumer	0	105	337
Total	232	145	3,694

In real life, it often shakes out something like this: Of the 15 SMPs we're interested in, Magnetek competes in five of them. They're clearly weak in one, medium-strong in two others, and strong in the final two. Let's say that in the AC-Industrial SMP that adds up to $954 million, Magnetek is a strong player, which we guesstimate to translate into a 15 percent market share. In another, slightly smaller SMP—AC-RHVAC, adding up to $530 million— Magnetek is relatively weak, which we say translates into a 5 percent share. You basically need to tweak the six SMP numbers until they add up to something like $232 million in sales, in a way that best approximates everything that you've learned about Magnetek.

With this information in hand, you have in effect a picture of Magnetek's portfolio of strategic market positions. Finally, as the dotted horizontal lines in Figure 3.7 indicate, you want to calculate a weighted average of those SMPs to come up with an overall SMP for Magnetek (and, of course, for all the other companies you're studying). In other words, if your subject company has $50 million in sales in one SMP and only $25 million in two others, you weight the $50 million SMP twice as high as the others.

With all the weighted averages in hand, you can start to ask and answer some important questions. Are we better than our competitors, or worse? Why? Do we have weak positions in some very large markets that are dragging us down? What SMPs look most promising for us to develop further? Which look like candidates for a quick (or gradual) exit?

Step Five: Test Your Conclusions

The final step in our five-step process is to test your conclusions against the known reality out there. By the logic outlined in previous chapters, companies with better SMPs ought to be performing better—growing faster, earning higher profits, and building more value for shareholders.

Well, are they?

If they are, that is a strong indicator that you have determined the industry segmentation correctly, and you have a good strategic framework to work within. If they aren't, then one of two things must be true:

1. You don't have the segmentation right and you need to revisit your assumptions.
2. There are other reasons why certain companies are underperforming relative to their SMPs.

Why might a company underperform? Bad management is an obvious—and sometimes too easy—answer. Extraordinarily good management by that company's key competitors might be another. One reason why Southwest Airlines looked so good in recent years against its competitors was that its managers wisely hedged their fuel costs for a number of years. Every airline had the opportunity to do so; only Southwest had the foresight (call it luck, if you prefer) to do so. Still another reason for underperformance despite relatively good SMPs might be legacy costs—for example, high labor costs resulting from generous long-term contracts granted in better times before strong international competition came on the scene. Similarly, an older company may have pension obligations that a younger competitor does not.

Assuming that reality seems to support your competitive portrait of your industry and the players within it, continue the discussions that you began in the previous step. Where should we grow, and—possibly—where should we shrink? As you tackle these all-important questions, be aware of two closely related psychological traps.

The first trap is what might be called the "one sneaker for every person in China" trap. Suppose you have a leading position in several modest-sized segments, but no position at all in a *huge* strategic segment. "If we could grab even a 2 percent share in that segment"—you're likely to hear—"that would mean a *30 percent increase* in our sales! How hard would it be for a high-performing company like ours to grab a measly 2 percent? Let's go for it!"

Don't go for it—unless, of course, you have a carefully thought-out plan to leverage strength in adjacent strategic markets that gives the potential to achieve a 20 percent share of the new strategic segment. If all you can manage is 2 percent share, then the chances are that you will be at a big disadvantage against other competitors. Your SMP will be weaker overall, and the chances are that your profitability will decline in line with your SMP.

The second psychological trap might be called the "bad report card" trap. Say you have a healthy 30 percent share in each of three markets, and a 3 percent share in the other two. Human nature (reinforced by 20 years of schooling, plus or minus) pushes us to *get those bad grades up*: "Can't we fix those two laggards? What are we doing wrong? Is it our products? Our sale force? We're a successful company. We've got to find ways to *succeed* in those two markets!"

Maybe yes, maybe no. Maybe there are good reasons why your company is not well aligned with what is needed to compete in those segments. Investing more to find ways of succeeding there—driving up sales—may actually translate into failure. In business, unlike at school, investing in failure is rarely a winning proposition.

Uncovering Value in the Health-Club Game

Now, after our extended five-step detour and with your new detective tools in hand, go back to the health-club industry. If you're a player in this industry and you want to understand and improve your SMP, how do you go about it? What kind of detective work must you do?

As we discussed earlier in the chapter, the critical first step in determining your SMP is correctly deriving the Value Map for your industry. If you use guesswork rather than facts, there is a good chance you will get it wrong. In this example, I describe a more rigorous approach to deriving the Value Map, based on a build-up of operating costs and how these vary with different types and levels of scale.

Let's start by looking at Bally Total Fitness, the nation's leader in health and fitness, with more than 400 health club locations and $800 million in annual revenues.[1] Bally's began as a tennis and health club in 1962 and grew to become the largest publicly held health-club operator in the United States.[2]

As a result of bad investments, a 2003 earnings restatement, and a misguided growth strategy, Bally's stock price has plummeted from a high of $36.62 in 1998 to a price (as of this writing) of something more than $8.00 a share.[3] After posting losses in 2003, the company continued its "turnaround" process, trying to undo many of the bad strategic decisions of years past. Paul Toback, chairman and CEO of Bally, put it this way:

> Almost three years ago, Bally was in the midst of an operational decay . . . my predecessor refused to acknowledge the competition as a business factor, or to develop a strategy to address competitive forces . . . We invested millions of dollars on bad club locations and ill-conceived club design, and narrow and unfocused strategies. . . .[4]

How can a leading health and fitness club with great national market share and a strong brand lose so much value? The answer is clear: bad Strategic Market Position. Unfortunately for Bally, national market share is not where value hides in the health-club trade.

Now look at a different kind of competitor. The parent company—Town Sports International Holdings, Inc. (TSI)—has been around for more than 30 years. With annual revenues of $365 million, it is one of the two leading operators of fitness clubs in the Northeast and Mid-Atlantic regions of the United States.[5] Never heard of TSI? If you live in a major city in the Northeast, you may know TSI by one of its many regional brands: New York Sports Clubs, Boston Sports Clubs, Washington Sports Clubs, and Philadelphia Sports Clubs. In fact, with a focus on metropolitan areas in the Northeast, TSI's top three regional markets—New York, Boston, and Washington—comprise more than 90 percent of the company's locations.

What's the equivalent number for Bally's? Based on the analyses of SMP that I've presented up to this point, you can probably figure out where this argument is going. Bally's top three locations—New York, Chicago, and Los Angeles—account for only 21 percent of their club locations. With that figure in mind, now look at Table 5.4.

Perhaps most striking about this table is the Rest of U.S. figure for TSI: Only 11 of the company's 139 facilities are outside its top

TABLE 5.4 Bally and Town Sports International

	Bally Total Fitness	Town Sports International
NYC	36	89
Boston	12	19
Washington, DC	8	20
Rest of U.S.	308	11
Total	364	139

three metropolitan markets. TSI refers to this strategy as "regional clustering":

> Regional clustering strategy [is] designed to maximize revenues and achieve economies of scale. We believe our regional clustering strategy allows us to maximize revenue and earnings growth by providing high-quality, conveniently located fitness facilities on a cost-effective basis while making it more difficult for potential new entrants into our markets. Regional clustering has allowed us to create an extensive network of clubs in our core markets, in addition to a widely recognized brand with strong local identity.[6]

At this point, it would probably be helpful to examine those economics and economies of scale a little more closely, since this kind of analysis is at the heart of SMP. It provides another answer to the question posed previously: *Where do those scores for benefits of scale on the Value Map come from?*

Look at Table 5.5. Suppose you knew enough about the health-club industry to know that the revenue and expense items in the column entitled Club Details are the critical drivers in this business. Suppose the question you want to answer is, *What happens along each of these expense items as I go up in scale?*

What's going on in Table 5.5? From the first column, you can see that salaries account for about 25 percent of revenues for a single club and rent constitutes another 15 percent. You can see advertising and marketing on top of that. Add depreciation, other operating expenses, and then the administrative overhead to operate the business as a whole, and you can see that, for a single club, it's a pretty tough business. My company's research indicates that very few single clubs approach a 5 percent operating margin. So all in all, it's a pretty thin operation.

TABLE 5.5 Health Club Cost Structures

Club Details	Single		Local (5 locations)		Regional (30 locations)		National (150 locations)	
	Thousands	% of Rev.	Thousands	% of Rev.	Thousands	% of Rev.	Thousands	% of Rev.
Revenue	$1,350	100%	$6,750	100%	$40,500	100%	$202,500	100%
Salaries	337	25.0	1,688	25	10,125	25	50,625	25
Rent	200	15.0	1,000	15	6,000	15	30,000	15
Adv. & Mktg.	150	11.1	450	6.7	1,575	3.9	7,875	3.9
Depreciation	86	6.3	407	6.0	2,314	5.7	11,250	5.6
Other Exp.	202	15.0	1,012	15	6,075	15	30,375	15
Total Op. Exp.	975	72.3	4,557	67.5	26,089	64.4	130,125	64.3
Overhead	338	25.0	1,321	19.6	6,038	14.9	30,188	14.9
Profit	37	2.7	872	12.9	8,373	20.7	42,187	20.8

Now think about how that changes if you operate more than one club all within the same city. If you have five clubs instead of one, you will need five times as many fitness instructors, five times as many receptionists, and so on. Salaries will therefore be the same proportion of revenue. Rent is the same situation: If you have five facilities instead of one, you most likely will have five times the rent. Other expenses—such as laundry and cleaning services—will also just go up in proportion to revenue, so you won't find much advantage there.

Advertising and marketing, though, are a different story. You can leverage a lot of your advertising costs across multiple locations, which has the effect of reducing your advertising and marketing costs as a percentage of revenue by something over one-third.

You may also see a bit of improvement in depreciation, because now you're buying five times as much equipment and you can probably negotiate a little better deal with the equipment suppliers. So you see some improvement there.

In overhead, too, you should show some improvements. Whereas you need to have one general manager for a single operation, with five operations you will be able to have one more senior general manager at the top to oversee the five clubs and get away with a more junior supervisor at each location, so there are some savings to be had there. And similarly, you need to have only one person thinking about human resources (HR) issues, one person thinking about recruitment, one person thinking about management policies, and so on. Our estimate is that having a five-location operation, versus a single operation, reduces overheads by about 20 percent.

We immediately see that margins for a five-location operation—*provided those five locations are all closely located within a single city*—are much higher. Most likely, you've gone from low single-digit profitability to low double-digit profitability.

Next, move one level further up the hierarchy to the status of regional player. Here, we're talking about an organization with perhaps 30 locations. Again, we are assuming that all are within a closely packed geographic region. What happens to costs, in this case? Well, again, salaries, rent, and other expenses are likely to stay constant in proportion to revenue, so there are no real benefits to be found there. But you will get some further economies on advertising and marketing, and maybe now you can afford to advertise in radio and TV or in the larger newspaper, which you might not otherwise be able to do. And you can probably further leverage your overheads, in terms of supervisory staffing. The result? Now we see your operation's profitability going up from the low double digits to something around 20 percent or more.

Now look at a national operation, with something like 150 locations. What does that do to the economics? You won't really get any improvement in advertising and marketing benefits, because in all likelihood you will be buying across different media markets. And so the fact that you've got scale in Los Angeles as well as scale in Chicago doesn't really help you. You're not buying national TV; you're buying local TV or local newspapers and radio.

In terms of depreciation, you're already pretty much there. You might get a few pennies of extra discount from your suppliers, but if you already have 30 locations as a regional player, you're probably already getting excellent discounts from your suppliers. And in terms of overheads, it's not really reasonable to expect that someone based in Chicago will be able to do much for you, in terms of overseeing an operation that's on the West Coast or in the Southeast. So you need to replicate a lot of that regional overhead.

Here's the interim punch line: When you go from a regional player to a national player, you remain strongly profitable, but you don't get any more profitable. And this assumes that the way you get from being a regional to a national is by having a number of strong regions. If you're a national player with, say, five regions where you have many locations in each, you're going to have excellent economics.

Consider another, somewhat more visually appealing way of presenting the same basic concepts (Figure 5.7). Look what happens in the last column. Here, you're a national-scale player, but instead of having 150 locations concentrated in four, five, or six regions, you're spread out in many different regions. So you're operating in 20 or 30 states. What do the economics look like?

You've actually lost ground. In your advertising and marketing, you can't get the same economies, because you're buying in so many different media markets. You can't get the overhead savings because, again, you're going to have managers in all the different locations where you compete. You still do get the benefits from low depreciation from more effective equipment buying, but as noted earlier, those savings aren't that great anyway because you've

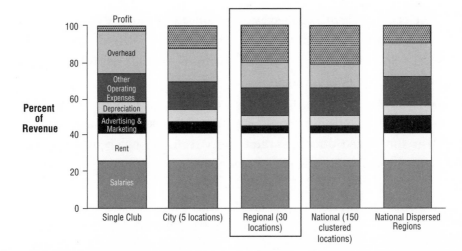

FIGURE 5.7   Health-Club Economics

already rolled down the discount curve by the time you get to be a regional player. What you see is that the profitability for a national player with dispersed regions is actually substantially less than for a strong regional player.

Obviously, the goal is to grow the profit segment (at the top of each bar in Figure 5.7) as much as possible. Note how the economics of the Regional (30 locations) bar—the one I've highlighted with a box around it—are almost identical to National (150 locations). This is good news for TSI, which is something of a hybrid of these two columns: a collection of regional players amounting to significant scale, but not a true national player. But it's bad news for Bally's, which is somewhere off the right end of this table: 364 locations, widely dispersed on a national basis.

Earlier in the chapter, we looked at alternative Value Maps that reflected positions of the two groups at (imaginary) American Fitness. The Value Map of the group favoring regional intensification of the company's footprint looked like Figure 5.8.

This is, in effect, TSI's Value Map. Again starting with geography, we conclude that national market share (assuming wide geographic dispersal rather than collections of concentrations) is of extremely low value in terms of the economic and consumer benefits of scale or scope. Simply spreading yourself out thinly across the country does you very little good. A focused national strategy, or—just as good—a concentrated regional strategy, produces far better economics. And while health clubs often compete (especially locally) on the basis of their specialized offerings, these don't really do much to affect the economics of scope/scale.

The bottom line: TSI's regional clustering strategy has had a powerful and positive impact on company profitability, giving it operating margins of 11.2 percent from 2002–2004. Mighty Bally's comparable figure is –1.3 percent.

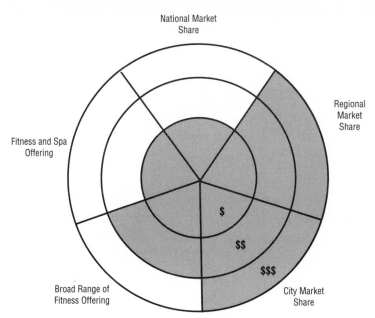

FIGURE 5.8 Value Map: Health Clubs (c)

GEOGRAPHIC SEGMENTATION IN OTHER BUSINESSES

In many service businesses, understanding the right way to compete and grow across geographies is a critical driver of profitability and growth. We have already seen examples in retailing and airlines. Another example is TV and radio stations. The major TV networks make most of their money not from the network itself, which has come under tremendous pressure from increasing costs and declining viewers, but from the local stations that they own and operate.

Within the local stations business, operators have begun to discover the savings that are available from operating multiple stations under the same ownership. Infinity Broadcasting was one of the first to take advantage of this in radio broadcasting. Over the past 10 years, TV operators have taken the same lesson to heart. Between 1996 and 2003, the number of TV stations owned by the top 15 operators more than doubled (from 200 to 438). Companies such as NBC and Univision have emphasized owning multiple stations in the major markets, whereas Tribune and ABC have a more "spread it thin" approach, owning just one station per major market.

Do you want to hazard a guess as to which is the better strategy? If you chose the former, then you are starting to develop an intuitive understanding of the principles of SMP. Table 5.6 shows the economic impact of owning two stations in a single market.

TABLE 5.6   TV Multiple-Station Ownership Benefits

	Stand-alone	Stand-alone × 2	2 Stations
Revenue	$100	$200	$200
Operating Expenses			
Engineering	$ 6.5	$ 13.0	$ 7.8
Programming	$ 17.6	$ 35.1	$ 26.3
Local News	$ 16.9	$ 33.8	$ 16.9
Sales Force	$ 7.2	$ 14.3	$ 14.3
G&A	$ 12.4	$ 24.7	$ 14.8
Other	$ 4.6	$ 9.1	$ 9.1
Total Operating Expenses	$ 65.0	$130.0	$ 89.2
% of Revenue	65%	65%	45%
Contribution	$ 35.0	$ 70.0	$110.8
% of Revenue	35%	35%	55%

Source: Prior L.E.K. casework, L.E.K. interviews, Merrill Lynch, Deutsche Bank.

MANY PATHS THROUGH THE WOODS

In laying out the five steps to determining SMP, I have tried to be as methodical as possible. In practice, the approach will be somewhat different for every industry. The critical insight that can change the way you think about your business, and how you should invest for growth, can come from many different sources. Having applied this approach to hundreds of different businesses and industries, my advice is:

- *Be methodical.* Work through the process and be wary of jumping to conclusions too soon or blindly accepting established wisdom.
- *Be rigorous.* As we showed for motors, health clubs, and TV stations, there are ways to quantify the economic effects of different types of scale and avoid relying on guesswork.
- *Steal ideas from everywhere.* Look at other industry examples and successes. Look overseas. Spot patterns and identify similarities and insights you can apply to your own business.
- *Draw it out.* By plotting the "strategic chessboard" for your business, you will be in a better position to test hypotheses and develop strategic pathways.

We have one more chapter in this how-to section of *Where Value Hides*. Chapter 6 builds on the lessons of this chapter, showing you how to apply SMP in ways that both make future sales easier and improve your long-term profitability.

6

Applying SMP to
Sales and Marketing

Some of the most important decisions that business leaders have to make involve *what* to market and *how* to market it. What products is the company going to put promotional resources behind? Which distribution channels is it going to emphasize? If choices have to be made—and they almost always do—how will the company make them? Will choices made regarding one product line or channel have unexpected reverberations elsewhere?

Is there some way to know *ahead* of time?

As I explained in Chapter 4, there's almost never a shortage of ideas bubbling up within your company, especially if yours is a culture that emphasizes growth. You may have your board or corporate strategy group coming up with Big Ideas. You may have marketing or business development groups constantly on the prowl for new product ideas or synergistic additions to the portfolio. And, of course, you have your sales teams, whose "feet on the street" put them in close contact with customers. (Those customers are usually more than willing to tell your troops how your company should reorganize itself to serve them better.) In most cases, your salespeople are quick to bring back this intelligence from the field—intelligence that frequently boils down to adding a new product or service to your mix. Adding new lines tends to make life easier both for your customers and for your salespeople, so there's always pressure from the sales and marketing end of the business to expand into new areas. When combined with the overall corporate imperative for growth, this pressure can be overwhelming.

But as the exercises laid out in the previous chapter amply demonstrate, you can't and shouldn't do everything. Sometimes a lost sale is not a bad thing, but a *good* thing. In this chapter, we look at ways to apply SMP to your company's product portfolio, and—by extension—to its sales and marketing activities. If anecdotal evidence (like reports from the field) tells you that something needs to be added to your product line, how do you figure out if adding that missing product is going to be good for the company? And although it's far less common for anybody out there—customers, marketing, salespeople—to propose doing away with an existing product, that's obviously a piece of the larger picture, as well. How do you figure *that* out?

As you will see, the discipline of SMP can help with both of these challenges. To illustrate the key points of this chapter, we call upon a venerable and successful milling and food-processing company: C.H. Guenther & Son, Inc., based in San Antonio, Texas.

Introducing Our Central Character: C.H. Guenther & Son, Inc.

Guenther was founded in 1851 by a German immigrant, Carl H. Guenther.[1] He built his first mill in the small Central Texas town of

Fredericksburg, and relocated his business to the fast-growing community of San Antonio in 1859.

The arrival of the railroad in San Antonio in 1876 brought new and ample supplies of Midwestern grains, pointing the company toward growth. And since trains run in both directions, they also enabled Carl Guenther to start supplying customers well beyond the geographic confines of South Texas. At that point, Guenther started building its position as a strong regional player in the national milling business—a niche that, defined broadly, the company still occupies today, with successive generations of the extended Guenther family maintaining the tradition of family involvement in the business.[2]

Guenther made its first move into consumer convenience foods in 1932 with the introduction of Breakfast Treat wheat cereal. From that point forward, Guenther made regular investments in an applied form of research and development. Six months of work in the company test kitchen, for example, led to the introduction in 1948 of Pioneer Biscuit Mix, one of many value-added products that Guenther successfully introduced over the decades. The expansion of the product line, as well as sales growth across existing lines, meant regular investments in new facilities. After only two years of selling Pioneer Biscuit Mix, for example, Guenther had to put up a new building specifically for the manufacture of prepared mixes, which soon included cake, pancake, and cornmeal mixes.

The company's distribution network grew in parallel. By the late 1960s, Guenther had a well-established, 12-state marketing area that extended west to New Mexico, east to Tennessee and Alabama, north to Kansas, and south into the northern sections of Mexico. Beginning in the early 1980s, Guenther ran regional advertising campaigns (for example, "Southern Success Since 1851") to reinforce its retail sales.

New product introductions continued and reshaped the direction of the company. In 1985, for example, Guenther introduced

Old-Fashioned Country Gravy Mix, the first in a line of flour-based Guenther gravies, which soon emerged as one of the company's best-selling products. Acquisitions also helped reshape the company. In 1987, in a purposeful related-diversification move, Guenther acquired Dallas-based Texas Custom Bakers, which put the company into the frozen baked goods and biscuits markets.

Bringing the story up to the present, Guenther is still a family-owned milling company, headquartered in San Antonio and operating four mills in the South and Southwest.[3] Its retail market has expanded to 22 states in the South and Southwest. Under its San Antonio River Mill Store brand, the company markets gourmet mixes both to specialty stores and by direct mail. Guenther manufactures flour-based products under its Pioneer, White Lily, and White Wing brands, which it sells through distributors. The company also has an increasingly important trade with chain restaurants, ranging from Bob Evans to mighty McDonald's. "Today," reports the company's web site, "the company produces everything from biscuit mixes to gravy to frozen dough to fully baked products." I discuss these various product lines and distribution channels at greater length shortly.

In 1993, Scott Petty, chairman of the board of Guenther, decided that it was time to sort through its strategic choices in a systematic way.[4] The material contained in the following pages is largely borrowed from that strategic review.

The Problem Statement: 1993

From the vantage point of 1993, Guenther's top executives were proud of their company's greatly increased scale and scope, and of its diversified product and channel base. They believed that their high market share within their regional base, as well as high levels of consumer brand loyalty, positioned them to compete effectively in the future. Figure 6.1 shows a typical Guenther product's strong market-share position within the company's regional base.

In the previous half-decade, moreover, Guenther had enjoyed gratifying levels of growth—better than many national players and ranking not far behind the industry leaders. At the same time, however, Guenther's senior managers were concerned about trend lines that seemed to be taking shape. Most troubling was the fact that, while sales were growing at a healthy double-digit rate, profits were growing significantly more slowly, and the company was finding it difficult to fund all of its growth initiatives. Instead of achieving economies of scale and higher margins as the company grew, it seemed that each new growth initiative took the company into lower-margin activities.

Based on publicly available data, Guenther knew that national players like General Mills consistently enjoyed higher margins than the relatively small player in San Antonio. What was unclear, though, was whether this was an inescapable structural problem—the natural outcome of being a smaller player in a competitive industry—or

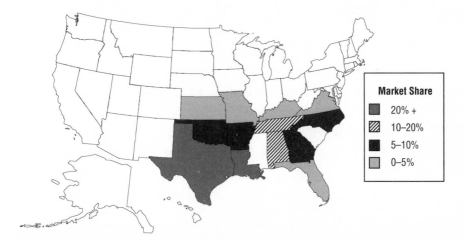

FIGURE 6.1   Representative Market Shares for C.H. Guenther Retail Products

whether something else was going on. In other words, was the company permanently stuck in its lower-margin position, or were there things that Guenther could and should do differently? Were there products or channels that were particularly good performers or, conversely, especially poor performers? If so, would that argue for changes in the company's product offerings or channel emphases?

How would those choices be defined and made?

NUMBERS AND WHAT TO DO WITH THEM

Guenther's sales and marketing organization was grouped into three divisions, each representing a different sales channel for its products:

1. Retail.
2. Food service (through distributors).
3. Chain restaurants (casual dining and quick-service restaurants).

Each division was headed by a vice president with responsibility for the sales in his or her respective division. Naturally enough, each VP felt that his or her division was the mainstay of the business and deserved more sales resources, more R&D to develop new products, and more manufacturing investment to increase capacity for the products their customers needed.

To help resolve these conflicts, the company undertook an extensive activity-based cost analysis for all of the products sold through each of the three channels. When the company looked at the results, products were all over the map. The company produced more than 150 different products, and there were huge differences in profitability among the various products. To make sense of this, the company then looked at how various costs were linked to key factors, including

Contribution/Selling Costs, Freight, General and Administrative (G&A) expenses, and Production facility. The results, reproduced in Figure 6.2, included some startling findings.

To their surprise, Guenther's senior executives found that their retail trade—long the company's mainstay—was actually its least profitable business. With the 0 point in Figure 6.2 indicating average companywide profitability, retail was on average six points below that company standard. Food service, by contrast, ranked six points higher than average, and the chain-restaurant trade (at eight points above average) was the most profitable business of all.

The other findings summarized in Figure 6.2 were less surprising, but still contain food for thought. Shipping locally within Texas was obviously cheaper than shipping farther afield. Similarly, shipping full truckloads to one destination (as was often the case with the larger chain-restaurant customers) was ideal. Making multiple stops to service smaller customers was less ideal. Both the chain restaurant and retail businesses required a significant investment of G&A time, while

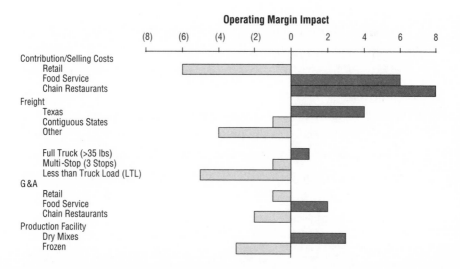

FIGURE 6.2   Profitability Impacts by Channel and Geography

the food-service channel was less demanding in this regard. (In this channel, distributors took responsibility for much of the administrative burden of moving product, whereas the other channels, by definition, did not.) And finally, the production margins on dry-mix products were above average, while those on frozen products were below average.

Production capacity remained a point of confusion. As suggested earlier in the chapter, Guenther had tended to expand its manufacturing capability in an opportunistic manner over almost a century and a half of growth: *If customers in Location X want more of Product Y, then we should find a way to increase capacity.* Add onto an existing facility, build a new one, or acquire a competitor with the needed capacity.

But as at many other companies in a wide range of industries, once that capacity was in place, the great temptation was to *keep those machines running*. Whenever someone from accounting attempted to point to a particular product and question its viability, the head of manufacturing would respond by saying that the company had to keep that product alive just to *keep those machines running*. The result was a self-fulfilling prophecy: You need machines for the products, and then you need products for the machines.

Investment hurdles for proposed capital investments were not consistently applied. The rationale was that only after a new machine was in place would the sales force be able to sell products to use the new capacity. As a result, the people who proposed these kinds of investments rarely thought in terms of ROI.[5] Capital investments tended to be made on a sort of tacit rotational basis: If the Chain Restaurants division got their investment request last time, it was probably the turn of Food Service or Retail next time around.

The company also identified another challenge—seemingly tangential to SMP, but actually at the heart of the company's operations, and therefore important to any future SMP implementation. This was the executive incentive structure. Stated simply, executives at Guenther were rewarded on the basis of both top-line growth and bottom-line returns. But since revenues were measured for each division but profits were measured only for the company overall, the VPs for each division focused much more on sales growth than on earnings. Until that incentive system was changed, the company most likely would continue to see a gap between sales growth and earnings growth. Any SMP intervention, therefore, would need to be linked to a new incentive structure.

It's fair to say that up to this point—that is, in the early stages of its 1993 investigation—Guenther was basically doing what any other skilled and experienced company above a certain scale does on a periodic basis. It was employing standard cost accounting procedures to pin down the costs and benefits of doing certain kinds of business in certain kinds of ways. Similarly, it was looking at production capacity, and—like most other businesses—planning as best it could for a systematic expansion of that capacity to accommodate anticipated growth. It was examining the appropriateness of its incentive system and asking whether a different system would produce markedly different results.

Simply by continuing in this vein of standard business procedures, Guenther could have begun to adjust its mix of channels and products: less of this, more of that. It could have changed its capacity planning accordingly. And, of course, it could have tweaked the executive compensation system to include more profit and value-related incentives.

It was at this point, however, that Guenther began exploring the principles of SMP. Based on the information summarized in Figure 6.2, it would have been easy enough, for example, to emphasize dry-mix products and deemphasize frozen products. But as

CFO Janelle Sykes recalls, Guenther wanted to move carefully, even cautiously:

> First of all, your average 150-year-old company is inclined to move in conservative ways. But equally important, it just wasn't obvious to us *which ways* we should move. At that time, we had something like 150 SKUs [stock-keeping units, or individually tracked products] out there in the field. Maybe they interacted with each other, and supported each other in the marketplace, in ways that we didn't really understand. Maybe our channels interacted in ways that weren't obvious. So changing our mix of products or channels was not something we were going to do lightly.[6]

By stating the problem in this way—*interactions that we might not understand*—Sykes and her colleagues were intuitively embracing the principles of SMP.

WHAT ARE THE REAL SEGMENTS?

To restate the problem just defined: Guenther realized that it needed to get a better understanding of the strategic segments in which it competed. Simply stated, suppose that the cost-accounting exercise showed conclusively that frozen biscuit dough was a low-profit item. By the logic of SMP, you can afford to discontinue (or deemphasize) frozen biscuit dough if it doesn't lie within one of your strategic segments. If frozen biscuit dough *does* sit within one of those strategic segments, however, you have to think very carefully about deemphasizing that product since you may weaken a strong position with a certain production facility or a certain set of customers. At the very least, you might be spreading many fixed costs over a smaller base— which may mean that instead of making your profits go up, dumping frozen biscuit dough could make your profits go down. At worst, you would be driving away some of your most important and profitable customers.

Look at Guenther's three distribution channels using the Value Map tool, and see what we can determine about where the company's strategic segments lie. In this case, I plot all three channels on Figure 6.3, which will help throw into sharp relief both the overlaps—and more important, the *lack* of overlaps—among these channels.

In this case, as with previous Value Maps, I've started it at the top with some geographic entries: national and regional. (Along which geographic dimension do we need to achieve scale, channel by

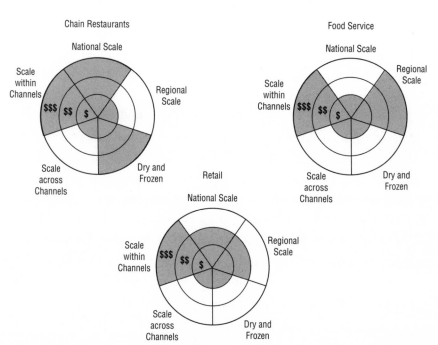

Economic and Customer Benefits of Scale or Share

FIGURE 6.3   Value Map: Baking Products

channel?) Then I've added a "dry and frozen" dimension. (Is it important to achieve scale in *both* dry and frozen, or is that not a significant factor?) Finally, I've included "scale across channels" and "scale within channels." To be successful in the channels of retail, food service, and chain restaurants, do you have to be successful in more than one of these channels? Do you need to achieve a certain scale to succeed in them?

The plotting of the three channels—which is more or less how Guenther viewed its distribution channels at this point in their investigation—immediately highlights some interesting dissimilarities across channels. This, in turn, implies that the strategic segments will be different within each of the three channels.

Look at the geographic entries, for example. Food service is about providing products to hundreds of thousands of individual restaurants and institutional catering facilities. Some of the distributors are national, but the restaurants themselves are all local businesses. Contrast that to the chain restaurant channel, in which most of the customers are national companies that require the same products to be available for their restaurants all over the country. In other words, scaling up to become a national player in the food service channel is not a requirement for success. There are many examples of successful food service suppliers that succeed by focusing on only a single region, catering to local tastes and building a reputation among local restaurants. For Guenther, the cost accounting summarized in Figure 6.2 showed that food service does best when it services local establishments within and near Texas. On the other hand, serving chain restaurants absolutely demands a national presence. Any steps that Guenther might take that would undermine its ability to serve this channel on a national scale would definitely be counterproductive.

Retail—as the Value Map implies—sits somewhere in the middle, with a shading toward national scale. There are many examples of regional retail brands that exist around the country, but it is hard for them to compete against nationally advertised brands with all the merchandising and marketing support they have behind them. Simply put, it's increasingly difficult for, say, regional pancake mixes to compete with the likes of Bisquick. Either you commit to huge investments to build toward national scale or you reset your expectations for growth and start planning how best to defend your business cost effectively in the geographic markets where you are strongest.

The "dry and frozen" dimension again highlights some sharp distinctions. For both the food-service and retail channels, it was not particularly important for Guenther to be in both businesses. But for the increasingly important chain restaurant channel, "covering the waterfront" was all-important. Some restaurants (for example) like to buy biscuit mix and do the baking from scratch in their own kitchens; others in the same restaurant chain may prefer to buy frozen biscuits to eliminate the extra labor. The corporate buyers want product consistency and will require that both the dry and frozen versions have the same product formulation. If Guenther were to provide only dry-mix versions without frozen, then it would be both disappointing its customers and providing an entrée for competitors to serve the account.

The last two scale dimensions on Figure 6.3 show consistent benefits of scale for each of the three channels. For no channel was it important to achieve scale *across* channels. Conversely, for all three channels, it was extremely important to achieve scale *within* that channel.

Summing up, the last two scale dimensions on the Value Map in Figure 6.3 tell us that the Retail, Food Service, and Chain Restaurants channels are separate strategic segments; the Dry and Frozen dimension tells us that there are separate dry and frozen strategic segments within Food Service and Retail, but that for Chain Restaurants these are one combined segment; the two geographic dimensions tell us that Chain Restaurants are best thought of as a single national market, Food Service is a collection of regional markets, and Retail is mixed but becoming more national. So the strategic market segments that Guenther competes in for baking products are:

- Chain Restaurants: one national segment for dry and frozen.
- Food Service: separate dry and frozen segments, each broken down further into regional market segments.
- Retail: separate dry and frozen segments, regional markets becoming more national.

This is not an academic exercise. Many companies face difficult decisions about which products or channels to emphasize and invest in. An understanding of the strategic market segments in which you compete gives you a framework for understanding the linkages between different parts of your business so that you know when you can cut back in one area without damaging another.

The need to make decisions about different parts of the business was a very real issue for Guenther back in the early 1990s. As CFO Sykes recalls:

Like every other business I know of, our business had to make choices. There are never enough resources to do everything that might be worth doing. And human nature being what it is, it's often easier just to dole out the available dollars on a more or less equal basis. You have four groups with a valid claim on resources, and you have four dollars? Fine. They each get a dollar. Everyone will complain a little, and no one will complain a lot. But are you doing the best thing for the overall health of the business? Almost certainly not.[7]

"Making choices," of course, implies action. With a clearer sense of the boundaries of the company's relevant SMPs—intersected with the earlier cost-accounting findings—Guenther was in a position to act and make some adjustments to its product and channel mixes.

A PRESCRIPTION AND RELATED CHALLENGES

Having defined its strategic segments, Guenther was now in a position to start making decisions about where to invest for growth. A major input was the cost and profitability analysis outlined in Figure 6.2. However, management also took time to survey customers and develop a view of their unique set of strengths:

- Skilled R&D group with proven track record of meeting customer requirements.
- Ability to deliver both dry-mix and frozen versions of the same product.
- Growing awareness and reputation among national chain account buyers.
- Low overhead costs compared to most national-scale competitors.

There was a lengthy process to gather the information and weigh the findings. But at the end of that process, the preliminary SMP-oriented strategic prescription that Guenther arrived at looked something like the following.

- *Emphasize the national chain-restaurant business.* Because national scale helps us, target the national-scale chains. Take advantage of the fact that we have both dry-mix and frozen products of a high and consistent quality and many of our competitors don't. Keep our full trucks making only one stop:

at the Bob Evans or McDonald's loading docks. Yes, it's true that frozen drags down your dry-mix margins to some extent, but here's a case where shutting down a lower-margin product line would amount to shooting yourself in the foot. Looking for growth? At last count, McDonald's had something like 30,000 restaurants serving 50 million people in 120 countries every day. Selling more products into an enterprise on that scale is a challenging avenue toward growth, but one that is a great fit with our capabilities.

- *Emphasize the food-service and dry-mix businesses in Texas and contiguous states.* Any way you slice it, this is a local/regional business. Concentrate on serving your nearby customers as well as possible—taking full advantage of favorable transportation costs—and don't worry about serving people up in New England or other distant parts of the country. (New England doesn't know you aren't serving them and Texas cares only about the quality of your products and service in Texas.)

- *Deemphasize the frozen food-service business.* Assume that there's no such group outside the immediate region that you can serve in an effective and profitable way. If someone comes up with a plan for serving a local constituency leveraging products that have already been developed for chain-restaurant accounts, then we should consider that, but otherwise we make our sales and our manufacturing resources available for other opportunities that offer better prospects.

- *Deemphasize the retail business outside Texas and contiguous states.* This was, in a sense, our starting point: Smaller regional players will always have a hard time competing with larger national players—the General Mills and Pillsburys of the retail world (now merged into an even more formidable competitor). The prescription was to cut back on costly advertising campaigns, new product launches, and slotting fees. Either find a way to support higher prices outside the proximate region or pull in the outside perimeter enough so that only the higher-margin retail businesses remain.

Of course, for Guenther in 1993, getting from here to there would be far from obvious or easy. Take the last point, for example: deemphasizing retail. This prescription seemed to fly in the face of brand theory and the company's place in the world. Guenther was known mainly for its brands, which commanded high degrees of consumer loyalty within the company's regional base. (As noted, the "Guenther" name was far less well-known than "Pioneer" and the other leading Guenther brands.) Did it make sense to do less to support and promote these established brands?

From an SMP perspective, the answer was a selective yes. This is not to say that Guenther had to start pulling its venerable brands off the shelves. But the company could certainly raise prices on a systematic basis to try to achieve satisfactory and consistent margins. If the customers stayed with the company, fine; both the seller and the buyer would be happy. If they *didn't*, then the company had to be prepared to let that business go away.[8] Sometimes a lost sale is a good thing.

But there were other significant obstacles to changing the patterns of business as usual. Almost inevitably, someone's ox would get gored. As I said before, each of the three existing channels had a vice president overseeing its activities. If the emphases and deemphases listed earlier were indeed carried out, did that mean that the VPs for food service and retail would be demoted? Would they be put under the wing of the favored chain-restaurant business?

And what about R&D? According to Janelle Sykes, directing these efforts was another point of contention for the company.

What we had were a group of food scientists and technicians who were accustomed to pursuing ideas that intrigued them, although, again, with roughly equal allocation of R&D dollars across the three divisions. In other words, for every dollar spent on R&D that might be applicable to chain restaurants, we tended to spend another dollar on food-service R&D, and another dollar on retail-related R&D.

Nor was there any clear directive that new R&D should be aimed at extending existing product lines. We were just as likely to move off in a direction that wasn't directly related to products that were already out there. And while there's certainly something to be said for breaking new ground, there's also a lot to be said for concentrating your R&D firepower on urgent and known needs.[9]

Customer surveys underscored the ambiguous results of Guenther's R&D efforts. "They have excellent R&D," commented one national player. "They always have the answer to problems." But another major player added an important qualifier. "They need to be more flexible as far as what they can do," this customer volunteered. "I'm sure they could supply us with other stuff. They have the technological capability."[10]

The tentative prescription just described was worked out by the top half-dozen executives at Guenther, who kept their cards close to their vests during the planning process. Again, I present only the outcome of that process here. Obviously, there were a great many interim steps along the way and—in light of the kinds of sensitivities outlined earlier—senior management saw no advantage in floating ideas that were still in the speculative stage and that might never get beyond that stage.

Eventually, though, it came time to announce, explain, and implement the plan for a substantially recast Guenther.

IMPLEMENTING SMP AT GUENTHER

Several months into the planning process, the senior managers began laying out the elements of the new plan to the company's managers and employees. This was accomplished through a series of workshops, which were characterized by a substantial give-and-take. At the end of this process, however, the fundamentals of the plan remained largely unchanged.

Central to the plan, of course, was a substantial reorientation of the company's product offerings along the lines suggested previously. The adjustments, as Janelle Sykes recalls, were "far-reaching and far-ranging."[11] A significant number of products would be dropped outright. In fact, by the time the last dust had settled several years later, the overall product count had dropped from 150 to approximately 60. For a second group of products, either prices would be increased, promotional spending would be cut, the sales-force effort would be decreased, or some combination of these three moves would be embraced. Either these products would come to make a greater contribution to profits or they would fall by the wayside.

Future investments in plant and equipment would be held to a demanding internal rate of return: 15 percent.[12] Part of the workshop process revolved around helping managers at all levels understand exactly how this worked. The point was *not* to discourage people from coming forward with great ideas; the point was to help people understand ahead of time exactly which ideas were great and which weren't.

One constant refrain throughout the workshop exercise—which was designed in large part as an educational experience—was that *value created by a 1 percent increase in margins is significantly greater than value created by a 1 percent increase in sales growth.* Figure 6.4 is a modified version of one of the slides shown at the workshops.

In this same spirit, management announced that the tail-chasing exercise of adding capacity and then adding products to take advantage of that capacity would end. A careful study of the company's real manufacturing capacity revealed that, even though Guenther's plants were close to capacity, the elimination of certain product lines would create ample capacity for growth in the near term. By the same calculation, there was no compelling reason to prop up a low-performing product simply to keep machines running. Except in the case of very specialized equipment, those machines could run on new growth alone.

The executive incentive structure was revamped along similar lines. Additions to the top line (i.e., sales growth) received reduced emphasis; additions to the bottom line received substantially greater emphasis.

So what were the results?

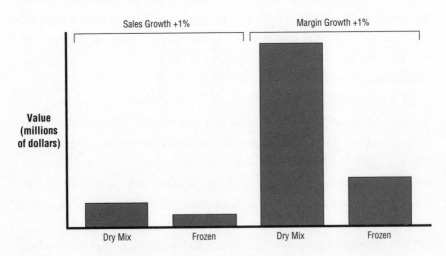

FIGURE 6.4   C.H. Guenther: Value Created by One Point Improvement

On the negative side of the ledger, there were some frustrated customers on the retail and food service sides who could no longer get some of the products they were accustomed to getting—at least at their former prices. "Yeah, it was a number of years before those kinds of letters stopped coming in," admits CFO Sykes. "Giving things up is never easy, either for the seller or the buyer."[13] There were a few executive departures, none of which (Sykes says diplomatically) were entirely unexpected. Certainly, some of those individuals in the company whose job descriptions and accustomed ways of doing business changed unexpectedly—for example, in the sales force or in manufacturing—felt somewhat bruised by those changes.

On the positive side of the ledger, *operating margins doubled within 12 months.*

Guenther's shareholders were obviously thrilled at this strong performance. And this created more running room for management. Based in part on the shareholders' renewed confidence in the business—and, of course, on cash in the bank—Guenther was able to acquire (in 1995) the Knoxville-based White Lily Foods Company, which effectively doubled the size of Guenther overnight. Based on this acquisition and on ongoing improvements to operations, the overall profits of the business *quadrupled* within a three-year period.

As noted, some people in the R&D operation worried that the company was straying from its longtime tradition of investing in "pure" R&D. But in fact, for many years prior to the 1993 intervention, relatively small players like Guenther had had little luck launching new brands. The 1985 success of Old-Fashioned Country Gravy Mix notwithstanding, the established national players and their well-advertised brands were, as a rule, already far too potent to overcome. (Meanwhile, the food-service buyers were too fragmented a channel to be of much help in supporting a new brand.) After the 1993 changes were implemented, a full 90 percent of the company's R&D dollars were directed into initiatives mounted on behalf of chain-store customers and the remaining 10 percent went into leveraging existing product lines.

The result, not surprisingly, was a set of far more collaborative relationships with key players in the chain-restaurant industry. In May 2003, for example, McDonald's proudly announced the introduction of its new McGriddles breakfast sandwiches—a product that had been jointly developed by the Oakbrook, Illinois-based chain and its small-but-focused partner in San Antonio. "These new breakfast sandwiches," boasted a McDonald's spokesperson, "are some of the most unique in the breakfast category."[14]

THE IMPLICATIONS FOR SALES AND MARKETING

At the outset of this chapter, I promised to talk about the implications of SMP for sales and marketing. By now, I hope, those implications are clear.

Prior to the 1993 planning exercise and its aftermath, C.H. Guenther's sales and marketing efforts were effectively balkanized—by product line, channel, and region. Within each channel, the philosophy was, "Every sale is a good sale!" Executive compensation reflected that philosophy. So did capital investments: If we have the money and we can define a (possible) need, the investment is justified. The result, not surprisingly, was strong sales growth but sagging margins.

By embracing the principles of SMP, Guenther was able to determine *where value hides*. It was able to break its business down into strategic segments and see which of these had been creating value in the past and which had the potential to create even more in the future. It was able to make tough decisions about which products and channels to emphasize and which to deemphasize. Equally important, it was able to put in place a clear system of screens and hurdles against which to test proposed new initiatives, which in turn helped people across the organization take more responsibility for the company's success.

For Guenther, higher margins meant more funding to support bigger growth initiatives. Whereas before the salespeople spent most of their time pursuing business in increments of $10,000 or $20,000 orders, now the team was able to go after $200,000 or $2,000,000 orders. In the company's priority strategic segments, Guenther was able to offer its best pricing because it knew how well this business fit with its capabilities, and it understood the cost-benefit trade-offs of doing this. What was more, the salesforce could now bring the right level of R&D resources and manufacturing commitments to win the business. The result for the sales organization was that average proposal size went up *and so did the win rate for turning proposals into firm sales.* By becoming a more focused player, Guenther was able to serve better the kinds of large customers who populated the company's most lucrative SMP. The result was bigger, more successful and more profitable sales and much higher growth and value creation for the company's shareholders.

This brings us to the end of the how-to section of *Where Value Hides.* In the third and final section of the book, we look at some of the most important specialized applications of SMP: finding new and profitable markets, improving low-growth or low-margin businesses, and identifying (and putting the right price on) acquisition opportunities.

III

KEY APPLICATIONS OF STRATEGIC MARKET POSITION

7

USING SMP TO FIND NEW MARKETS

I F SMP IS all about playing to your strengths—which, of course, tend to concentrate in those sectors where you've been doing business for years—how do you ever do anything *new*? How do you break the mold, leapfrog over the competition, and achieve that double-digit growth that your strategic plan anticipates and that your shareholders are clamoring for?

The short answer is: *You use your existing strengths as the jumping-off point.* You build SMPs that are related in significant ways to your existing SMPs. Yes, new markets are always there to be conquered, but they are most likely to be conquered by companies that already know how to compete in this new space.

In Chapter 2, I made reference to the Growth-Share Matrix, which was popularized by the Boston Consulting Group back in the 1970s. According to this model, companies were supposed to "milk their cash cows" while keeping an eye out for new "stars" to invest in.

That was one strategic perspective, now largely discredited for reasons I described in that chapter. But other strategic fads have inevitably followed. A business book that has generated a lot of buzz in recent years is *Blue Ocean Strategy*, by W. Chan Kim and Renée Mauborgne.[1] The central premise is that companies are better off competing in "blue oceans," that is, new and uncontested market spaces, rather than in "red oceans." Red oceans, it seems, are the bloody battlegrounds in which existing companies slug it out for existing market share. "The only way to beat the competition," Kim and Mauborgne write, "is to stop *trying* to beat the competition."[2]

I've already made the case that Henderson and the Boston Consulting Group got it wrong. You don't set out to *milk* your cash cow. Your goal, instead, should be to *feed* and take care of that cow, so that it grows bigger and, if possible, bears calves.

As for *Blue Ocean Strategy*, well, I have problems with some of the hyperbole. (In the real world, companies don't get very far when they stop trying to beat the competition.) And the image of a tranquil blue ocean—full of fat and slow-moving fish, where no one has thought to fish before—is very appealing. But in the real world, life mostly isn't like that. True, sometimes a genius stumbles upon a blue ocean, but that's a dangerous plan to bet the company on.

That said, some of the principles in *Blue Ocean Strategy* do dovetail quite nicely with SMP. Take the very first in-depth example in the book, in which Kim and Mauborgne celebrate the success of Casella Wines (best known for their Yellowtail brand), which have enjoyed exceptional growth in recent years. Casella Wines, Kim and Mauborgne write,

> created [yellowtail], a wine whose strategic profile broke from the competition and created a blue ocean. Instead of offering wine as wine, Casella created a social drink accessible to everyone: beer drinkers, cocktail drinkers, and other drinkers of non-wine.[3]

Well, yes and no. From my perspective—the SMP perspective—Casella did a great job of identifying an underserved *market* segment—customers looking for an easy-to-drink, mid-priced wine with a strong brand. But we know that only in hindsight. In other words, we now have the benefit of looking backward at the success the wine has achieved in a highly competitive industry.

But did Casella "break out of this red ocean of bloody competition to make the competition irrelevant"?[4] I argue that Casella is still competing in the same *strategic* segment as Gallo, Mondavi, and the other volume wine companies in the United States. The product has the same ingredients, the same production economics, and competes through the same distribution channels for the same precious shelf space in retailers.

You may ask, "What does it matter if Casella is still in the same strategic segment? Doesn't the company's success prove that the competition is irrelevant?" Again, looking retrospectively, it is easy to spot successful hit products that have created tremendous value. The question is, How do you improve your success rate in identifying successful product launches and new strategic initiatives *before* they are launched?

Consider Figure 7.1. This shows the number of new product launches for a range of food and beverage categories, and indicates how many of these launches were by leading segment competitors versus smaller or newer players. As you can see, the leading companies accounted for only around 25 percent of the new product launches for the period.

Now look at Figure 7.2. This shows the value of sales achieved by those product launches. The leading players accounted for only 25 percent of the new product launches, but around 85 percent of the sales achieved by all those product launches. Put another way, the average sales achieved by a new product launch from a well-established competitor were *17 times higher* than for a company with a weak SMP.

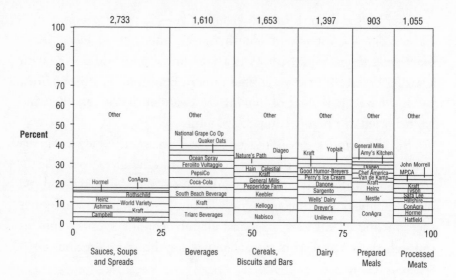

FIGURE 7.1   U.S. Number of Product Innovations (1997–2000)
Data Source: Mintel, winDatamonitor.

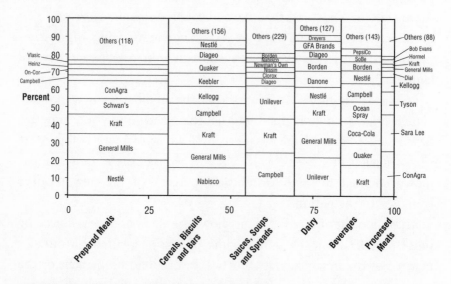

FIGURE 7.2   U.S. Innovation Value (1997–2000E)
Data Source: Mintel, winDatamonitor, Productscan.

That doesn't mean that the smaller guys can never achieve a big hit. It can happen—and when it does, people tend to notice it and talk about it. But it is easy to forget that, of the thousands of failed product launches that simply disappeared, most were from companies that were at a big disadvantage against segment leaders in terms of resources, distribution, logistics, and efficiency.

Now, return to the Casella example. Yes, they scored a hit despite having limited presence in the United States prior to the launch. This was supported by a strong marketing campaign and was helped by the fact that alcoholic beverages are unique among U.S. consumer packaged goods categories in having government-mandated, independent distributors that deal with retailers and thereby dilute the influence of the larger drinks companies. But did Casella really make the competition irrelevant? No. And looking more generally, you'll find that the best track records of long-term success are put together by businesses that understand not only how to identify unmet market needs, but also how to improve their odds by leveraging strong SMPs.

In this chapter, I explain how the SMP Test can be applied to challenge conventional market boundaries and can be used as a screen for assessing—and perhaps embracing—exciting new opportunities. And as in previous chapters, I use real-life examples to introduce and underscore my points.

BAXTER: A TALE OF TWO VENTURES

Let's begin with two stories about Baxter International, Inc., an Illinois-based medical products and services company with 2005 sales of $9.8 billion and some 47,000 employees worldwide.[5] Baxter has done some very smart things in recent years, and it has also done a few not-so-smart things.

Start with a not-so-smart example: a diversification into the "health water" field.

Taking a Pounding on PULSE

In 2001, the year both of our Baxter stories begin, the company had three divisions: *Medication Delivery*, which manufactured and marketed a range of intravenous solutions and specialty products used for fluid replenishment, nutrition therapy, pain management, and antibiotic and chemotherapy; *BioScience*, which developed biopharmaceuticals, biosurgery products, vaccines, and blood-collection, processing, and storage products; and *Renal*, which developed products and services related to end-stage kidney disease.

Each of these divisions was actively engaged in expanding its lines of products and services, both through internal development and acquisition. In addition, however, Baxter also supported an innovation incubator called Non-Traditional Research and Innovation, or NTRI. Baxter launched this formal program in early 2001 to incubate and harness nontraditional growth opportunities across its businesses, and to leverage related technological expertise that did not neatly fit within Baxter's existing businesses.

Sometime early in its first year of existence, NTRI started looking into the possibility of steering Baxter into what might be called the "nutritional water" market. On the face of it, this probably seemed like a good idea. The bottled water market was (and still is) one of the fastest growing beverage segments. More than $25 billion in bottled water was sold in the United States in 2000, and this volume was expected to keep growing at more than 5 percent annually.

Meanwhile, nutritional supplements were growing at rates of between 7 and 15 percent annually. Once mainly targeted at those with real nutrition needs—like low birth-weight babies and the elderly—nutritional supplements in liquid, powder, and bar form increasingly were aimed at broader populations. At the same time, these supplements were expanding beyond their traditional distribution channels—drugstore chains and health-food stores—and were consuming more and more space in the grocery store aisle.

Seduced by these alluring statistics and trends, many companies—ranging from beverage manufacturers to pharmaceutical companies—introduced new products aimed at grabbing a piece of this growing market. One of these companies was Ross Products, an Abbott Laboratories company, which had created a liquid nutritional supplement called Ensure a quarter century earlier. Formerly targeted toward hospital and nursing home populations, Ensure (later joined by its sister product, ZonePerfect) was increasingly being marketed to the active and healthy adult. Available in five flavors and multiple packages, Ensure could be found on the shelves not only at Walgreens, but also at Wal-Mart, Target, and your local grocery store.

Ensure and ZonePerfect, moreover, were only part of Ross's growing nutritional supplement empire. Ross also made Similac Advance and Isomil Advance for infants and small children, and Glucerna for people with diabetes.[6] It appeared that the nutritional supplement market was only waiting for the right market-segmentation genius (see Chapter 4) to come along and carve out new segments.

The innovation incubators at NTRI decided that Baxter, too, could play in this game. After all, the company had extensive experience in nutritional solutions and knew how to formulate non-water-soluble ingredients into a water-based solution. Baxter also knew how to develop containers that would protect solutions' contents and give them a long shelf life. It had a distinguished history of producing therapeutic fluids for more or less complicated applications. *Obviously*, Baxter could jump into this market.

And so jump the company did. On May 28, 2002, Baxter launched a line of what it called "water + nutrients" supplements called, collectively, PULSE. The new line of supplements—introduced in test markets in Arizona and Chicago—were billed as a "convenient way to receive nutrients and other nutrient-related ingredients, specifically targeted for areas of health and wellness." In particular, Baxter claimed, the PULSE supplements would meet key nutritional needs of Baby Boomers between the ages of 38 and 56. According to Baxter, the initial PULSE product offering contained specific ingredients that provided benefits for women's health, men's health, and heart health.

If nothing else, it was a triumph of velocity: PULSE had gone from an idea to a product line in just 14 months. And the torrid pace continued. Five months later, on October 7, 2002, Baxter unveiled PULSE "water + nutrients" supplements in 34 additional states across the United States. "Baxter is uniquely positioned to launch this product given our knowledge and history in nutrition, and our experience developing health-related products," said Arline McDonald, Ph.D., senior project manager at Baxter. "PULSE is another first from a company that is a recognized innovator in the health care industry."[7] Baxter's ambitious plans for the PULSE product launch included staged regional retail rollouts, with full national distribution by mid 2003.

To make a long story short, PULSE was a flop. Walk into your grocery store today and you're very likely to find other leading "nutritional waters," including Dasani Nutriwater from Coca-Cola, Veryfine Fruit$_2$0 from Kraft, and Propel and Aquafina Essentials from PepsiCo. You're very unlikely to find anything called PULSE. If you go to the former PULSE web site (www.pulsenutrition.com), you encounter an "under construction" sign.

What went wrong? Simply put, Baxter was leaving behind its strengths and entering an entirely new strategic segment—a strategic segment of ready-to-serve water and soft drinks that was crowded with established players that already understood the retail channel in a way that Baxter never would. Skill in packaging water—other than the purely promotional aspect of packaging—was mostly irrelevant in this market. There was almost no chance that Baxter would achieve economies of scope or scale or would provide a compelling enough menu of benefits to consumers for PULSE to dislodge the other entrants in the field.

In fact, there was something vaguely unseemly, even distasteful, about having Baxter in the drinks business. "You know you're getting older," reads the first line in the *Arizona Republic*'s article about the arrival of PULSE in Phoenix, "when your favorite drink comes from a company that makes IV fluids."[8] Or prepackaged doses of vaccines, for that matter, or dialysis delivery systems.

But before digging any deeper into the significance of the PULSE story, look at a far more successful Baxter acquisition.

A Home Run in Bloomington

Of course, it's very easy to get everything right in hindsight, and you can't put a halt to innovation when the first skeptic pops up. But there were clues along the way that Baxter might have picked up on, if it had been open to negative internal feedback on PULSE. One clue came when Baxter asked its existing businesses if they wanted to take PULSE under their wing. Everyone said, "No, thanks."

One of those businesses was the parenterals group. ("Parenterals" are simply drugs that enter the body by a route other than the mouth, e.g., through an injection.) At about the same time that NTRI was cooking up PULSE, the Medication Delivery division, of which parenterals were a key part, was finalizing a deal to buy Cook Pharmaceutical Solutions, a Bloomington, Indiana-based contract parenteral manufacturer. Cook manufactured prefilled syringes used to inject drugs intramuscularly and subcutaneously, almost always under contract to pharmaceuticals companies that had reduced their in-house manufacturing capabilities.

Looking at Cook, Baxter realized something interesting: Baxter did something very similar to Cook's business in its own core Medication Delivery business, working with pharmaceuticals to package drugs in intravenous containers (IV bags) and other specialized delivery systems. Looking forward from 2001, Baxter saw enormous growth potential in its own drug-delivery systems—thanks in part to the arrival of new biotechnology-derived drugs—and saw a natural fit between its own established product lines and the syringes from Bloomington. "The acquisition of Cook Pharmaceutical Solutions," said David F. Drohan, head of Medication Delivery, "will broaden the range of delivery options Baxter is able to offer our pharmaceutical partners around the world."[9]

Although the numbers are not public, all available evidence suggests that the acquisition was an immediate success. Between 2001 and 2003, for example, the Bloomington facility—renamed Baxter Pharmaceutical Solutions, or BPS—doubled its employee base as Baxter embarked on a seven-year, $100 million investment program in Bloomington. Baxter retained and grew the kind of business that Cook had been cultivating before 2001. "Outsourcing specialized services is becoming a more efficient solution for many of our pharmaceutical partners, especially biotech companies," explained one Baxter manager.[10] It appears that, if anything, that manager was guilty of understatement.

THE SMP TEST

Obviously, these two Baxter initiatives—PULSE and BPS—are asymmetrical in all kinds of ways beside their relative success. PULSE, as noted, was an orphan from Day One. It didn't fit into any existing corporate categories. Neither the Baxter annual reports nor the analysts' reports from the 2001–2003 period made any mention of

PULSE. In fact, if you look at those annual reports from this period—which are consistently organized in terms of the company's three main divisions—it's hard to imagine how an oddball product line like PULSE could *ever* find a home there. This, too, is a clue: If you can't imagine how you're going to represent this new venture to the owners of the company, it may be a loser.

There's another asymmetry that we shouldn't overlook: the basic issue of financial insignificance. In the context of a $9 billion corporation, any business unit that does less than, say, $100 million in annual sales (around 1 percent of the total company) is almost certain to be overlooked. In fact, it will always risk being axed in some round of corporate housecleaning. Here's the unpleasant truth for a tiny division in a huge company: Unless you appear to be the uncontested wave of the future, and unless you can ramp up with extraordinary speed, you're unlikely to stick.

I mention these asymmetries in part because they're the real world—which I'm trying to stay focused on in this book—and in part because they help introduce the basic principles that add up to what I call the SMP Test. The SMP Test includes four questions:

1. What strategic segment are we entering and who is the competition?
2. Will the new business improve our SMP in segments where we already compete?
3. If we are entering a new strategic segment, can we leverage our SMP in adjacent segments to ensure we achieve a strong SMP in the target segment?
4. Bottom line, will the new business make the weighted average SMP for our overall company better or worse?

Let's assume that your company is reasonably good (or expert) at idea generation. You're accustomed to casting a broad net and you're accustomed to finding a range of interesting ideas in that net when you pull it into your corporate boat.

Let's assume, too, that you and your colleagues are wise enough to concentrate your fishing in oceans where you already have strengths and where you're in a position to leverage either (1) your existing operations, (2) the scope of your customer solutions, or best of all possible worlds (3) both.

So when that seemingly good idea hits the table, the first question you should ask is, *What strategic segment are we entering and who is the competition?* It's always tempting to congratulate yourself and say, "We're creating a new strategic market segment." (This is blue ocean thinking, although with my vocabulary overlaid on top.) But most often, you're not. You may *think* you're going to be plowing virgin turf, but in the real world, someone's very likely to say, "Hang on, pal; that's *mine*."

So you have to think through this question with an open mind: What strategic segment are we entering? Is it truly a new strategic segment? If so, great. Go for it. Or is it a new market segment within a broader strategic segment in which competitors already exist? Those competitors are likely to have advantages in scale and scope if they turn their attention to the new market segment. Baxter wanted to believe that PULSE's competition was likely to be small and disorganized players with minimal channel clout, and so they believed it. But in fact, the real competition for PULSE was likely to be giants like Coke and Pepsi, who understood (and to a certain extent, controlled) the vital distribution channels. Who are your real competitors, current and potential?

The second question in the SMP Test is, *Will the business improve our SMP in segments where we already compete?* If the new business will add scale in a strategic segment where we are already competing, then according to the Value Maps depicted in earlier chapters, we should be able to ramp up our activities in such a way that we can achieve either increased economies of scale or scope, or expanded customer benefits that—in the reasonably near term—will lead to higher profitability and growth.

If the answer to the second question is no, then we must apply the next part of the SMP test: *Can we leverage our SMP in adjacent strategic market segments to achieve a strong SMP in the target segment?* Up to this point, we've considered strategic market segments and SMPs in a relative vacuum—that is, as if they were freestanding. In the real world, a strong SMP in one strategic segment will often provide some benefit when competing in an adjacent strategic segment. Not enough to overwhelm the advantages of a strong competitor in the adjacent strategic segment (otherwise the two businesses would be best thought of as one combined strategic segment), but enough to tip the balance when we are going up against more fragmented competitors.

The final question for the SMP test is, *Given what we know about the strategic segments and competition, is the new business likely to make our company's overall weighted-average SMP better or worse?* If the answer is "better," then we will be not only making our business bigger, but also creating increased competitive advantage that should translate to higher profitability and growth.

In the case of Pulse, Baxter did a good job of uncovering a blue-ocean opportunity with market needs not being met by other competitors. But the strategic segment of water and soft drinks was one where Baxter could not hope to be successful against the huge-scale incumbents. The initiative, to the extent it succeeded in gaining sales at all, was destined to *weaken* Baxter's overall competitive position and average SMP.

The Cook acquisition, by contrast, was a less innovative strategy that expanded on services that Baxter and others were already providing. Leveraging its sales force and reputation with pharmaceutical companies enabled Baxter to build leadership quickly in an adjacent strategic segment that lacked strong competitors. The result was an increase in Baxter's overall SMP and what became one of Baxter's fastest-growing business units over the next three years.

To underscore this point, let's look at another example of a company that figured out how entering an adjacent market could reinforce and expand its core business and add extraordinary value to the enterprise.

BEST BUY BUYS GEEK SQUAD: PUTTING ADJACENCIES TO WORK

The protagonists in this story are big-box retailer Best Buy—which has a core specialization in PCs and other consumer electronics—and a computer-support service firm called Geek Squad.

The Two Protagonists

Best Buy Co., Inc., the acquirer in our story, was and is a specialty retailer of consumer electronics, home-office products, entertainment software, appliances, and related services. Incorporated in the state of Minnesota in 1966 as Sound of Music, Inc., the company changed its name to Best Buy Co., Inc. in 1983. Although it began life as an audio components retailer, in 1983 the company revised its marketing strategy and began employing mass-merchandising techniques that included offering a wider variety of products and operating its outlets under a "superstore" concept. In 1989, it dramatically changed its method of retailing by introducing a self-service, non-commissioned, discount-style store concept designed to give the customer more control over the purchasing process (and to protect him or her from the badgering that has been associated with audio components retailers in the past).

What about the other company? Geek Squad, also based in Minnesota, was founded in 1994. Although a relatively small operation—with a payroll of approximately 60 people—it was nevertheless one of the larger players in a very fragmented field. Offering 24-hour tech support to both residential and commercial clients, Geek Squad had achieved some modest celebrity through a succession of clever marketing ploys. For example, it had its computer technicians don uniforms and badges that made them look like nerdy FBI agents. It put them in Volkswagen Beetles with distinctive paint jobs for their house calls. It used its offbeat corporate name—and image—to full advantage. By the time it was acquired by Best Buy in October 2002, it had operations in Minneapolis, Chicago, Los Angeles, and San Francisco.

Retailers into Services

At first blush, you might think that embracing Geek Squad represented an even odder departure for Best Buy than PULSE was for Baxter. But the logic of SMP—and, of course, the track record of this particular combination—argues strongly that this is not the case.

In fact, specialty retail is a sector in which a broader offering has proved to have a particular sort of power. For example: It may not be immediately obvious that services are an integral part of a product-based retail industry. But these distinctions have been blurred in productive ways over the years. When you think of carpet sales and installation services, or auto sales and repair services, you realize that bundling products and services has become common in many categories.

This distinctive migration has led some retailers to rediscover and define their offerings to include both the products and services. From home improvement to consumer electronics and personal computers, retailers are increasingly adding services to enhance core products, capture additional value, increase switching costs, and strengthen their strategic market position.

In this spirit, big box specialty retailers—who traditionally have grown by invading new geographies—have more recently turned to increased customer service as a differentiator to defend and grow share. They've realized that customer-centric services not only open up new revenue streams, but also attract new sources of customers.

Take home improvement as an example. Both Lowe's and Home Depot have been aggressively expanding their service offerings, installing everything in your home from the roof to the floor—and all the windows, doors, cabinets, siding, and finishes along the way. Obvious? Not when you remember that this is an industry that originally played, with great success, to the confidence and resilience of the do-it-yourself customer. But now the companies are using expanded installation and service offerings to attract customers who wouldn't have *dreamed* of entering a Lowe's or a Home Depot, opting instead for calling their local contractor.

There have been challenges, but it seems to be working. In a recent quarter, Home Depot's services business enjoyed a remarkable *28 percent* year-over-year sales increase.

Looking for Growth—and Finding It

Now let's hone in on our subject company. Best Buy's service performance in consumer electronics and PC services is an even more compelling example of a successful extension in a strategic market segment. From the late 1990s through 2002, Best Buy was adding new store locations at an accelerated rate. (In fact, new store openings grew from 13 in 1998 to more than 60 in 2002.) But like almost all other established big-box retailers, Best Buy was seeing the limits on its ability to grow through geographic expansion.

But Wall Street never sleeps, and the pressure to grow was not abating. So where could the company look next for growth opportunities?

Best Buy turned to the service sector. In October 2002, the company bought Geek Squad. Best Buy paid a total of $3 million for the

Geek Squad name, 30 Volkswagen Geekmobiles, and the contracted services of 60 technicians.

The 30 Volkswagen Beetles were together worth only around $300,000, so this might seem like a steep price to pay for assets that are mainly intangible—goodwill, a staff of highly mobile technicians, and existing customer relationships. But if you consider the acquisition in SMP terms, you can understand how Geek Squad naturally complements Best Buy's core business of PC and consumer electronics product sales.

First of all, consumers can bring their PCs into a Best Buy store for drop-off repair. Or, if they're concerned about networking or security issues, or they don't want to be bothered with the sometimes intimidating process of packing up the equipment and dropping it off, they can schedule an in-home service visit from a Geek Squad technician, also known as an "Agent." (As with the FBI, "Agent" tends to be capitalized.) For consumers in this mindset, there doesn't tend to be a lot of price resistance: *My lifeline has been severed! Fix it!*

Meanwhile, back at the Big Box, new PC purchasers are being referred to the conveniently located Geek Squad counter for the installation of software and—frequently—for up-selling of additional higher-margin accessories.

By the end of fiscal 2005, Geek Squad's services were available through all Best Buy stores in the United States and Canada, as well as through 10 standalone Geek Squad stores. Best Buy has announced plans to open between 20 and 50 standalone Geek Squad stores in the coming years, which we can take to be a pretty reliable indicator that the economics of this new service-centric business are quite favorable, indeed. As I write this chapter (in 2006), Geek Squad is forecast to bring in more than *$650 million* in revenues and more than $50 million in net income.[11] Based on Best Buy's price-to-earnings multiple of ~27×, Geek Squad is worth more than *$1 billion*: not a shabby performance for a business that was purchased four years earlier for $3 million.

Meanwhile, of course, Best Buy has greatly improved its competitive position in PCs. Across the industry, PCs as a category are essentially a breakeven proposition for retailers. Retailers make money in this business by managing the "attachment rate"—that is, by driving up the ratio of higher-margin accessories sales relative to PC sales. With Geek Squad, Best Buy is realizing significantly higher attachment rates, as customers are "upsold" on additional accessories.

At the same time, of course, Best Buy gets the added benefit of another revenue stream through higher-margin services. Service gross margins are in the neighborhood of 50 percent, which is something like 25 percent higher than Best Buy's core business of retailing electronics.

Geek Squad's tremendous success has put Best Buy in an increasingly strong position in the electronics retail market. Since the acquisition, Best Buy has experienced consistent double-digit growth and has gained *eight points* of market share. Stealing 8 percent of the market from your competitors in any established industry is cause to celebrate; in the ferociously competitive field of consumer electronics, it's cause for a sustained victory dance. As noted, Geek Squad's revenues alone are projected to exceed $650 million annually and are also projected to keep right on growing. People are likely to remain technophobic, even as computers assume an ever more important role in their lives. In fact, Best Buy believes that the "do-it-for-me" trend is here to stay and that the technical-services market alone is a multibillion-dollar business opportunity.

Applying the SMP Test to Best Buy/Geek Squad

Think about Best Buy and Geek Squad in light of the SMP test I described earlier.

1. *What strategic segment are we entering and who is the competition?* Is technical service for PCs a separate strategic market segment from computer and electronics retailing? Is in-home technical

service a separate strategic segment from in-store technical service? Certainly, they are different market segments, serving different customer needs and situations. Many customers will buy the product without the service, or vice versa. But remember, the ultimate test for whether two market segments are part of the same strategic segment is whether a company playing in only one market segment would be at a substantial disadvantage to a company with strong shares in both.

I argue that in this case, product retailing and service are best thought of as one strategic segment. So much of the service is related to new product setup that there is a real benefit to the consumer from being able to buy both from one company. In addition, PC retailers need to be able to provide technical support in their stores, which means they cannot avoid being in the technical-services business to at least some degree. As we saw with other retail businesses, there is probably a geographic segmentation. In terms of products versus service, though, they are one strategic segment.

With respect to competition, Best Buy was already the market leader in consumer electronics retailing, with around 11 percent national market share in 2002, ahead of Circuit City, which had around 5 percent. On the service side, the market was served by thousands of independent operators along with mostly disinterested retailers and OEMs. Best Buy, with its 3,500 in-store technicians, was probably the largest provider of PC service and setup advice in the United States even before it entered the market for these services.

2. *Will the new business improve our SMP in segments where we already compete?* The answer is a clear yes. First, the acquisition of Geek Squad had a small but positive impact on Best Buy's share of the combined retailing and services segment. Since we determined that they both compete in the same strategic

segment, we can simply add the sales and share of each company. Second, the added convenience to consumers should create the opportunity for further gains in market share.

3. *Can we leverage our SMP in adjacent strategic segments?* This does not apply because we have already determined that we are expanding into a new market segment within the same overall strategic segment.

4. *Bottom line, will the new business make the weighted average SMP for our overall business better?* Based on the preceding answers, the combination looks strongly beneficial. In fact, in the first three years since the Geek Squad acquisition, Best Buy rolled out the service operations across its whole network. The result has been that Best Buy's U.S. market share for consumer electronics retailing (including services) has almost doubled, from 11 percent to 19 percent, with a corresponding increase in market share city by city. See Figure 7.3.

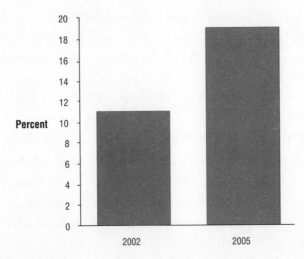

FIGURE 7.3 Best Buy Estimated Market Shares (2002–2005)
Data Source: IBIS World.

LINK TO FINANCIAL HURDLES

When it comes to investigating a new business, most senior management will ask a more fundamental question: *Does it meet our investment criteria?* Am I suggesting that the SMP Test should replace this? The answer is no. In fact, SMP analysis should *complement* traditional financial criteria.

The most widely used financial metric for major investments is discounted cash flow analysis. This is Finance 101, and I don't go into it at length here.[12] Simply stated, you look at the incremental costs and revenues that will be associated with this strategic move over time. Then, using your weighted average cost of capital, you discount future cash flows to reflect your risk and the time value of money. This gives you the value of the future stream of cash flows that would result from the investment. As long as the value of that future stream is greater than the upfront investment you need to put up to enter the business, you're creating value and you should move ahead.

The drawback with discounted cash flow is that it involves a lot of assumptions. For example: *What will we actually achieve, in terms of revenue? What costs will we incur?* I referred to temptation and wishful thinking earlier in the chapter; here's where they tend to turn up again. The temptation is to overstate potential returns and downplay potential costs. Time to get real: Why is the market going to allow you to pull off such a low-cost miracle? Given that there's lots of capital chasing new investment opportunities, and given that there are lots of smart people standing behind that capital—doing the very same kinds of analyses that you are—why should you assume that you can do better than the rest of that talented pack?

This brings us back to the logic of SMP. In order to earn returns above the weighted cost of capital, you have to have some special advantage that isn't open to other competitors. What *is* that advantage? Will you grow faster? Will you leverage some costs from within the same strategic segment and therefore enjoy lower costs? Will you share some of the same manufacturing infrastructure across your businesses (current and proposed) so that you have lower investment thresholds than other investors would? Exactly what—in terms of either higher revenues, lower costs, or lower investment requirements—enables you to achieve returns above the cost of capital and find hidden value for your shareholders?

If you understand your business' Value Map and SMP, you should be in a much better position to make accurate financial forecasts that reflect your competitive advantage (or lack of it). You will also be in a better position to explain to top management or directors why your proposed initiative makes strategic sense and how financial targets will be achieved.

General Electric Steps into an Adjacent Strategic Segment

I imagine that over the course of his illustrious career at GE, Jack Welch very often played the role of the skeptic, forcing his planners to paint compelling pictures, both with numbers and narratives.

GE can be seen as the "best practice" model for many strategic concepts. I argue that effective use of the logic of SMP is one of many explanations for GE's success. In fact, one of the most important factors in the resurgence of GE under Welch was its comprehensive-service business model, pursued by GE Capital in tandem with the company's product businesses.

An example of this new focus was GE's strategy in the aircraft engines sector. In the 1980s, GE served mainly as an OEM in the aircraft-engine sector, but soon realized the revenue and profit opportunities of integrating the maintenance, repair, and overhaul (MRO) function into their aircraft engine manufacturing business. For every dollar spent on aircraft components, 66 cents is spent on MRO. See Figure 7.4.

In 1991, GE began building their MRO offering through the £272 million acquisition of a British Airways aircraft engine overhaul plant. Through further acquisitions at home and abroad, GE's share of the nonairline owned engine overhaul market went from 20 percent at the beginning of the 1990s to more than 50 percent in 1997, as the company expanded from simple engine repair to parts management and on-wing support.[13]

Not only did GE's share improve, but—as implied earlier—it enjoyed greater profit margins on the service side. Engine services provided just 40 percent of the combined revenues of the Aircraft Engine division in 1996 but yielded approximately 75 percent of the division's net profits. Against its largest competitor, Pratt & Whitney,

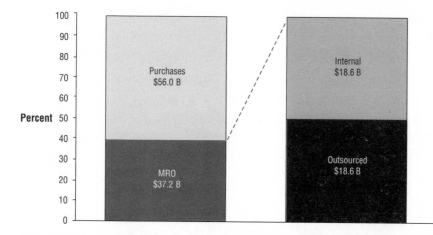

FIGURE 7.4 Worldwide Commercial Aircraft Purchases and MRO (2005)
Data Source: Frost & Sullivans, Boeing Investor Relations.

GE's Engines Division was able to gain substantial share while at the same time enjoying higher margins. See Table 7.1.

Realizing that it was lagging behind, Pratt & Whitney mimicked GE by forming its Eagle Services Division, joining in the profitable trend of downstream initiatives. Moves like this one from GE and competing OEMs practically eliminated the third-party service share of the engine overhaul sector.

But GE's move into aircraft MRO was only part of a bigger picture. Under standing orders from Chairman Welch to "participate in more of the food chain,"[14] in the 1980s GE began acquiring financial-service businesses to build its financial leasing unit, GE Capital. Through a joint venture between GE Capital Aviation Services and GE Engine Services, GE Engine Leasing provides a comprehensive array of financing and operational solutions that cater to any type of customer. Included are short-term rental programs, operational leases, structured finance for longer-term transactions, and component management services, as well as guaranteed availability. Although these programs vary in their specific terms to fit the needs of a specific customer, the common trend among these programs is the inclusion of service and finance with the product.

The integration of services and finance continued to evolve over the decade, further expanding the breadth of offerings to customers. One such evolved program is the Component Management Service,

TABLE 7.1   G.E. Engines Division versus Pratt & Whitney

	GE			Pratt & Whitney		
	1995	2005	Change	1995	2005	Change
Revenue ($M)	6,098	11,904	14.3%	6,170	9,295	8.5%
Market Share	36.2%	40.9%	4.7%	36.6%	31.9%	(4.7%)
Average Operating Margin (1995–2005)		18.2%			13.1%	

Note: Revenue change shown as 1995–2005 CAGR; market share is PPT change.

introduced in 2004. Geared toward commercial airlines, GE offers the aircraft engine, financing, servicing, and management of parts for one fixed price per flight hour. Imagine how compelling this proposition is from the vantage point of a commercial airline, which is now able to convert a lumpy fixed cost into one that varies with their own business activity.

GE THROUGH THE SMP LENS

Are engine servicing and aircraft financing in the same strategic segment as engine manufacturing? I argue that they are not. The technology barriers in producing aircraft turbines are so great that these have to be thought of as separate strategic segments. The continued success of Rolls-Royce engines, built on technology leadership without a large service business, is proof of this.

If servicing (and aircraft financing) are separate strategic segments from engines, then we have to consider the SMP Test: *Can we leverage our strong SMP in engine manufacturing to achieve a strong SMP in the target segment?* In other words, to be successful, it was not enough for GE just to enter the services market. It needed to achieve leadership in the strategic segment. A look at the competition for engine repair and overhaul would have shown GE that while there were some mid-sized competitors, the industry was mostly fragmented, with no multibillion dollar corporations capable of giving GE a run for its money. When GE began making acquisitions in the sector, it was quickly able to build the global leadership that enabled it to offer attractive integrated offerings to customers.

The bottom line from GE's push into engine servicing was a market-leading SMP in a new strategic segment. For the engines business overall, the result was higher weighted-average SMP that was reflected in both faster growth and higher profitability.

Much has been written about how Chairman Welch began pushing for a "boundaryless company" that would "remove barriers among engineering, manufacturing, marketing, sales, and customer service."[15] I translate this into the need to look at adjacent SMPs—that is, new areas of business that would take advantage of existing strengths in new ways. People marvel at the success of GE Capital. My take is that this success grew in part out of the close ties to the company's successful manufacturing arm through its growing service divisions.[16]

Even Bigger Challenges

This brings us to the end of our explorations of ways to use SMP to find new markets. Throughout much of this chapter, our implicit assumption has been that you enjoy the great blessing of a vital core business (e.g., Baxter, Best Buy, or GE) that you're trying to leverage through SMP. Nothing succeeds like success, and it's arguably easier for a world-class company—with resources, momentum, and the skills to implement the heck out of something—to step sideways into new areas of endeavor and succeed.

But what about the less happy circumstance in which your core business is anemic? Can SMP help in that situation as well? The answer is yes, and that's the focus of our next chapter.

8

SMP Strategies for
Low-Growth or
Low-Margin Businesses

So far in this book, I've tended to focus on either *really good* or *really bad* situations. This has been mainly for narrative reasons: It's easier to illustrate a point with a tale from one extreme of the business spectrum or the other. In some cases, as in Chapter 1, I paired companies to illustrate both ends of the spectrum at once. If you're an airline, for example, you'd rather be soaring like Southwest than struggling like America West. For similar SMP-related reasons, you'd rather be Wal-Mart than Kmart. You'd rather be Nintendo than Sega.

But what about the situation in which most companies actually find themselves—that is, slugging it out in the middle of the pack? Or worse, what if you're in a low-margin, low-growth business? What if you're making only, say, 5 percent on sales? What if you're making less than a 10 percent return on your invested capital, for example? What if certain constituencies, say, your shareholders, are starting to ask out loud whether their resources might be better off pulled out of this company and parked in an index fund somewhere—with generally lower risks and the likelihood of a higher return? Can SMP help in this kind of scenario?

The answer is yes. In this chapter, we focus on the kind of diagnostics that you should run on an underperforming business and the kinds of steps that you should take based on the results of your diagnosis. As you will see, there are a number of decision points in this kind of diagnosis. There are also a number of endpoints, ranging from revival (through focused SMP-building) to exit. I include real-world examples illustrating both key decision points and endpoints.

THE STARTING POINT: YOU, YOUR INDUSTRY, AND YOUR SMP

Start with a branching diagram—a simple decision tree—that I use as the organizing device for this discussion. See Figure 8.1.

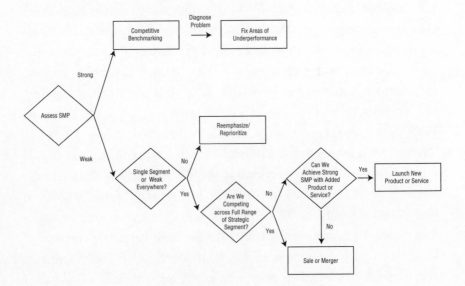

FIGURE 8.1   Decision Tree: Addressing Weak Performance

The first question that this diagram is designed to help us answer—the left-hand side of the chart—is, *Why is this business not doing well?* (The right-hand side answers the question, *What do we do about it?*)

We're assuming that your business isn't performing at a high level. Well, why *is* that? Contrary to much of what you read in the business press today, underperformance is rarely the result of management not trying hard enough. In fact, if it were possible to try too hard, most managers today could be convicted on that charge easily. In my experience, this is *particularly* true when things aren't going well. People get up earlier, try harder, stay at work later, and otherwise flog themselves, all in the name of turning in a better performance.

In many such cases, you wind up running hard just to stay even. You're dealing with the day-to-day requirements of running the business, while at the same time fending off the dark clouds of uncertainty and frustration that seem to blow in when results are below expectations. Rarely, if ever, can you carve out the time to think through and implement fundamental changes in the way you position your business.

In such circumstances, it's always tempting to blame the industry as a whole for your own company's underperformance. One refrain that I hear very often, for example, is, "Competitors are bidding for work at below cost. There's no way *anyone* in this industry is making money now!"

But most likely, that's not true. In Chapter 1, I referred to a study that my firm conducts every year that is printed as a special section of the *Wall Street Journal*, usually in late February. As you may recall, the analysis is called the "Shareholder Scoreboard," and it presents a tally of how the top 1,000 companies in the United States performed for their shareholders in the preceding year.[1] Year after year, two interesting things have consistently emerged. First, there's *no such thing as a bad industry*. Sure, you can point to the extreme cases thrown up by Big Changes in the real world. (In recent years, these extreme cases have included home construction on the high end and fixed-line telecoms on the low end.) But, by and large, most industry groups tend to perform consistently in a band of between 0 and 20 percent over a five-year period or 5 to 15 percent over a 10-year period.

Frequently, people don't buy this conclusion because it's counter-intuitive. How can a stodgy industry perform as well as a sexy one? But it's true. If you look at five-year industry-group returns, stodgy railroad properties (18.3 percent) did almost exactly as well as sexy Internet properties (18.4 percent).[2]

There's a corollary argument that probably needs a sideways glance here. At this point in the discussion, people often say something to the effect that, "Yes, but you can make a *whole lot more money* in pharmaceuticals than footwear." This is true only if you don't take into account the cost of developing or buying a pharmaceutical drug. Sure, everybody would like to be in a business with 90-plus-percent gross margins and with unbreachable patent walls all around you. But developing a marketable, patented drug is hideously expensive—somewhere between $800 million and $1 billion, with no guarantees of success—and buying someone else's successful pharmaceutical is another extraordinarily expensive proposition. In other words, the sexier the industry, the higher the cost of entry and the harder it will be to create value for your shareholders, at least in the near term. Remember Boardwalk and Park Place in our Monopoly game in Chapter 1? They cost a lot to acquire, and therefore dollars invested in them don't necessarily give you a better rate of return.

So for the sake of argument in this chapter, we assume that your company is in the huge group of industries that perform in the middle range.

The second interesting thing that emerges from the "Shareholder Scoreboard," year after year, is that *there are spectacular differences across companies within industries.* In the same five-year period that Dean Foods turned in a 22.6 percent performance, Sara Lee registered negative 1.9 percent.[3]

Those are the kinds of differences that we're trying to get at in this chapter. If you're in one of those industries that include both losers and luminaries, how can we get you out of the former category and into the latter?

This process begins, therefore, when you agree to worry less about overall industry conditions and dynamics and more about your position within your industry. As Figure 8.1 indicates, your first step should be to *assess the overall SMP* for your company or business. As we have described in earlier chapters, this involves first determining the boundaries for the *strategic segments* you compete in (using the Value Map tool) and then assessing your strategic market position for each strategic segment where you compete and for your business overall.

I can't emphasize too strongly how important it is to get this step right. First, if you don't understand what strategic segments you are competing in, you're almost certain to attack the wrong problem. And second, depending on how weak or strong your SMP is, you will have to consider very different strategies for improving your performance.

STRONG SMP, WEAK PERFORMANCE

If you have a strong SMP but you're underperforming, then by definition you are not taking full advantage of your potential scale or scope benefits. Perhaps you've achieved strong market share through a series of acquisitions, but these acquired companies have never been effectively integrated to achieve the savings that should be realized in manufacturing or distribution. Maybe you're operating several divisions, each with an autonomous sales organization, that are missing opportunities to present an integrated solution to customers—in other words, a single customer-facing point of contact. Here, again, your Value Map ought to be useful. Where are the benefits of scale in your particular industry and what opportunities aren't you taking full advantage of?

One approach for an underperforming company with a strong SMP is to identify opportunities for improvement through competitive benchmarking. This involves importing the well established techniques of benchmarking into the SMP realm.[4] Examining competitive practices and researching competitor expense levels can uncover opportunities for improvement that may have been overlooked in the past.

This is rarely easy. (See Chapter 5 as well as the Appendix for tips as to how to "do the detective work.") The research needs to be conducted through reviews of public filings, published information, and various other sources, and—depending on the industry—should focus on things like plant locations, head count data, wage levels, work practices, equipment used, and so on. Although this information is hard to develop, it can provide invaluable clues for improving performance. In fact, it can serve as a wake-up call for managers and can give them the confidence needed to shoot for much higher levels of profitability and value-creation.

How so? Well, perhaps your competitors have been more aggressive in relocating their manufacturing capacity or sourcing product from low labor-cost countries. Perhaps your competitors have done a better job of employing new technologies to streamline their operations. Perhaps they've simply done a better job of designing a leaner, flatter organization.

Maybe they've *had* to do this, and—up to now, at least—you haven't. Sometimes it's the company with the strong SMP that is the last to adopt the latest practices—such as offshore manufacturing or disruptive technologies—because their greater scale means that they have more invested in traditional ways of doing business. Sometimes that scale provides a cushion that enables the company to postpone making the difficult decisions.

One of my firm's clients, a manufacturer of portable cardiac monitoring devices, found that it was losing share to a new competitor that was pricing lower and was still able to make money. Our client's response—and this was *before* they were our client, by the way—was to position their device as a premium-priced product, emphasizing the unique benefits of their product's real-time data interpretation and nonproprietary recording media. The pricing policy didn't work very well, and this was the point when we were called in.

We talked to cardiologists and hospital technicians and we soon discovered the problem: They said that these features were nice to have but did not justify paying a substantial premium for our customer's product. That was the bad news. The good news came when we benchmarked our client's costs against those of the new competitor and found that our client's direct manufacturing costs were actually lower than the competitor's. The competitor, as it turned out, was using outsourced manufacturing and contract sales reps. This meant that they had very low fixed costs but much higher variable costs. The reason our client was struggling to match the competitor's prices was that our client was trying to cover a hefty burden of selling and administrative costs with a shrinking base of sales.

Armed with this benchmarking-derived knowledge, our client cut its prices to a level close to those of the competition. With their higher variable costs, the competition was unable to cut their prices further. Meanwhile, our client had a similar product with better features. You can guess where the market went: Our client's sales more than doubled and profits increased dramatically.

In other words, accurate competitive benchmarking had enabled our client to achieve the higher growth and profitability that was warranted by its strong SMP.

It's a little like a star athlete suddenly proving unable to compete in the majors, even though his or her talent hasn't diminished. What are the winners in that sport doing that the underperforming star isn't? To cite a case in point: In 1999, tennis star Andre Agassi found himself knocked out of the Australian Open in the fourth round. As he reflected on this rude awakening, he reminded himself that it had been four years since he had won a Grand Slam title. He had to ask himself: Could he still compete, or was it time to retire?

Part of the answer came when Agassi looked at what the winning tennis players in 1999 had in common: *physical fitness*. Agassi committed himself to a regimen of physical conditioning—and began winning Grand Slam titles again.

Benchmarking at Samsonite

Now look at another example of a high-SMP business that was not achieving its full potential in a tough market and used benchmarking to help increase its profitability and growth.

The Samsonite brand name has more than 95 percent consumer brand recognition.[5] (This high recognition factor was greatly aided by its legendary 1980s TV ad campaign, which featured an exasperated gorilla failing to damage the Samsonite luggage that it was hurling around in what appeared to be a behind-the-scenes airport baggage-handling area.) Including its Samsonite, Samsonite Black Label, and American Tourister branded products, the company is estimated to have around 20 percent share of luggage sales in Europe, the United States, and Asia.[6]

Samsonite has a strong SMP in the strategic segments it serves—arguably the strongest of any luggage manufacturer. However, it also carried a heavy debt load, and despite its strong competitive positions, Samsonite posted four straight years of net losses between 1999 and 2003.[7]

To be sure, part of the problem was external to the company. Following the terrorist attacks of September 11, 2001, the travel industry went into a tailspin. Travel expenditures dropped 6 percent year-over-year between 2000 and 2001 and an additional 3 percent between 2001 and 2002.[8] The luggage industry—and Samsonite sales—followed suit. The company did better than some competitors but suffered a 6 percent decline between the fiscal year ending January 2001 and that ending in January 2002.

As part of a strategy review and in conjunction with a series of related restructuring efforts, Samsonite undertook an industry benchmarking study in 2001. The study made it clear that, relative to industry benchmarks, Samsonite suffered from poor cost positions in manufacturing, warehousing, other variable costs, and selling, general, and administrative (SG&A) costs. The summary results of that study are reproduced in Figure 8.2.

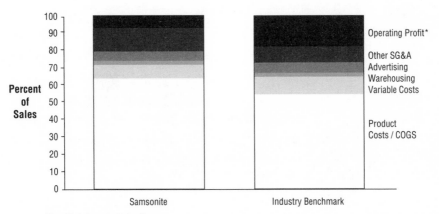

Note: *Excludes restructuring charges.

FIGURE 8.2   Samsonite Benchmarking (FY2002)
Data Source: Company financials, annual reports.

As you can see, Samsonite was performing significantly worse than industry benchmarks, mainly due to excessive product costs. But there were other issues to attend to. The company's warehousing expenses were reputed to be something like 20 percent above the industry average.

The problem was that Samsonite was being run as two separate companies (U.S. and European divisions) without leveraging its global scale. In some cases, the two divisions were sourcing U.S. and European products from the same supplier without knowing it. No wonder Samsonite was not enjoying profitability consistent with its global SMP. In response, Samsonite rationalized sourcing with global product lines. In addition, proposed changes to Samsonite's U.S. warehousing capacity promised to yield an additional $3 to 4 million in annual savings.

The company successfully implemented these and other cost-reduction plans. As a result, its gross margins improved from 39.8 percent in FY2002 to 46.1 percent in FY2005. See Figure 8.3.

Interestingly enough, the benchmarking exercise also highlighted areas in which Samsonite was spending *too little*. For example, it became

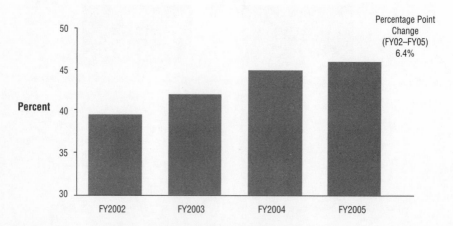

FIGURE 8.3   Samsonite Gross Margin (FY2001–FY2005)
Data Source: Bloomberg, annual reports.

clear that the U.S. arm of the company was suffering in part as a result of a curtailed advertising effort. Due to its poor operating results, the company had been decreasing its advertising expenditures in the United States from nearly 6 percent of sales in FY1999 to barely 2 percent of sales in FY2002. The benchmarking study underscored the need to free up dollars to support the brand in the U.S. luggage marketplace.

This brings us to another SMP-related point. Normally, a strong SMP business is exactly the kind of business you should be investing in and growing. But you will have a hard time justifying investments in the business if it is not earning according to its full potential. Take a look at Figure 8.4.

This shows how much value is generated for shareholders by

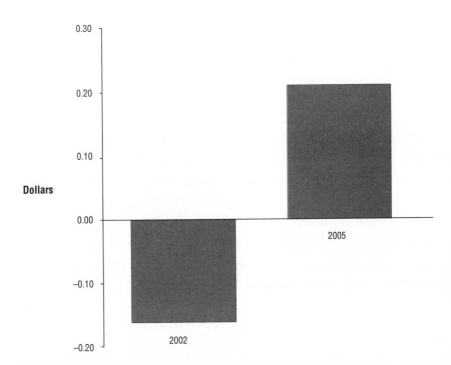

FIGURE 8.4   Samsonite: Shareholder Value Impact of $1 Sales Increase
Data Source: Bloomberg, annual reports.

increased sales. It is calculated as the perpetuity value of the profit from increased sales less the capital investment required to support increased sales. With Samsonite's level of profitability in 2002, increased sales resulted in a value loss for shareholders and it was hard to justify increased advertising spending or other investments to build sales. By 2005, the value of each dollar of sales growth was up to 20 cents. Now that it is performing at a level more consistent with its strategic market position, Samsonite has earned the right to grow its business and strengthen its SMP still further.

WEAK OVERALL SMP

As you might expect, weak overall SMP is a far more common circumstance than the scenario that was just described and that was exemplified by Samsonite (strong SMP/weak performance). The first question that needs to be answered is, *Are we weak everywhere or only in some areas?* Do we have a weak SMP in some strategic market segments and a strong one elsewhere? If so, can we emphasize the strong SMP(s) and deemphasize or exit the weak one(s)?

Think back to the example of C.H. Guenther, described in Chapter 6. As you recall, Guenther discovered that it had different strategic market positions (and different profitability) across its portfolio of products and customers. What was needed was to focus efforts on some areas and "de-market" products and customers in strategic segments where C.H. Guenther was weak. The result? Operating margins doubled within 12 months.

Dean Foods

Another example of the benefits of reemphasis and reprioritization of strategic segments is Dean Foods. In the food products industry sector, where multibillion-dollar companies such as ConAgra, General Mills, and Kraft play, the average five-year shareholder returns hover around 5 to 6 percent.[9] Over the past five years, however, the relatively small Dean Foods has beaten the best of this elite group, posting an amazing 22 percent annual shareholder return.[10] What has Dean done to generate this success? They have grown by improving their SMP—gaining share in stronger and well-defined strategic segments while also systematically exiting from weaker segments.

Our story begins in December 2001, when Suiza Foods acquired rival Dean Foods for $2.5 billion. The new company operated under the name Dean Foods, with annual sales of around $9 billion.[11]

With the acquisition, Dean focused subsequent moves on strengthening its position within its core SMP, that is, fluid dairy products and in particular, milk products. Dean's first move was to increase its 36 percent ownership in WhiteWave, the leading producer of soy milk (branded "Silk"), by purchasing the remaining 64 percent of the company for approximately $189 million.[12]

Soon after, Dean sold off its noncore boiled peanuts and contract hauling businesses and all its Puerto Rican operations. In October 2002, the company completed the sale of its 94 percent interest in EBI Foods Limited, a U.K.-based developer, manufacturer, and marketer of food coatings, stabilizers, bakery ingredients, and blended products. "Completing the sale of EBI Foods is consistent with our strategy of focusing on our core businesses and divesting non-core assets," said Dean Foods CEO Gregg Engles.[13] Dean also exited some frozen dairy segments through the divestiture of its frozen nondairy topping and frozen creamer business.

With an eye on the trend toward organic products, Dean purchased 13 percent of Horizon Organic in 2003 and acquired the remainder of the company in 2004 for $216 million.[14] Horizon Organic, with 2002 revenues of $217 million, was the leading organic food player in the United States. Along with the Silk brand in soy milk and Lactaid brand for lactose-intolerant consumers, the addition of Horizon Organic ensured that Dean had a prominent presence in every subsegment of the milk market. Throughout this period, Dean continued to purchase regional milk processors to gain share and production in the dairy milk marketplace.

In 2005, the company sold Dean's Dips and Marie's Dressings to Ventura Foods. Continuing in this vein, Dean spun off its specialty foods group, TreeHouse, to shareholders. Referring to this unusual divestiture, Engles commented that the parent company was divesting products that were "not core to our mission going forward."

To summarize: Over the course of more than five years, Dean focused on its core, thereby building its overall SMP—and it paid off. You recognize Figure 8.5 as the less important market-share

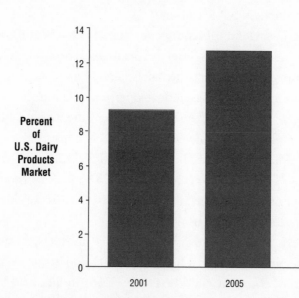

Market Shares

FIGURE 8.5   Dean Foods (2001–2005)
Data Source: Euromonitor, company annual reports.

measure (in this case, aggregate market share of the U.S. dairy products market).

Now look at Figure 8.6, which—in a slight twist on our previous versions of this all-important chart—captures Dean's weighted-average market share in both 2001 and 2005.

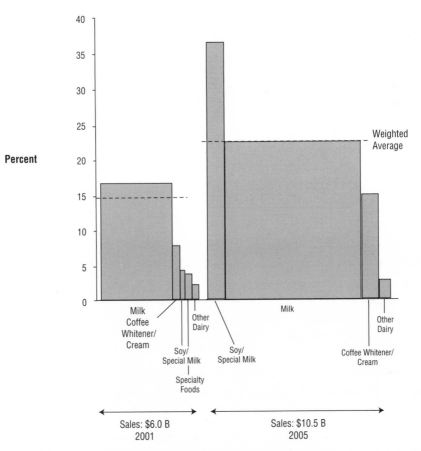

FIGURE 8.6 Dean Foods: U.S. Dairy Products Market (2001–2005)
Data Source: Euromonitor, company annual reports.

Look at the most obvious difference between the left side of the figure and the right: the width of the Milk band. As Dean grew in its largest strategic segment, it was able to realize increased economies of scale. After eliminating more than $100 million in costs in 2002, Dean was able to stabilize and even grow its margins, despite increasing raw milk costs.[15] At the same time, Dean's growth in specialty milks has enabled it to achieve strong SMP in a smaller but higher margin segment. The combined result has been improved shareholder returns, as seen in Figure 8.7.

More significantly, the company is poised to generate ongoing shareholder value, as it is expected to trade at a 10 to 12 percent premium to large-cap food stocks. As a February 2006 analyst report put

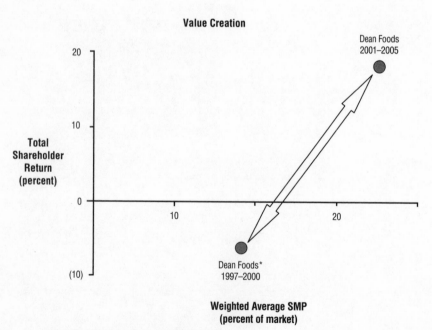

Note: *1997–2000 shareholder return based on Suiza Foods stock prices.

FIGURE 8.7   Dean Foods (2001–2005)
Data Source: Bloomberg.

it, "Looking longer-term, we continue to believe [Dean Foods] has one of the strongest franchises and best managements in the entirety of the food industry. We believe they will continue to create value for shareholders."[16]

WEAK SMP EVERYWHERE

What if we have no strategic segments where we are strong? What if we compete in only one strategic segment—or we compete in multiple segments but have a weak SMP in each? We can begin to answer this question by asking another one: *Are we competing across the full range of the relevant strategic segment?* In other words, are our offerings sufficiently broad that we are covering the needs of the market? If not, there may be competitive spaces within our strategic segment that have been neglected or haven't yet been occupied by strong competitors.

If this is the case, we should ask ourselves whether we can achieve a strong SMP in our strategic segment by adding one or more product lines, either organically or by acquisition.

Palm Computing, Inc.: An SMP Rebound

Let's look at a case in point. What happens when a company with a formerly strong SMP—overwhelming market share, high brand recognition, strong customer loyalty—suddenly discovers that its position has weakened and a new strategy is needed? The story of Palm Computing, Inc., manufacturer of the PalmPilot and the Treo, provides a compelling example of how a creative response to the challenge of a shifting SMP can not only protect a company from losing value, but can also create substantial value in a changing strategic market.

Palm was founded in 1992 by Jeff Hawkins and Donna Dubinsky. With the launch of the PalmPilot in 1996, Palm effectively created the market for personal digital assistants (PDAs) and achieved a dominant position, with more than 60 percent share.[17] PalmPilots—basically, handheld electronic organizers containing a calendar and contact list that could sync with an individual's PC—became a household name. This fueled strong revenue growth, first for U.S. Robotics, Palm's owner, and then for 3Com after it acquired U.S. Robotics.

Over time, though, Palm leaders clashed with 3Com management over issues such as operating system (OS) licensing and budget allocations. In May 1998, Hawkins and Dubinksy resigned, convinced that they did not have the freedom or control that they needed to maximize Palm's growth. They then formed Handspring, Inc., where they continued their track record of strong technological innovation by launching the Visor in October 1999. The Visor ran on the Palm OS but added new functionalities that appealed to high-end PDA users.

Meanwhile, Palm continued to release a series of products whose development Hawkins had overseen: the Palm III, Palm V, and Palm VII. In part through skilled marketing, Palm was able to use these products to solidify its market leadership. But this market is characterized by extremely rapid change—with agile innovators like Handspring bringing new products to market at an accelerating pace—and after the introduction of the Palm VII, the company began to suffer from its inability to bring forth next-generation products.

Had Palm rested on its laurels at this point and continued focusing on PDAs, it most likely would be remembered today as a flash in the pan—a point along the evolutionary trail of handhelds. Consumer demand started shifting away from simple handheld organizers to BlackBerry e-mail devices and "smartphones," that is, devices that integrated some combination of PDA, mobile phone, and e-mail/Web terminal.

For Palm, this shift was nothing less than catastrophic. Figure 8.8 shows the market loss Palm was facing, with an average annual decline of 9.1 percent.

Bad as this was, I argue that this figure overstates the strength of Palm's position in 2002. This is because the strategic segment had evolved beyond standalone PDAs to include the more complex integrated devices. Consider the Value Map in Figure 8.9.

As recently as 1999, customers had been happy to buy standalone organizers that lacked phone or e-mail capabilities. That was because the devices that had tried to integrate these functions were hard to use and unreliable. All that changed with the successful launch of BlackBerry portable e-mail devices. Almost overnight, integrated e-mail functionality became a required feature. The strategic segment that Palm was competing in was no longer standalone PDAs, but executive organizer and mobile communication tools. In this larger strategic segment, Palm faced a strong emerging competitor (BlackBerry) as well as established mobile phone companies that were adding functionality to their handsets. In SMP terms, Palm went from having a greater-than-60 percent market share in a

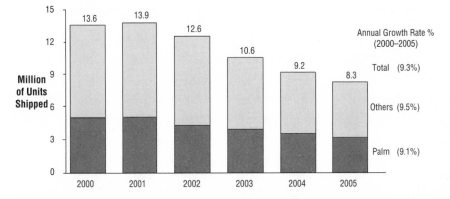

FIGURE 8.8   Palm Market Share in the Global PDA Market
Data Source: Gartner Dataquest, IDC.

Economic and Customer Benefits of Scale or Share

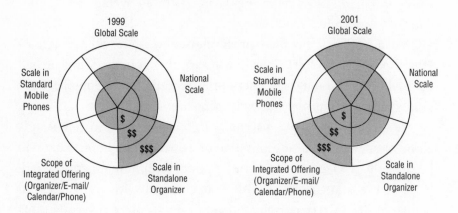

FIGURE 8.9   Value Map: Executive Organizer/Communication Tools

strategic segment that was declining (PDAs) to something like a 30 percent market share in a strategic segment that was growing rapidly (PDAs + e-mail + smartphones).

Facing a dismal future for their existing products (PDAs) and anticipating the enormous growth potential in the broader strategic segment, Palm made the fateful decision to reorient its focus away from the PDA and toward the e-mail/smartphone.

Palm's first attempt in this space—the Tungsten W, introduced in early 2003—was a complete failure. The company did not give up. Instead they looked, not surprisingly, at corporate offshoot and rival Handspring, which in October 2001 had introduced its first-generation smartphone. This device, called a "Treo," merged three devices (a trio) that had formerly been separate: a PDA, a mobile phone, and an e-mail/Web terminal.[18] Palm recognized that it lacked the innovative capability represented by the Treo and had to take dramatic steps to turn its fortunes around. Palm entered into discussions with Handspring, and those negotiations ultimately culminated (in August 2003) in Palm's strategic acquisition of the company for $169 million.

Palm Solutions Group President and CEO Todd Bradley commented on the deal in a Palm press release:

> This is a merger of leaders—the world's leading marketer of handheld computers and a global leader of Palm OS-based smartphones. Having the best and broadest portfolio of innovative products that deliver what matters most to customers, sold by a robust channel and built from a foundation of operational excellence, is the best formula to expand our young, promising markets.[19]

Good SMP-driven language, in my estimation. But was it a good move? Consider the following:

- Revenues increased 23 percent annually from 2003 to 2005.
- Net income moved from a $443 million loss to a $66 million profit.
- Palm's stock price has rebounded from a low of $3 in April 2003 to levels (at this writing) of over $23.
- The market equity value for Palm rose from $316 million to $2.1 billion.

To reiterate: Palm found its formerly unassailable SMP fading quickly. It asked the right (and tough) question: *Are we competing across the full range of our strategic market segment?* The answer, obviously, was no. So Palm took the expensive step of bringing its runaway offshoot, Handspring, back into the fold, creating a strong offering in a rapidly evolving strategic segment that lacked strong competitors with the track record of Palm. Yes, this strategic move cost Palm $169 million—and probably a certain amount of embarrassment, internally—but it created more than a *billion dollars* in shareholder value.

CREATING VALUE BY SELLING OUT: VICURON

The remaining option for unlocking value involves selling all or part of the company. This is by no means necessarily a failure; if the price is right, this may be by far the best way to unlock value for shareholders.

Take the case of Vicuron Pharmaceuticals, based in the Philadelphia suburb of King of Prussia, which was acquired by Pfizer in 2005 for $1.9 billion. In this case, we will adopt the point of view of the acquired company, rather than the acquiring company.[20]

Just prior to the Pfizer transaction, Vicuron was a publicly held company with a market capitalization of about $800 million. Vicuron was well-known in its industry for pursuing a disciplined, integrated approach to discovering next-generation compounds to treat both hospital-based and community-acquired infections. As a result of those efforts, the company had submitted new-drug applications to the Food and Drug Administration (FDA) for its two lead products: dalbavancin, a novel intravenous antibiotic for the treatment of serious Gram-positive infections; and anidulafungin, a novel antifungal agent. Although neither drug (nor any medicines based on them) had yet been approved by the FDA, analysts concluded that the drugs could eventually generate annual combined revenue of $1 billion.

Vicuron and Pfizer already knew a lot about each other. In fact, they were already collaborating on the discovery of next-generation oxazolidinones, the first new class of antimicrobial agents in three decades. Jointly, the two companies were searching for compounds that could become candidates for clinical trials for treatment of drug-resistant infections like penicillin-resistant pneumonia and "flesh eating" staphylococci bacteria.

For its part, the giant Pfizer needed to beef up its portfolio. The company had seen sales of its antibiotic Zmax fall 8 percent in 2004 as the result of competition from generic drugs. Although Pfizer had antifungals on the market, the patents for these drugs would soon run out and Pfizer would face still more competition from generics.[21]

Vicuron knew it had potentially valuable properties on its hands, but it also knew that it lacked the distribution system necessary to make those properties succeed in the marketplace. Perhaps even more frustrating, it was clear that Vicuron couldn't justify building a new network from scratch just to market its antifungals. (A pharmaceutical sales rep costs something on the order of $250,000 just to put in the field, and he or she generally needs more than one product line to sell to justify that kind of investment.) And for the moment, at least, Vicuron didn't have any products.

Just as the company began exploring its options, the FDA weighed in, giving only limited approval to one of Vicuron's drugs. The company's market capitalization tanked almost overnight: from $1.5 billion to $800 million.

At this point, Vicuron began thinking seriously about selling itself to a larger pharmaceutical. The company still had valuable late-stage, Phase 3 products in its pipeline and it was possible that more favorable FDA rulings were in the offing. But the company was still living off its cash and the prospect of putting 100 sales agents in the field—at a cost of perhaps $25 million a year—was daunting.

Vicuron began systematically thinking about potential buyers. It researched leading pharmaceutical companies to answer the question, "For which company will our technology provide the greatest boost to their strategic market position?" This is effective SMP thinking: If you know the answer to that question, then you are a long way toward knowing who is likely to put the greatest value on your business and what aspects of your business you should be emphasizing to them.

Through this process, Vicuron was able to secure serious interest from several bidders. When the Pfizer deal closed, Vicuron's CEO, George Horner III, declared that it would "enable Vicuron's two near-term products to utilize Pfizer's capabilities in order to fully achieve their potential."[22]

As noted, Pfizer paid $1.9 billion for Vicuron. This is one of the most clearcut examples of finding hidden value for your shareholders that you're likely to come across: a *billion-dollar* premium (and then some) over the pretransaction market capitalization. Or, stated more precisely, an 84 percent premium over Vicuron's closing price the week before the deal was announced, and a 74 percent premium over the stock's three-month average closing price.[23]

Sometimes the highest-value application of SMP is letting you know when and how it makes sense to sell off or merge a business that would find it difficult to achieve a strong strategic market position on its own.

DIGGING OUT OF A HOLE

Much of this chapter has been about a relatively unglamorous challenge: digging out of an underperformance hole.

Many of the tools and tactics I've pointed to—for example, benchmarking and selective expansion and pruning of the corporate portfolio—are thoroughly familiar to people who are already in the trenches. What I've tried to do, though, is talk about those familiar tools and tactics in the logic and language of SMP. How do you get better and uncover hidden value? What do you do if you can't find hidden value within the organization? What do you do if you find that value—as in the Vicuron example—but you can't exploit it on your own?

In the next and final chapter, I return to the area of mergers and acquisitions, sometimes thought of as the fast lane of corporate life. But I ask you to keep your SMP hat on. As you will see, this area has the potential for huge losses and wrecked careers, as well as rapid growth and value creation when approached correctly.

9

WHEN DO
ACQUISITIONS MAKE SENSE?

LET'S BEGIN TO answer the question posed in this chapter's title with a blunt statement that will annoy the M&A industry: *Organic growth is generally better.*

It's true. As a rule, you're better off growing it yourself. Why? First, there's the logic of SMP, as described in the previous chapters. You're more likely to increase the value of your company if you can find a way to expand your existing business and achieve increased benefits of scale or scope within your existing strategic segments.

There is also the issue of the price of acquisitions. Every successful corporation is feeling the same growth imperatives that you are. All are looking for growing, profitable companies to add to their portfolios of businesses. So you have strong competition from corporate buyers.

You also have strong competition from financial buyers. There are thousands of private equity firms looking for good companies to buy—financial buyers that weren't in the game 20 years ago or even a decade ago. It takes only one or two such buyers with an inflated sense of their own management capabilities to drive up the cost of a potential acquisition past what you should pay for it.

And finally, there's the problem of all that cheap money floating around out there. The convergence of all these factors means that valuations of good companies, and even some not-so-good companies, have been steadily creeping upward since the market recovery began in 2001. (See Figure 9.1.)

The upshot: You may have to pay 20 times earnings, or even more, to acquire a good property. This means that, even ignoring the time value of money, you need 20 years of profits at the current level to get your money back.

But as I've already shown in previous chapters, there certainly are situations in which an acquisition makes good sense. (Think back to the examples in Chapter 7 of Baxter buying Cook Pharmaceutical Solutions or Best Buy acquiring Geek Squad.) So how can you use

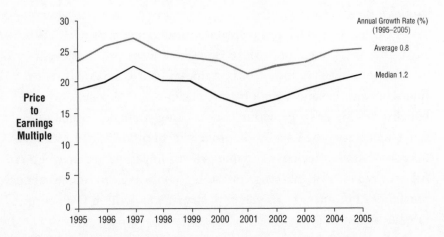

FIGURE 9.1   Transaction Price-to-Earnings (P/E) Ratio Offered (1995–2005)
Data Source: Mergerstat.

the logic of SMP to figure out when an acquisition makes sense? And more specifically, how can you figure out whether the acquisition premium that you're almost certain to pay, in today's competitive M&A environment, is worth it?

That's the subject of our final chapter. Again, we will apply the SMP Test just as we did when considering new business opportunities in Chapter 7, using real-world examples of both happy-ending stories and not-so-happy-ending stories. I also include an example of applying the principles of SMP to an "acquisition," of sorts, in the non-profit sector. As you'll see, SMP sometimes can be very useful outside the confines of the for-profit universe.

QUAKER BUYS SNAPPLE: A COSTLY MISTAKE

Our first cautionary tale is the ill-fated acquisition of the Snapple Beverage Corporation by the Quaker Oats Company.

I know this is a story that's familiar to many in the business community, in part because it was such a costly mistake, both for shareholders and management. But reinterpreting a well-known story through the SMP lens may help you understand better what happened and how it could have been avoided. In the early 1990s, Snapple was an innovative, fast-growing drinks company that seemed to be doing everything right. Then, in 1994 Quaker acquired Snapple for $1.7 billion. Snapple's sales skidded and actually declined for the year after the purchase. Two years after that, Snapple was sold for 82 percent less than the original purchase price. Quaker CEO William Smithburg, architect of the Snapple deal, departed soon afterward.

My argument, as you will see, is that applying the logic of SMP to this proposed acquisition could have headed off this disaster.

Snapple: Healthy, Wealthy, and Wise

Snapple Beverage Corporation was founded in 1972 as the "Unadulterated Food Products, Inc." by three New York City natives with a shared interest in healthy foods. They began selling all-natural beverages to New York health food stores in 1986, and their small company experienced rapid growth, especially in the relatively untapped market of ready-to-drink (RTD) tea.[1] The company pioneered a new "hot package" process for teas that quickly became the industry standard—and for good reason. "We made the first ready-to-drink tea that didn't taste like battery acid," explained Snapple's co-founder Arnold Greenberg.[2]

Meanwhile, Snapple's advertising created an individualistic image and a cult-like following. (Market segmentation at work.) Beginning with the company's immodest motto—"Made from the best stuff on earth"—Snapple marketed its product to health-conscious consumers as an alternative to carbonated beverages and other "unhealthy" drinks. The company used quirky advertising that portrayed Snapple as a fun, offbeat, even wacky kind of brand.

But lurking just behind this zany public façade was a hard-nosed and opportunistic business. Take distribution, for example. Recognizing the futility of going up against giants like Coca-Cola and PepsiCo in their wheelhouses, Snapple made only minimal efforts to fight its way onto already-crowded supermarket shelves. Instead, it purposefully targeted alternative distribution channels, primarily relying on the "cold channel" network of small, independent co-packers and distributors. These distributors serviced hundreds of thousands of mom-and-pop stores, lunch counters, and delis.

Consider the first question of the SMP Test we saw in Chapter 7: *What strategic segment are we entering and who is the competition?* For soft-drink manufacturers, as well as for other producers of packaged goods, the cold channel network has very different attributes from the supermarket channel that serves mass merchants and grocery stores. Table 9.1 underscores some of the key differences from a drink manufacturer's point of view.

Snapple made only 20 percent of its 1993 sales in the supermarket channel, where Coke and Pepsi brands dominated. But using the cold channel, it more than made up for those lost sales in higher-margin retail "neighborhoods" where the competition wasn't so ferocious.

I maintain that these two channels aren't just a little different; they are fundamentally different strategic segments. Why? Because *the infrastructure and requirements to be successful in one are so very different from what is required for success in the other.* Snapple succeeded in large part because it cultivated its cold-channel network assiduously and because it stayed out of the supermarket channel.

So, to revive the market-segmentation language that I introduced in earlier chapters, Snapple used market segmentation to target and sell to a particular group of health-conscious consumers. (Having a product that didn't taste like battery acid was a great starting point, of course.) Simultaneously, the company developed a distribution strategy that kept it out of the *strategic segments* dominated by the Coke and Pepsi juggernauts. It built scale by playing to its own strengths and resolutely avoided going toe-to-toe with the industry giants. In other words, by combining market segmentation with a strategic view

TABLE 9.1   Comparison of Cold Channel versus Supermarket Channel

	Cold Channel	Supermarket Channel
Size	$2–3 B	$20–30 B
Distributor margins	$4/case	$1–2/case
Inventory turns	Weeks	Days
Typical retail pricing	$2/serving	$0.40/serving
Packaging	Single serve	Case or six-pack
Basis of competition	Product differentiation	Cost and differentiation

of the competition and the implications of that competitive context for distribution, it created a powerful SMP in the cold channel segment, within which it could compete quite successfully against other specialty drinks companies and the carbonated drinks behemoths that were not focused on this channel.

The market took note. In 1992 Boston-based Thomas H. Lee Company led a leveraged buyout of the company and took it public a year later. The offbeat marketing intensified. For example, employee Wendy Kaufman was cast as the "Snapple Lady." She preached the gospel of Snapple to the common person and read customer letters on air, many of which detailed customers' fantasies about their favorite Snapple products. Pitchmen as diverse as Howard Stern and Rush Limbaugh were called upon to sing Snapple's praises.

But not all was well in the RTD tea industry. Yes, Snapple was the second-largest seller of single-serve juices and was the fastest-growing entrant in the field, having grown from $4 million in sales to $674 million in the decade between 1984 and 1994.[3] But competition was intensifying. Unseasonably cool weather in the summer of 1994 cut into Snapple sales and led to an oversupply. Snapple's stock sank a full 50 percent from its 1993 high of $60 a share. Snapple's owners were ready—even eager—to cash out.

The Quaker Acquisition

Now, turn to Quaker, which in 1994 made the decision to buy Snapple.

By that time, depending on where you want to dip into the company's history, Quaker was already more than a century old. Henry Parsons Crowell—a devout Christian who had gone into business to serve God after recovering from a childhood bout with tuberculosis—bought the run-down Quaker Mill in Ravenna, Ohio in 1881. One of the first manufacturers to start packaging and selling oats directly to consumers, beginning with "Pure Quaker Oats" in 1884, Crowell created one of the nation's most successful branded cereals. In 1901, he joined forces with three other cereal magnates to formally found the American Cereal Company, headquartered in Chicago.

In subsequent years, Quaker (as the company became known) expanded its product line to include specialty cereals (such as puffed rice and puffed wheat, introduced as novelties at the 1904 World's Fair in St. Louis), and—over subsequent decades—clothing, eyewear, pet food, toys, and beverages.[4] In the 1960s, Quaker became an international company when it established a successful beachhead in Europe. The old oat miller had become a highly diversified multinational, with irons in many fires.

One of the company's most successful acquisitions came 1983, when Quaker purchased Gatorade. The sports drink had been invented in 1965 to rehydrate athletes at the University of Florida and had since been acquired by Stokely–Van Camp. William Smithburg, then two years into his tenure as Quaker's CEO, had been drinking Gatorade himself for a decade. When Stokely–Van Camp came up for sale, Smithburg paid a premium for the lackluster company, thereby beating out archrival Kraft Foods, mainly to get his hands on Gatorade.

Gatorade enjoyed double-digit sales growth every year for the first decade that Quaker owned it. This growth, although welcome, occasionally made Smithburg and others at Quaker nervous. When were Coke and Pepsi going to wake up and start competing with Gatorade? As Smithburg later recalled:

> We didn't want to wake up a sleeping giant. We were always watching what their response was to Gatorade's growth, but it's amazing that we had it for about 10 years before they got into Mountain Dew Sport (later All Sport) and POWERade. . . . We were most worried about POWERade. Coca-Cola was the 800-pound gorilla, because they had such a tremendous distribution system.[5]

Quaker's 1994 acquisition of Snapple seems to have been inspired, in large part, by the company's previous resounding success with Gatorade. Smithburg and his top lieutenants made a series of optimistic pronouncements about their ability to create synergies between Gatorade and Snapple and to recreate the Gatorade magic:

> Right after some discussions started, it was so obvious that Snapple had an interest and we had an interest and these two great brands, Gatorade and Snapple, would benefit from a put-together, and it just snowballed from then.
>
> (William Smithburg, former CEO, Quaker Oats)

> We have an excellent sales and marketing team here at Gatorade. We believe we do know how to build brands, we do know how to advance businesses. And our expectation is that we will do the same as we take Snapple as well as Gatorade to the next level. . . .
>
> (Don Uzzi, president, Quaker Oats Beverage Company, North America)

The truth, however, was that Quaker did not understand the true source of Snapple's success: its unique SMP. The staggering $1.7 billion acquisition price reflected Quaker's conviction that it could take Snapple into the much larger supermarket channel—leveraging the Gatorade distribution system—and at the same time have Snapple's distributors take Gatorade into the cold channel.

How to Lose $1 Billion in Three Years

Quaker was wrong on both counts: It's hard to extract substantial synergies by integrating companies operating in different strategic segments. The independent distributors would not sell Gatorade and lose Snapple volume, because Snapple's $4-per-case margins were almost double those of Gatorade. Snapple's undisciplined manufacturing process—which could take weeks, rather than days, to churn out product—proved impossible to merge with Gatorade's large-scale packing and distribution channels. In the meantime, Lipton/PepsiCo had recognized the opportunities in the tea segment. They increased advertising, gaining back share from Snapple. Other tea competitors, including Coca-Cola's Nestea and Arizona Iced Tea, also increased spending and gained share.

Quaker also thought that Snapple's strength in certain market segments provided a defensible position from which it could attack Coke and Pepsi. Quaker even launched a Spike Lee–directed campaign of TV advertising called "Threedom is Freedom," to position Snapple as the number 3 drinks brand, challenging Coke and Pepsi. This was a disaster.

On balance, CEO Smithburg was inclined to blame the victim:

> When we bought Snapple, we bought it on a down slope. We knew it wasn't going to die and we felt we could turn it around fast. We were wrong. The down slope was steeper than we thought and it took longer to turn around.[6]

Yes, Snapple had its problems and may even have been on the down slope that Smithburg describes. But the real fault lay with Quaker, which took Snapple from a strategic segment in which it was competing successfully and forced it into the giant supermarket segment, where it could be nothing more than a minnow competing against sharks. In this channel, the Snapple brand was simply not strong enough to overcome competitors' superior marketing clout and operating efficiencies.

Instead of showing increased profits, Snapple lost $100 million under Quaker's management. The recriminations flew. Longtime

Quaker managers began referring to Snapple as a "cancer." *Business-Week* called the Snapple acquisition one of the 10 worst mergers of the decade. Quaker's board withheld Smithburg's bonus and salary increase two years in a row (1995 and 1996).

The outcome was inevitable, but nonetheless stunning when it arrived. In 1997, Quaker sold Snapple to the Triarc Company for a meager $300 million. Triarc wisely redirected the company back to its original strategy and positioning—its original cold channel strategic segment—and, as a result, losses were halted and market share was stabilized. In 2000 Triarc sold Snapple to Cadbury Schweppes for $1 billion, more than tripling its investment in three years. Cadbury Schweppes has since attempted to combine the business with its portfolio of drinks brands (Dr. Pepper, Schweppes, 7-Up, Canada Dry). Snapple's troubled history, combined with the logic of SMP, suggests that this will prove a tough slog.

What about Quaker, which—depending on how you credit the associated write-offs—lost between $1 billion and $1.5 billion on the Snapple fiasco? Smithburg resigned as CEO shortly after the 1997 sale to Triarc. Quaker wound up being acquired by PepsiCo in December 2000 for the hefty price of $13.4 billion in stock.

PepsiCo's purchase of Quaker was actually the second of two great acquisitions that were overshadowed by the oversized Quaker/Snapple train wreck. (The first, of course, was Quaker's long-ago acquisition of Gatorade from Stokely–Van Camp.) Why? Because by acquiring Quaker, PepsiCo got its hands on the still potent Gatorade brand, and Gatorade soon proved a spectacular fit with PepsiCo's capabilities in the supermarket channel. In other words, Gatorade found a natural home within PepsiCo's core strategic segment, the supermarket channel. Bolstered by its parent company's clout, Gatorade has continued to run rings around its competition.

HP AND COMPAQ: INVESTING IN WEAKNESS

Our next acquisition story is even more notorious than the Quaker/Snapple fiasco. In the summer of 2001, Hewlett-Packard (HP) and Compaq formally announced their plans to merge. In effect, the proposed merger was a takeover of Compaq by HP. The combination would create a new and substantially larger HP, with projected total revenues of $87.4 billion.

The immediate reaction was negative: On the day of the announcement, HP's stock closed at $18.87, down sharply from $23.21 the day before. At first blush, at least, the Street didn't like what it was seeing.

To understand where this merger came from and to assess its chances of success in terms of SMP logic, you need to understand the two companies separately and decide how well they might fit together. You also need to understand their industry context (or more accurately, in SMP terminology, their strategic segments).

The Company That Hewlett and Packard Built

Founded in 1939, Hewlett-Packard had grown to become one of the world's leading providers of computing and imaging solutions and services. With 87,000 employees, operations in 120 countries and revenues of nearly $45 billion in fiscal 2001, HP competed in nearly every major information technology (IT) product segment.

HP sought to be the category leader with respect to each of the specific products and categories in which it competed and it actively expanded into new and adjacent markets. As of October 31, 2001, HP's three major business segments included Imaging and Printing Systems, Computing Systems, and IT Services.

Although HP had enjoyed considerable success over the years, there were no guarantees that the success would continue. In fact, during the late 1990s, HP's sales growth had declined to a 15-year low. Though management blamed this decline in earnings on a weakened macroeconomic environment and competitive price pressures, industry observers also criticized management's inability to keep pace with changing market conditions. The analysts specifically faulted HP for its failure to come up with a substantial recasting of its long-term corporate strategy—a recasting that companies like Dell and IBM had already gone through.

In response, HP began to initiate far-reaching changes. To ride herd on those changes, the board hired a new CEO, Carly Fiorina, in 1999. Fiorina carefully scrutinized the IBM model, which had included a significant investment in the services/consulting side of its business in the previous decade. By the turn of the century, IBM was generally considered to have the best consulting arm of any high-tech company—a resource that helped Big Blue provide one-stop shopping to its customers, which in turn increased the stickiness of its customer relationships.

In this service realm, HP trailed well behind IBM and Sun Microsystems, with a relatively modest team of 3,500 consultants. To remedy this problem, HP briefly considered an acquisition of the consulting arm of PricewaterhouseCoopers (PwC). (The large U.S. accounting firms were then under pressure from the regulators to divest themselves of their consulting arms, and most did so in this period.) An HP acquisition of PwC's 31,000 consultants—a deal that would have been in the $17 to $18 billion range—would have vaulted HP ahead of Sun and would have gone a long way toward closing the service gap with mighty Big Blue. Although the deal fell through, Fiorina continued to invest in HP's consulting arm, which (in a typical quarter in 2000) registered $178 million in profits on $1.8 billion in revenues.

During Fiorina's reorganization efforts, the company posted improvements in top-line performance and revenue growth. But HP soon found itself dealing with a significant slowdown in business and consumer spending in 2001. In part because management failed to heed signs that tech buying was waning, the company experienced a major earnings shortfall. Despite renewed cost-cutting initiatives, HP's 2001 net earnings declined a full 89 percent, precipitating a 35 percent decrease in stock price.[7]

From the Compaq Side of the Ledger

Founded in 1982, Compaq Computer started out as a manufacturer of portable IBM-compatible computers. In its first year of operation in 1983, the company recorded $111 million in sales, the greatest first-year sales record in the history of U.S. business. Adopting a price-setter strategy in 1992, Compaq became the world leader in PC sales by 1994.

But the success was short-lived. Although Compaq's dealer network had originally supported the company's rapid growth, the expense put Compaq at a cost disadvantage to Dell. In 1997, amid heightened PC price competition and diminishing margins, Compaq sought to remain competitive by emulating Dell's direct Internet sales channel strategy and IBM's full-line provider model. Toward the latter end, Compaq acquired Tandem Computer and Digital Equipment Corporation (in 1997 and 1998, respectively).

Although its acquisitions briefly improved operating results, Compaq struggled with its new model and experienced difficulty maintaining profitability during the integration. With the tech market softening in 2001—leading to price competition and declining margins—Compaq's revenues continued to fall. Despite ongoing efforts to cut costs and transform itself into a full-service enterprise computing company, Compaq still faced significant strategic and financial challenges and ended the year with a $785 million loss. In that same year—2001—Compaq shares fell more than 35 percent.[8]

"Compaq needs to dramatically reduce its cost structure," observed one Wall Street analyst, "or it may never be able to fend off Dell in the PC and industry standard server markets."[9]

To Merge or Not to Merge?

In short, in the early years of the twenty-first century, both HP and Compaq found themselves rocked back on their heels. Faced with a slowdown in business and consumer spending due to the 2001 recession, price competition, and an evolving market, both companies were under increasing pressure to find profitable growth. Their separate quests ultimately led them to consider a merger.

According to HP management, while neither HP nor Compaq alone was in a position to provide customers with full-line, end-to-end hardware and services, together they could replicate IBM's model. Furthermore, the argument went, not only would HP enjoy top market share in printers, PCs, and storage, it would also have the second-largest server business and the third-largest tech-services organization.

Management cited several potential benefits from the merger:

- *Improved economics and innovation in personal systems.* HP and Compaq needed to improve the economics of their PC business to compete effectively with Dell. Management predicted that the combined company would have a lower cost structure, due to economies of scale.
- *Complementary leadership in key markets.* Complementary strengths in servers and storage would make the combined company a leader in both segments. In addition, the company would be better positioned to provide integrated solutions that

would meet the needs of customers as a result of having a broader portfolio of products and services.

- *Strengthened business in IT services.* As noted earlier, service was very much on the minds of HP's leaders. They evidently believed that the merger would significantly strengthen HP and Compaq's combined services businesses, adding critical mass that would help accelerate growth.
- *Financial benefits.* According to management's plan, the merger would yield $2.5 billion in annual cost savings by mid 2004. In theory, at least, the cost savings would significantly improve overall profitability.[10]

The proposed merger had the support of a number of powerful players, including the CEOs of HP and Compaq, their respective boards, consultants McKinsey and Accenture, and financial advisors Goldman Sachs and Salomon Brothers. But the proposed deal also faced powerful opposition. The most outspoken critic was Walter Hewlett, HP director and son of co-founder William Hewlett. Although Hewlett agreed with Fiorina's assessment of the changing marketplace, he argued that acquiring Compaq was not the solution. Instead, Hewlett favored strengthening HP's profitable image printing business and shedding all noncore businesses.

Hewlett (who led a group of dissident stockholders) offered the following reasons for voting against the merger:

- *HP's business portfolio would get worse, not better.* The proposed merger would dilute HP stockholders' interest in the profitable imaging printing business and increase their exposure to an unprofitable PC business.
- *The integration risk of the proposed merger was substantial.* No significant combination involving a computer company had ever met expectations, and the odds appeared to be stacked against

this merger—particularly in light of the fact that HP's management described the transaction challenge as "a massive integration effort . . . in the midst of reinvention."

- *The financial impact on HP stockholders had been, and would continue to be, negative.* When stock prices tumbled in the wake of the announcement, the market sent a clear signal—that the proposed combination would destroy value for HP shareholders.

- *HP's strategic position would not materially improve.* The proposed merger would dramatically increase HP's market position in an unattractive, lower-end commodity business (PCs). Further, neither company had successfully transitioned to a direct distribution model to become more cost-competitive with Dell. Finally, the deal would divert management's attention and financial resources from HP's preeminent imaging and printing business.[11]

Many analysts, including several from UBS Warburg and JP Morgan, agreed with Hewlett and opposed the merger.[12] One analyst made the salient observation that this proposed merger posed only a minimal threat to Dell. "Dell is efficient," he observed, "because they are Dell, because of the way they go to market—the direct model—and because of the way they do build-to-order manufacturing. Putting together two weakened PC companies—Compaq and HP—is not going to yield a Dell competitor."[13]

Assessing the Damages

I've already revealed the punch line of this story: The deal went through (being formally closed on May 3, 2002). Although the stock of the combined company continued to sag, initial reports from within the company were positive. The integration went faster than anticipated and the cost savings were higher. At the one-year anniversary, most analysts—even the skeptics—were concluding that the merger had been successful.

But in reaching that conclusion, unfortunately, they were wrong. Let's revive our market-share charts from earlier chapters. First, look at an industry market share chart (Figure 9.2).

Figure 9.2 makes the Compaq acquisition look good, in that it seems to say that the acquisition increased HP's share of the U.S. computing industry. But as you recall from earlier chapters, gross market share is often not a true picture of a company's competitive situation. Figure 9.3 presents HP's *strategic* market position—its

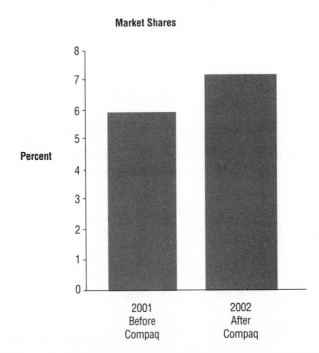

FIGURE 9.2 Hewlett-Packard: U.S. Computing Industry (2001–2002)
Data Source: CIBC, Gartner, company annual reports.

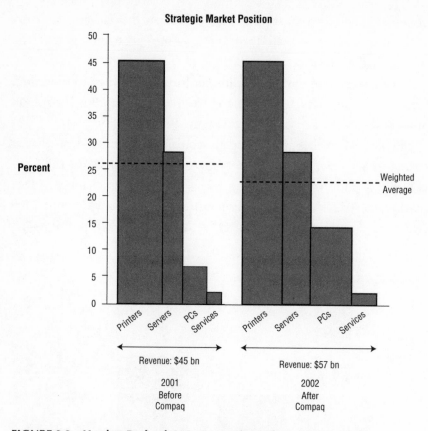

FIGURE 9.3 **Hewlett-Packard: U.S. Computing Industry (2001–2002)**
Data Source: Bloomberg, U.S. Census Bureau, U.S. Economic Census.

SMP—with its weighted average market share indicated by the horizontal dashed line.

Figure 9.3 demonstrates convincingly that Walter Hewlett and his fellow dissenters were right: The merger would only *weaken* the company by growing a weak part of the business (PCs) while ignoring a far stronger and more important part of the business (printers). Figure 9.4 presents another view of the same problem. Yes, HP improved its SMP in PCs (although I argue that the true picture was

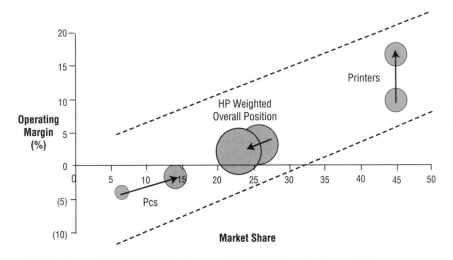

FIGURE 9.4   Hewlett-Packard: Operating Performance (2001–2002)
Data Source: Company annual reports.

worse than this, given both companies' downward momentum in market share), but by investing heavily in low-margin PCs, HP actually dragged down its overall weighted position (from "northeast" to "southwest").

I don't recount in equal depth the four difficult years that followed the acquisition. Very briefly stated, HP's fortunes rose, but then they sagged badly. By 2005, while rivals Dell and IBM were flourishing, HP's shares had fallen 50 percent in five years.[14] While its revenues had grown, its gross profit as a percent of sales had declined by an average of 4.5 percent. On February 7, 2005, frustrated with the company's continuing inability to dig itself out of its deepening hole, the HP board asked Fiorina to step down as CEO of HP.[15]

There is an old military adage: Never reinforce failure. Unfortunately, that is a perfect description of what happened with HP. Through the acquisition, HP made a huge investment in its weakest business (PCs) while diverting resources and distracting attention from its strengths in printers and servers. It is hard to imagine what move HP could have made that would have played more to Dell's strength. Even worse, the distractions at HP enabled Dell to grab share away from HP—not just in PCs, but in servers and printers as well.

Walter Hewlett intuitively thought about the business in SMP terms when he suggested abandoning the deal and instead divesting the PC business:

> *Hewlett-Packard's Business Portfolio Will Be Worse.* The proposed merger would dilute Hewlett-Packard stockholders' interest in the profitable imaging and printing business by over one-third, and increase the percentage of revenues derived from a currently unprofitable PC business from 20% to 31%. The combined company would be weaker, not stronger, than Hewlett-Packard.[16]

If only Carly Fiorina had thought about the business along the same SMP-related lines and avoided the pressure from advisers to do the deal, then a great company could have avoided a very costly diversion.

NORTHROP: GETTING IT RIGHT

Maybe having read two accounts of unhappy acquisitions in a row, you're wondering if I think that acquisitions *ever* make sense from an SMP point of view. The answer, of course, is yes. So it's probably time to include a few examples of highly successful acquisitions, with an emphasis on transactions in which the hidden value in the acquisition—the SMP-derived value—was substantial.

Our first such case concerns Northrop Grumman, which since the late 1990s has used a number of targeted acquisitions to strengthen its SMP and, by extension, its profitability and value.

Northrop was founded in California in 1939 by entrepreneur Jack Northrop, who had previously founded three other aviation-related companies (including Lockheed). During World War II Northrop produced the P-61 fighter and the famous Flying Wing bomber, which famously failed to win a production contract. In the 1950s, Northrop depended heavily on F-89 fighter and Snark missile sales.

By the early 1990s the company was a major defense contractor that was still looking for further growth. Northrop and private investment firm The Carlyle Group bought Vought Aircraft in 1992 and in 1994 paid $2.1 billion for Grumman Corporation—a premier electronic systems firm and the prime contractor for the lunar excursion module used in the Project Apollo moon landings. Grumman then changed its name to Northrop Grumman. The acquisition gave Northrop a leader in airborne surveillance and electronics warfare systems.

Results in the late 1990s were disappointing. Northrop's margins in important programs remained anemic and annual revenue declined from $8.6 billion in 1996 to $7.6 billion in 1999.[17] The nation's fourth-largest military supplier, faced with a competitive battle, began looking for new ways to expand. On May 27, 1999, Northrop Grumman announced that it would buy Ryan Aeronautical from Allegheny Teledyne for $140 million, with the goal of expanding its reach into key niche markets. These included the emerging industry of "unmanned aerial vehicles," or UAVs.[18]

Ryan Who?

San Diego-based Ryan Aeronautical was then a relatively tiny firm, at least by defense-contractor standards: 300 employees and annual sales of about $100 million. Nevertheless, the company was a leader in UAV technologies, designing and manufacturing both the Global Hawk High-Endurance UAV for the Air Force and the Miniature Air Launched Decoy (MALD) for the Air Force and the Defense Advanced Research Projects Agency (DARPA).

From the perspective of a potential acquirer, Northrop looked at these capabilities covetously. Exploring the likely progression of modern high-tech warfare, the company's planners saw three key trends converging:

1. Mounting pressure from the public to reduce casualty levels (to an ideal of zero casualties).
2. An increased need for strategic and tactical surveillance to leverage a dwindling number of combat platforms.
3. An increasing availability of bandwidth for remote control and receipt of video surveillance.

This meant that, among other things, unmanned aerial vehicles (UAVs) most likely would play an increasingly important role in warfare. Independent analyses pointed in the same direction. The consulting firm of Frost & Sullivan, for example, predicted a 13 percent growth rate for UAVs between 1998 and 2005.[19]

Northrop's acquisition of Ryan for $140 million in cash was completed on July 16, 1999. Reaction in the analyst community, as well as within the defense community, was mixed. Some called the acquisition a "perfect fit" that would give Northrop "some major muscle [in] next-generation UAV programs."[20] Others concluded that Northrop had overpaid substantially for Ryan—perhaps by a factor of two or three times. A good way to start assessing whether the skeptics were right is by looking at SMP.

The SMP Test

Apply the same questions we developed in Chapter 7 to Northrop's Ryan acquisition.

1. What strategic segment are we entering and who is the competition?
2. Will the new business strengthen our SMP in segments where we already compete?
3. If we are entering a new strategic segment, can we leverage our SMP in adjacent segments to ensure we achieve a strong SMP in the target segment?
4. Bottom line, will the new business make the weighted average SMP for our overall company better or worse?

Were the UAVs made by Ryan part of the same strategic segment as the combat fighter aircraft produced by Northrop? I don't think so. In 1999 the systems in a modern combat aircraft were at least an order of magnitude more complex than in a UAV. If you had to construct the Value Map and apply the 50 percent rule we described in Chapter 5, you would find that much less than half of the manufacturing costs and support functions for combat aircraft were shared with UAV production. But the technologies for UAVs, particularly with respect to weight and endurance, were becoming more complex and harder for new entrants to emulate. Against the few other UAV competitors that existed, Ryan had already carved out a leading position in the nascent strategic segment.

Would Ryan strengthen Northrop's position in combat aircraft and other military systems? Again, I think the answer has to be no. Ryan was only 2 percent of Northrop's size, and it is hard to imagine how it would make much of a difference to Northrop in its competition for multibillion dollar defense contracts.

On the other hand, could Northrop leverage its strength in combat aircraft and large-scale defense contracting to help Ryan achieve a strong SMP in UAVs? Ryan had already shown the ability to secure funding and contracts from the U.S. Air Force and DARPA, but it was still a tiny voice in the context of overall defense industry contracting and lobbying. If UAVs really had the potential that some believed, then Ryan would need much more sophisticated lobbying and higher-level relationships to get its share of much larger contracts in the future. Perhaps Northrop could supply that and help Ryan realize its full potential.

This brings us to the crux of the SMP test. For Ryan's acquisition price to be justified, Northrop needed not just to maintain Ryan's leadership in UAVs, but also to grow the business sufficiently to have an impact on the SMP for Northrop overall. This is exactly what Northrop has done. Among Northrop's 2004 contracts were $1.04 billion for X-47B Joint Unmanned Combat Air Systems. That single contract was more than enough to justify the $140 million cost for acquiring Ryan. Other UAV business has followed, and the Global Hawk UAV has played a critical role in the Iraq War.

The Accounting

In terms of shareholder returns, it is hard to separate the impact of the Ryan acquisition from the string of other, mostly larger acquisitions that Northrop has completed since 1999. The company has also benefited from a steady upswing in U.S. military spending.

That being said, Northrop's revenues have shot up 26.2 percent annually since 1999, and net income has increased by 20.1 percent annually to $1.4 billion. Similarly, the stock price has grown at an average annual rate of 12 percent.

Today, Northrop Grumman is the world's leading shipbuilder and is the second-biggest U.S. defense contractor (behind Lockheed

Martin). Northrop's defense portfolio is highly diversified, which—in light of the Pentagon's increasing emphasis on one-stop shopping—probably gives the company an edge in future Defense Department purchases. That, combined with other favorable trends, has made industry observers pay a lot more attention to once-shaky Northrop. "All of a sudden," observed one economist, "Northrop Grumman is a major player, and they have a couple of aces up their sleeves . . . It's quite an amazing story. If Hollywood was interested in business stories, this is one Hollywood could make an interesting movie out of."[21]

As noted, when Northrop purchased Ryan, there was talk that Northrop had paid two or three times what it should have for the UAV maker. The skeptics were proven wrong, when—as part of Northrop—Ryan began generating *annual* revenues of more than 10 times its acquisition price. Just as we saw with the Best Buy and UPS examples in Chapter 7, the acquisition price became irrelevant in comparison to the amount of new business generated. I extrapolate from these specific experiences to make a broader point. Most likely, there are properties that your company *should* pay a substantial premium to acquire—assuming, again, that you have a clear view of the strategic market position you are trying to build. Successful strategic acquirers focus on understanding the *strategic value* of an asset, measured by stronger SMP and increased revenues or higher profitability for the combined organization. This strategic value is often very different from a fair price based on multiples of historic earnings or cash flow.

APPLYING SMP MORE BROADLY:
A NONPROFIT MERGER

Up to now, we've focused the SMP lens exclusively on the private, for-profit sector. But the logic that I've laid out in previous chapters also pertains in a variety of other contexts. For example, nonprofits also do better when they build a strong SMP for themselves, such as when they make acquisitions that increase their overall SMP in the strategic segments they serve.

Of course, instead of focusing on shareholder value, nonprofits are focused on building value for their constituents and stakeholders. That means most nonprofits have a different bottom line, more concerned with delivering more and higher-quality services. But their way of *getting* to that bottom-line improvement is remarkably similar.

To explore this point, look at the 2000 merger of two nonprofits that worked in the same arena: hunger relief in the United States. America's Second Harvest (ASH) and Foodchain, the two organizations involved in our story, merged their operations on April 18, 2000. As I recount the story, I describe the ways in which the logic laid out in previous chapters came to bear on this combination.

ASH, the larger of the two groups—with an operating budget of $14 million at the time of the merger—was started in 1980 to gather and distribute donations of surplus food. By 1999 ASH was the nation's largest domestic hunger-relief organization, with a national network of nearly 200 regional food banks serving all 50 states and Puerto Rico, which distributed one billion pounds of donated food and grocery products annually. The ASH network supported approximately 50,000 local charitable agencies that operated more than 94,000 food programs, including food pantries, soup kitchens, women's shelters, Kids Cafes, and other local organizations. Collectively, these organizations provided food assistance to 26 million hungry Americans, including 8 million children and 4 million seniors each year.[22]

But by the late 1990s, ASH was struggling. For one thing, it faced a steady decline in food supplies. The organization's strategy was to obtain food aid primarily in the form of canned ingredients that it was able to distribute using its extensive national network. But ASH was not prepared to adjust to changing trends in the industry. For example, new donors such as Pizza Hut and the Marriott Hotel chain were offering fresh, ready-to-eat foods rather than canned goods. Meanwhile, to accentuate this trend, the recipients of food aid also preferred hot meals to canned ingredients that they had to turn into meals themselves.

At the time of the merger, Foodchain—established in 1992 and with an operating budget of $900,000—was a network of more than 150 community-based hunger-relief programs that rescued surplus food from restaurants, caterers, cafeterias, grocery stores, and other food businesses.[23] The rescued food was delivered to more than 15,000 social service agencies providing meal programs or food assistance to the poor. In 1999, Foodchain programs rescued nearly 300 million pounds of food that was turned into more than 200 million meals for those in need. While Foodchain was the largest organization specializing in handling and distributing hot food, it did not have the staff, funding, or national presence to fulfill its potential.[24]

Conversations between the two organizations in the late 1990s soon turned into merger talks, and the deal was completed in the spring of 2000. Explaining the rationale behind the merger, Deborah Leff, the director of ASH, pointed out that her organization wasn't able to distribute prepared food from the hospitality industry: "[Prepared food] is the growth piece of the market, and it's also the piece that's really best for working poor people. It's a lot easier to take a prepared meal and feed it to a family than it is to take the food that you might get at a soup pantry and try to figure out how to put it together to make a wholesome meal."[25]

Christina Martin, founding executive director of Foodchain, assumed a vital role in the new organization as the director of Food Rescue—Affiliate Services. "Merging with America's Second Harvest is the right thing to do, at the right time," Martin said. "Foodchain brings to the organization an expertise in the food industry's fastest growing segment—prepared and perishable foods."[26]

Companies that worked with one or both of the nonprofits—including food donors like ConAgra, Sodexho Marriott, Kraft Foods, Pizza Hut, General Mills, and Pillsbury—also praised the merger, saying that it was an opportunity for the two organizations to combine their expertise and to achieve better results.

The SMP Perspective

Now let's look at this deal from the vantage point of ASH: Was Foodchain in the same strategic segment, and could it help improve the organization's overall SMP? Both organizations served the same customers and satisfied the same basic need for hunger relief. Merging these two complementary hunger-relief organizations provided better service to America's hungry people, while lowering overheads, improving distribution services, and combining the strengths of each organization. The merger produced the most comprehensive and efficient charitable food distribution in the country.

The merger's success, furthermore, is manifest in the continued growth of America's Second Harvest (as the merged organization was called) since 2000. In terms of food volume, for example, the combined organization distributed 2 billion pounds of food and groceries in 2005, up significantly from the 1.3 billion pounds that ASH and Foodchain distributed separately in the final year before their merger.[27] Figure 9.5 summarizes the impact of the merger on America's Second Harvest. As you can see, this is a great example of "one plus one equals three." As the organization's SMP increased, not only was the amount of food delivered by the two organizations together much greater than what they had handled separately, but they also be-

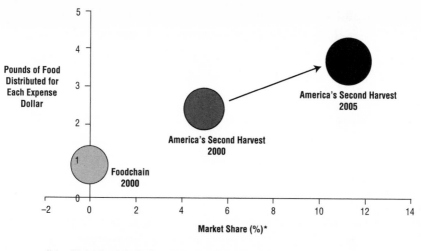

Note: *Market share defined as Second Harvest's share of total food needs of people facing hunger not met by the Food Stamps Program.

FIGURE 9.5   America's Second Harvest (2000–2005)
Data Source: Economic Research Service (USDA), America's Second Harvest Annual Report, *Forbes, Wall Street Journal.*

came more efficient, delivering 50 percent more food for each expense dollar.

THE VALUE OF SMP TO YOU

By now, after having read about how Strategic Market Position can be applied to more than two dozen corporate examples (as well as nonprofit organizations and board games), you should have a good understanding of these core principles of SMP:

1. Every business can be thought of as one or more *strategic segments*, defined such that increased scale or market share in any

segment will, other things being equal, always create the potential for higher profitability and competitive advantage. The boundaries for these strategic segments are determined by how different dimensions of scale or share impact economics for providers and benefits to customers (the Value Map). Strategic segments are often different from accepted market definitions and boundaries.

2. If you know the boundaries of the strategic segments you are competing in and can see the game board for your industry, you are in a great position to:

    • Find new businesses or acquisitions that enable you to build up a strong Strategic Market Position (SMP) in segments where you do not face overwhelming competitors.

    • Know when it makes sense to "overpay" for an acquisition opportunity (and when it does not).

    • Communicate the logic of your growth strategy to senior management and investors.

    • Know when your business is underperforming relative to its true potential, given your SMP.

    • Avoid dominant competitors by deemphasizing efforts to grow in strategic segments where you cannot achieve a strong SMP.

    • Know when it can make sense to sell off or merge a business that cannot easily achieve a strong SMP on its own.

3. If you increase the overall SMP for your business unit or company, you will increase your ability to achieve higher profitability and growth and unlock the hidden value of your business.

Yes, these principles are simple—so simple, in fact, that people grasp them intuitively and agree that they make powerful sense. But as we have seen, even among leading corporations, the principles of SMP are often only partially understood and—even more often—poorly applied. I hope this book helps remedy both problems.

Three ifs and a payoff: *If* this book has made you think about your own business decisions from the mindset of SMP; *if* you use the tools and tests I have described; and *if* you assess your business' SMP based on objective facts, rather than what you or your boss want to believe, then you will be well on your way to acquiring a level of business judgment and insight that most executives take decades to develop—*if* they get there at all.

Appendix

Guide to Information Sources for Competitive and Market Intelligence

IF YOU'VE GOTTEN to the Appendix, you must now be convinced of the power of SMP, understand the *who*, the *what*, and the *why*, and be keen to further understand the *how*. This Appendix is a valuable resource of techniques and sources to research and analyze SMP for your company and competitors within your industry. It begins with the process of determining what information you need, finding that information, and finally piecing the data together.

THE INFORMATION YOU NEED

To begin, identify the right strategic segment, for instance, why is product segmentation (e.g., luxury) the right strategic segment for BMW versus Mercedes? That is what the Value Mapping process is all about. Chapter 5 walked you through the Value Mapping process, a lot of which is based on industry knowledge. That said, the resources described in the following section can and will provide insight on strategic segmentation. Once you have determined the strategic segments, the challenge is to quantify both the market share and a measure of profitability or shareholder value within those segments. This will prove to be the most difficult aspect of your process—difficult, but not impossible.

Where to Find the Information You Need

Two fields of data exist to begin your search: market (or industry) data and individual company data. Company data may include your company, but this process is really about collecting intelligence on competitors. We work from the broad market data and move on to specific company information. A tabular summary, further explained in the text to follow, can be found in Table A.1.

Market Data   Industry information can be gathered from a variety of sources, but take care: Not all are legitimate! For example, if you run a Google search for the top five car companies in the United States, you might get a hit from a GM employee's blog spot, stating unequivocally that GM, Ford, DaimlerChrysler, Hyundai, and Fiat are the top five companies in the United States. Well, that's simply wrong, but no one is out there correcting misstatements on the Web.

The two best sources for industry information are market research reports and associations/trade journals. Market research reports have the potential to contain all of the specific information you need. A perfect market report will have done all of the research work for you, but chances are slim that you will find such a perfect report. Usually, a market report contains mostly analysis and words around the industry and industry segments (if it's broken down that far),

TABLE A.1   Summary of Sources for Market and Company Data

Data Type	Example Sources	Web Site (if applicable)
Market Data		
Market Reports	Datamonitor, Euromonitor, IBIS World, Frost & Sullivan, Freedonia	www.marketresearch.com; www.datamonitor.com; www.frost.com
Financials and Share Prices	Bloomberg, Yahoo! Finance	www.bloomberg.com; finance.yahoo.com
Industry Information	Government web sites	www.census.gov
	Standard and Poor's	www.netadvantage.standardandpoors.com
	Industry Organizations and Associations	Various
	General Business Publications, Regional Business Publications	www.wsj.com; www.ft.com; www.businessweek.com; www.fortune.com
Company Data		
General Company Information	Annual Reports, Press Web site, Management Presentations, Conference Presentations	Releases,
Financial Statements	10-Ks, 10-Qs, 8-Ks, S-1 (for IPOs)	www.sec.gov/edgar.shtml
Analyst Reports	Morgan Stanley, Credit Suisse, and so on	www.thomson.com
Business School Case Studies	Harvard Business School, Darden Business School, Sloan School of Management	www.hbsp.harvard.edu; store.darden.virginia.edu; www.ecch.com; cmr.berkeley.edu/cases.html; sloanreview.mit.edu/smr/
M&A Activity	Press releases, Mergerstat, Thomson Financial, Annual Reports	www.thomson.com

analysis of top competitors, and sales and/or market share of each participant in that industry (sometimes even in specific industry or market segments). Most market reports also include forecast growth of the overall market, and sometimes forecast growth of particular market or product segments.

The most general information you should take away from a market report is *the state of the industry*, that is, the top players, their sales, their strategies, and how the market is doing and where it is going. From there you can build your hypotheses as to what the Value Map might look like, and determine the strategic segments. You can further test these hypotheses as you collect company-specific data.

Potentially more valuable, but harder to obtain, is the information available through industry-specific organizations. This includes industry magazines, trade journals, conference proceedings, and the opinions and knowledge held by industry experts. An association or industry publication's sole purpose is to focus on their industry; thus they are more likely to provide the most accurate and up-to-date information. You do need to consider the audience, however: Industry organizations often try to put the best possible spin on current market conditions (or the *worst* possible spin, depending on what they are trying to achieve). Certain industries, like the U.S. automobile industry, are covered in great depth by many different organizations. Some offer quantitative information, while others offer market trends and forecasts. A phone call to senior people either employed or affiliated with industry organizations (e.g., senior editors, association presidents, speakers, etc.) is often the quickest means to gather information on the top competitors, their share, their relative profitability, and so on.

For example, in researching GE aircraft, the sheer magnitude of GE makes researching specific market segments difficult. To better understand GE and its offering, consider putting in a few calls to industry experts in the airline engine servicing market.

While market research reports and industry associations are your best sources for market intelligence, some other sources are still worth mentioning. In the United States, the government can be a very helpful resource. Besides keeping track of general economic indices (GDP, inflation, etc.), the government may also track activity in specific industries. Government information is almost always historic or a snapshot of a current situation and rarely includes a forecast of any kind.

As a rule, the government collects and synthesizes a lot of data for a wide variety of industries, but this information is sometimes not up-to-date. In addition, the government also conducts surveys, which are completed by the Census Bureau (U.S. Census 2000), the Department of Labor, and the Center for Disease Control. You can also find import and export volumes, commodity market activity, Medicare and Medicaid payment information, IRS returns for nonprofits, and Securities and Exchange Commission (SEC) filings of public companies.

In other geographies, country-specific government sources exist as well. When you span geographies, some good sources include the World Health Organization (WHO), the World Bank, and the Organization for Economic Cooperation and Development (OECD). Unfortunately there is no master list of all government information available, so the best approach is to go to a government web site and start searching.

Company Data   Hopefully, through your review of market data, you have become familiar with the competitors in the market. A good rule of thumb is to review and analyze the top five competitors, but this could differ depending on the level of concentration in the segments defined. In a very concentrated market, you could conceivably focus on the top three; in a fragmented market, you might want to include the top ten. Once the top participants are known, you can then determine the overall market share of a company and then more specifically their (and your) SMP.

Gathering company information can be the easiest research you'll conduct, but it can also be the most frustrating. Before you get into the nitty-gritty of company research, though, it's important to define clearly the type of information you are trying to collect. Your main goals are (1) to test your strategic segments hypothesis, (2) to develop a quantitative market share measure within that strategic segment, and (3) if possible, to develop an historical or future view on how share gain in the strategic segment impacts value.

Based on L.E.K. experience, there is probably a 5 percent chance that you will turn up a market research report that covers the key players and provides the necessary quantitative information, including not only on overall market share, but also on market share within the right strategic segment. For the other 95 percent, you must turn to company research.

Start with financial data, which are mainly found in annual reports and SEC filings. Be sure to look at the notes to financial statements, where—in some cases—revenues and profits are segmented by product, by channel, and/or by geography.

This can also give you clues as to potential strategic segments. For example, in its 10-K business overview, Samsonite breaks down its sales by product category: luggage, computer bags, casual bags, and so on. In the financial notes, it breaks down sales in the United States between wholesale and retail.

Which segmentation matters, and to what degree? Thinking about it in terms of the Value Map, product segmentation will have some quantification on the components of the circles, although it may not be a different strategic segment. In the case of Samsonite, however, it's safe to say that retail sales are an entirely different strategic segment from luggage wholesale. Uncovering segmentation is about finding the strategies and performance of competitors, deep in the text of the information disclosed, and thinking about it in SMP terms.

Company web sites are the next stop. In addition to the financials, which you already have in hand, the information you gather here may include the company's history (although sometimes this is not available on the web site), products, brands, channels of distribution, and notable news in their press releases. Press releases and historical notes really shed color on the company as a whole. They often disclose past and future strategies, including M&A activity and other important events, like plant closings or relocations, product line extensions, and so on. You may even be able to glean pieces of information on financials by product or channel financials. It is also helpful to look for competitive insights within investor call transcripts, management presentations to investors, newspaper articles, business periodicals, and conference proceedings.

Bloomberg is another great research tool for public, and sometimes private, companies. While annual reports contain the financial information for one company for one year, Bloomberg contains the financial information, including stock activity, for all public companies from the mid 1980s to the present. Bloomberg also does some of the work for you. For example, it accounts for inflation and currency differences and adjusts stock prices for dividends. Bloomberg is also a great source for M&A activity.

While company web sites and Bloomberg offer accurate, public information, a more in-depth look at companies is available in analyst reports. These offer an outside perspective on a company, especially as it pertains to the company's future. They are also a great source of past company information and how the financial markets react to strategies within the industry. For example, when Dean increased its ownership in WhiteWave (Silk soy milk) and sold off noncore businesses—which strengthened Dean's portfolio, in SMP terms—analysts praised the move.

Once again, though, be careful to consider the audience and intent of the analyst report. Investment research is typically generated to spur activity in trading and may not be entirely unbiased, and, of course, the analyst's reaction to company strategies is not always the correct one. Depending on the depth of the analyst report, you might also find information on industry trends and competitors. Look for reports of more than 10 pages; they often provide an industry landscape. An in-depth report might even analyze a company's market share and profitability in the overall market and in specific market segments. As in the case of associations and industry publications, you can always try to contact the analyst who wrote the report, to probe the depths that he/she may not have offered in his/her report.

Another source for more general company information and history is Hoover's (www.hoovers.com). Hoover's provides an overview and history of all public companies, in addition to some financial information and that company's competitors. Hoover's also includes information on selected private companies, which are almost always a challenge to research.

To state the obvious, private companies are more difficult to gather information for, as they are not required to divulge financial information. But this doesn't mean that no information is accessible, especially if the company sells any products or provides services to the public. The airline industry, for example, is highly regulated, and thus the government collects a lot of data on these carriers. And while an airline may be a private company and not publish its financial data, there is still other information available, such as load factors, which you can obtain through the government or associations.

Keep in mind, too, that while private companies are not *required* to share financial information, that does not mean that they can't. Some private companies do choose to publish information, although the extent and content varies greatly from company to company. Your best source to find private company information is Dun & Bradstreet (D&B). Second to them, as already mentioned, is Hoover's, and then sometimes Bloomberg.

Going Further

As you gather market and company intelligence, you are very likely to discover that the exact information you are looking for is unavailable. But this does not mean that it is unobtainable. Once you think you have gathered all the information you can from the earlier-mentioned sources and methods, and you still do not have the full picture, you have two more options. The first is primary research, and the second is creativity.

Primary research means conducting personal interviews with industry experts, competitors, and/or customers within a given industry. Primary research offers greater insight into an industry, specific industry segments, and the top competitors in that industry. While personal interviews can sometimes be difficult to obtain, conducting them will provide the most current views on the industry. These interviews are especially useful, as you can probe into the specific strategic segments that you are interested in, which may not be covered in published reports. For example: While you can learn from a published report that a widget company's total revenue was $20 million, an interview with a customer (e.g., a buyer) may reveal that the company's high-end widgets are selling horribly compared to a leading competitor's, but the company dominates the low-end widget market. Also take the opportunity in your primary research to test your SMP hypothesis, particularly with customers.

After primary research, it's time to get creative. If you could conduct a primary interview with every competitor and customer of your company—assuming they'd talk to you—you could perfectly paint the SMP picture. Of course, that is impractical. Even speaking to a fraction of those competitors and customers may seem infeasible. But there are other ways to gather information, most of which involve being creative. Unfortunately, there is no formula or list of options, but with some critical, outside-the-box thinking, you can find other ways to gather and piece together information.

Perhaps the best way to illustrate this point is to offer some examples of "creative analysis" used to develop the SMP perspectives within the book. These examples are also intended to provide a glimpse of the process in piecing the data together.

Example 1: Wal-Mart versus Kmart

The challenge: Market share not available by rural and urban markets.

The creative solution

- From annual reports, yellow pages, online maps, and phone calls to individual stores, identified Kmart and Wal-Mart stores as either rural or urban.
- Applied the store split percentage to revenue to get sales in rural and urban markets (the numerator).
- Researched a general merchandise spend per household, from the government economic census, and multiplied that by the number of households in rural and urban areas (the denominator).
- Divided company sales, split by urban and rural, by the general merchandise spend.

Example 2: Northwest Share of City Pairs

The challenge: Market share was not available by city pair.

The creative solution

- From the Official Airline Guide (OAG) determined Northwest's share of flights.
- Developed the share of economy seats based on the number of economy seats on each type of aircraft used in that city pair.

- Called agents to get comparable full-price fares of both Northwest and competitor airlines, and calculated revenue per available seat.
- Applied the company load factor for actual company revenue in the city pair.
- Divided the sum of Northwest's revenue over the sum of all airlines in that city pair.

PIECING IT TOGETHER

Pulling the available information together is really more an art than a science, hence the need for creativity. To analyze a company's SMP as it relates to competitors—which is what really matters—you need to follow the five steps outlined in Chapter 5:

1. Define the possible strategic segmentation dimensions (that is, the compass points of the Value Map).
2. Score those dimensions according to their relative values.
3. Define the relevant strategic segments based on the Value Map scores.
4. Plot your company's and your competitors' SMPs.
5. Test your conclusions and refine if needed.

The resources that are out there for piecing the SMP puzzle together are almost limitless, and—thanks to the Web—are growing every day. This Appendix should serve as a useful starting point for you to pursue market and competitor intelligence, and begin applying the logic of SMP.

NOTES

INTRODUCTION   *Where Value Hides and Why It Matters*

1. In this book, I use the SMP acronym to stand in for both strategic market position (the *outcome*) and the discipline of developing strong strategic market positions.

1   *Where You Should Compete*

1. Remember: We're talking ROI, here. Yes, you have to pay a lot more to the owner when you land on a built-up Boardwalk than when you land on a built-up Baltic. But it costs the investor far more to build up Boardwalk. The *rate of return* on investment is what counts—and that's very similar across all Monopoly properties.
2. John R. Wells and Travis Haglock, "The Rise of Kmart Corporation," Harvard Business School, July 1, 2005.
3. Ibid.
4. Bloomberg.
5. Ibid.
6. Vijay Govindarajan and Julie B. Lang, "Wal-Mart Stores, Inc.," Tuck School of Business at Dartmouth, 2006; Bloomberg Mergers & Acquisitions Search, March 2006; www.walmart.com, Wal-Mart web site.
7. John R. Wells and Travis Haglock, "Rise of Kmart Corporation," Bloomberg Mergers & Acquisitions Search, March 2006; www.kmart.com, Kmart web site.

8. "New Chapter of Growth—America West," *Airline Business*, January 1, 1996.

9. "Fit to Survive—Profile on America West," *Airline Business*, September 1, 1993.

10. Bloomberg Equity Fundamentals and Earnings Analysis, December 2005.

11. Sega's roots date back to the 1940s, while Nintendo is more than a century old.

12. "Power Play (B): Sega in 16-bit Video Games," Harvard Business School, July 12, 1995.

13. Ibid.

14. In 2003, one share of Sega stock was exchanged for 0.28 shares of Sega Sammy stock.

15. Bloomberg Equity Historical Prices; Bloomberg Equity Indices, March 2006.

16. This calculation is complicated by Sega's 2004 merger with Sammy Corporation, a maker of pachinko and slot machines, but the central point still holds.

17. See, for example, the 02.28.04 edition of the *Wall Street Journal*, pp. R1–R8. On a selective basis, other time periods (3-year, 5-year, and 10-year periods) are also included. All performance numbers cited in this section are from this 2004 edition.

2 *Bigger May Be Worse*

1. For this analysis, and for much of the discussion of the experience curve and Michael Porter's work that follows, I am indebted to "Competition and Business Strategy in Historical Perspective," an article by Pankaj Ghemawat in *Business History Review* 76 (Spring 2002): 37–74.

2. Ghemawat, "Competition and Business Strategy," 39.

3. Boston Consulting Group, "The Experience Curve—Reviewed," *Perspectives* 135 (Boston: 1973). Cited in *The PIMS Principles* by Robert D. Buzzell and Bradley T. Gale. (New York: 1987) The Free Press. 76. I have drawn on Buzzell's and Gale's analyses of BCG and Porter.

4. Buzzell and Gale, *PIMS Principles*, 77.
5. Ibid., 78.
6. Michael E. Porter. *Competitive Strategy* (New York: The Free Press, 1980).
7. Obviously, I'm greatly simplifying Porter's contribution. For an in-depth analysis, see Ghemawat's "Competition and Business Strategy," 53–57.
8. Porter's *Competitive Strategy*, 37 and 43.
9. See, for example, "What Is Strategy?," an interesting article by Porter that appeared in the November–December 1996 issue of *Harvard Business Review*. In this article, Porter goes much further in the direction of market segmentation, but not in the direction of SMP.
10. Buzzell and Gale, *PIMS Principles*, 86.
11. Ibid., 85–86.
12. Bloomberg Equity Fundamentals and Earnings Analysis; Equity Historical Prices, February 2006; L.E.K. analysis.
13. Ibid.
14. See, for example, "Pulling the Strings at BMW," BBC News, 03.16.00.
15. Stephan A. Jansen et al., "DaimlerChrysler Post-Merger Integration (A)," Harvard Business School Case #N9-703-417, 10.28.03.
16. Bloomberg Eqiuty Fundamentals and Earnings Analysis; Equity Historical Prices, February 2006; L.E.K. analysis.
17. Ibid.
18. Take the Economy Mid Car bar, for example. DaimlerChrysler sold 323,450 units in 1997 with six models across three platforms. The width of the Economy Mid Car bar is measured by this number of units sold relative to the total unit sales between DaimlerChrysler and BMW (2,548,553). To measure the height, we started with DaimlerChrysler's unit sales for Economy Mid Cars (323,450) and divided that by the total market unit sales in this class (4,151,584) to get DaimlerChrysler's market share in that class (7.8 percent). To take into account the platforms shared between models, we then divided this percent by the number of DaimlerChrysler platforms in that class to arrive at their U.S. market share by platform within the Economy Mid Car class of 2.6 percent.

19. Robert Slater. *Jack Welch and the GE Way* (New York: McGraw-Hill, 1999), 61.

20. In an 02.07.06 e-mail to the author, Stevenson elaborated on his comment. "Many a very profitable business has been built by trying to get 100 percent share among their current customers," Stevenson notes, "rather than 1 percent of the Chinese market for aspirin."

3   *Uncovering Where Value Hides*

1. "Fractional horsepower" simply means "less than 1 horsepower." Larger motors are referred to as "integral horsepower" motors.

2. Unless otherwise noted, the data included in this chapter are from internal studies conducted in the context of that L.E.K. engagement in the early 1990s.

3. Magnetek 2005 Annual Report.

4. Hoover's, Company Record Fact Sheet and Full Overview. Target Corporation, April 2006.

5. Peter Lowy, managing director of the Westfield Group, which has seven Targets in its U.S. mall portfolio and is building two more, quoted in *Women's Wear Daily*, 09.01.05.

6. See Scott McCartney, "The Middle Seat," *Wall Street Journal*, 04.04.06. McCartney's article contrasts two high-end airlines: Eos and rival Maxjet.

7. "Eos to introduce premium air service and experience for transatlantic travelers," from a 06.08.05 press release on the Eos web site, www.eosairlines.com/about_press0.html.

4   *Capturing Value*

1. This figure is the result of an unscientific—but systematic—sampling of some important and unimportant Northwest routes. In terms of our methodology, we asked the airline for the price of a Class Y ticket (to make sure we were comparing apples to apples), and subtracted Northwest's average costs per seat mile to get an indicative "profit." We then checked with the Official Airline Guide (OAG) to determine Northwest's share of departures on these routes.

2. Phillips got far larger after 1996 (the time of this comparison). In November 2001, Phillips and Conoco agreed to merge. After some difficulty obtaining the FTC's approval, the two companies merged successfully on August 31, 2002, creating the largest U.S. oil refiner, valued at $35 billion at the time.
3. See MBE's history at www.mbe.com/ambe/hi.html.
4. "UPS to Acquires Mail Boxes Etc. in Cash Transaction," press release 03.02.01, www.mbe.com/ambe/prpr_030201.html.
5. From the corporate history page of the FedEx web site, at www.fedex.com/us/about/today/history?link.
6. "UPS Builds Platform for Profitable Growth," UPS press release dated 10.30.03, online at www.pressroom.ups.com/mediakits/pressrelease/0,2300,4355,00.html.

5   Doing the Detective Work

1. Bally's related financial information is from Business Wire and Bloomberg Equity Fundamentals and Earnings Analysis, January 2006. Also useful is "Bally Total Fitness," Harvard Business School Case #9-706-450, November 14, 2005.
2. See the Bally's entry in Wikipedia at en.wikipedia.org/wiki/Bally_Tot, January 2006.
3. Bloomberg Equity Historical Prices, February 2006.
4. "Financial Results Call for 1st Nine Months 2005, Year-End 2004; Completes Restatement of Fiscal Years 2000 Through 2003—Final" Vox and FD Wire, December 1, 2005.
5. Town Sports International Holdings, Inc. S1, July 6, 2005.
6. Ibid.

6   Applying SMP to Sales and Marketing

1. This historical material is derived mainly from the historical section of the company's web site: www.pioneermills.com/about us. Also helpful was the Pioneer Flour Mills entry in the Handbook of Texas Online, at www.tsha.utexas.edu/handbook/online/articles.

2. According to the authorized corporate history—*C.H. Guenther & Son at 150 years: The Legacy of a Texas Milling Pioneer* (San Antonio: Maverick Publishing Company, 2001)—this balance started to be tilted back toward the formal company name in 1999. See the chronology on page 107 of the corporate story.

3. "Of the company's 100 shareholders [in 2001]," reports the authorized corporate history, "more than 90 remained descendants of Carl Hilmar Guenther," 95.

4. At that point, my company, L.E.K., was involved with this systematic study. The exhibits and commentary contained in this chapter are reproduced with the permission of Guenther. The company, which puts a high value on its privacy, releases very little financial information. Accordingly, the numbers in this chapter are presented only in relative and orders-of-magnitude terms. I am grateful to Guenther for their willingness to help out with this project.

5. Recently, in fact, the company had invested something like $8 million in specialized equipment for baking a particular kind of muffin—only to find that the market for that product at acceptable margins was nowhere near as robust as expected.

6. Interview with Janelle Sykes, 02.27.06.

7. Ibid.

8. I believe that the Guenther engagement was the first place where I encountered the word "demarket," a useful concept that the Guenther strategists used to describe their approach to a systematic deemphasizing of a product or channel.

9. Interview with Janelle Sykes, 02.27.06.

10. Quotes from customer surveys conducted in the spring and summer of 1993 for Guenther.

11. Interview with Janelle Sykes, 02.27.06.

12. This was a "stretch" hurdle, in the sense that the 15 percent figure substantially exceeded the company's true cost of capital. But part of the point of establishing a well defined hurdle was to get people across the organization to think in "stretch" terms: What's the *best* way to deploy our finite resources?

13. Interview with Janelle Sykes, 02.27.06.

14. From "McDonald's New *Sizzling* McGriddles Breakfast Sandwiches Are Truly Innovative," a press release issued by McDonald's on 05.30.03, online at www.rmhc.org/usa/news/2003/conpr-5302003a.html

7   *Using SMP to Find New Markets*

1. W. Chan Kim and Renée Mauborgne, *Blue Ocean Strategy* (Boston: Harvard Business School Press, 2005).
2. *Blue Ocean Strategy*, 3.
3. Ibid., 31.
4. Ibid., 25.
5. Unless otherwise noted, Baxter-related information is from the company's annual reports and web site. Although Baxter has been a client of my company in the past, this chapter does not draw on information derived from those engagements.
6. In 2004, Abbott further strengthened its position in the nutritional supplement category with the acquisition of Experimental & Applied Sciences, Inc. (EAS), the maker of AdvantEdge, Myoplex, and Body for Life brands. This acquisition accelerated Ross's entry into the increasingly important weight-management and sports-performance segments.
7. "Baxter Launches PULSE, New Water + Nutrients Supplement," Baxter press release, 05.28.02.
8. Maureen West, "'Vitamin waters' debut in Phoenix, nation's bottled water capital," the *Arizona Republic*, 05.29.02.
9. Gil Y. Roth, "Parenteral Dose Manufacturing," *Contract Pharma* 2002, online at www.contract pharma.com/articles/2002/11.
10. See "Acquisition Leads to Facility Expansion, Job Growth in Bloomington," from a Baxter promotional piece, July 2004, on the Web at www.baxter.com/about_baxter/sustainability/sust_stories/communities/comm_bps.html, 03.05.06.
11. Jefferies & Co. Analyst, 2002.
12. The best introduction to these tools is *Creating Shareholder Value*, by Alfred Rappaport (New York: Free Press, 1997). In the spirit of full disclosure, Rappaport has been closely associated with my firm in the past.

13. Much of this discussion comes from "Gently Down Stream—Maintenance Rationalisation," *Airline Business*, 10.01.97.

14. "Gently Down Stream—Maintenance Rationalisation," *Airline Business*, 10.01.97.

15. "GE's Two-Decade Transformation: Jack Welch's Leadership," HBS, 1999.

16. According to the HBS case cited at 15. GE Capital has become the "profit engine at the heart of the company, generating 41 percent of earnings."

8 SMP Strategies for Low-Growth or Low-Margin Businesses

1. See, for example, the *Wall Street Journal*, 02.28.04 R1–R8. On a selective basis, other time periods (3-year, 5-year, and 10-year periods) are also included.

2. *Wall Street Journal*, 02.27.06, R4.

3. Ibid., R6.

4. What you find, when you look at the benchmarking literature, is that much of it is specialized. If you're looking for an overview, this is unhelpful. On the other hand, you may find an industry- or function-specific book that can be quite helpful.

5. "Samsonite, Veteran Baggage Maker, on Comeback Trail Again," AP newswire, July 2003. Unless otherwise noted, the material in the section comes from internal L.E.K. analysis.

6. Global Industry Analysts, company financials, Bloomberg, L.E.K. analysis.

7. "Samsonite Insists It Is on Comeback Path," AP Online, July 2003.

8. "Travel Slump Forces Bentley's Luggage to Pack Up," The Travel Industry of America December 2002.

9. Weighted by market capitalization. *Wall Street Journal* "Shareholder Scoreboard," February 2006.

10. *Wall Street Journal* "Shareholder Scoreboard," February 2006.

11. Dean Foods press release, April 2001.

12. Dean Foods press release, May 2002.

13. Dean Foods press release, November 2002.

14. Dean Foods press release, January 2004.

15. From 2000 to 2004, the federally mandated purchase price of raw milk grew at a CAGR of 7 percent (USDA), whereas retail milk prices increased at a CAGR of just over inflation for the same time period. Euromonitor.

16. Credit Suisse analyst report, February 2006.

17. Other companies—most notably Apple Computer, with its ill-fated Newton—had ventured into this arena before, but Palm was the first to succeed in the PDA market.

18. See, for example, John Glynn's "Handspring and Palm, Inc: A Corporate Drama in Five Acts," Stanford Graduate School of Business, July 12, 2005. Also helpful in the preparation of this section was Lee Gomes's and Lisa Bransten's "Computers: Little Computers, Big New Marketing Battle," *Wall Street Journal*, 11.17.97.

19. Company press release.

20. Datamonitor News, August 2005.

21. Chimie Pharma Hebdo, June 2005.

22. The *Star Ledger*, June 2005.

23. FDAnews Drug Daily Bulletin, June 2005

9   *When Do Acquisitions Make Sense?*

1. "Quaker Oats and Snapple," case study no. 1.0041, Tuck School of Business, Dartmouth College, available online at mba.tuck.dartmouth.edu/pdf/2002-1-0041.pdf.

2. Ibid.

3. John Deighton, "How a Juicy Brand Came Back to Life," HBS Working Knowledge, 02.04.02, workingknowledge.hbs.edu/item.jhtml?id=2752&t=bizhistory&noseek=one, accessed 01.04.06.

4. The Quaker history is from Jeffrey L. Cruikshank, *The Man Behind the Curtain*, forthcoming from the Harvard Business School Press. Also helpful, again, is "Quaker Oats and Snapple," case study no. 1.0041,

Tuck School of Business, Dartmouth College, available online at mba.tuck.dartmouth.edu/pdf/2002-1-0041.pdf.

5. See the interview with Bill Smithburg on Darren Rovell's Gatorade blog, at firstinthirst.typepad.com/darren_rovells_blog_on_al/2005/11/interview _with_.html, accessed 01.05.06.

6. See the interview with Bill Smithburg on Darren Rovell's Gatorade blog, at firstinthirst.typepad.com/darren_rovells_blog_on_al/2005/11/interview _with_.html, accessed 01.05.06.

7. "Hewlett-Packard: The Merger Decision," *Harvard Business Review*, September, 14, 2004.

8. Ibid.

9. Bill Shope, "Compaq Computer," *ABN-AMRO*, 12.19.01.

10. "Hewlett-Packard: The Merger Decision."

11. Packard's position is derived from the 2001 Proxy Statement and from "Walter Hewlett: The Consequences of the HP-Compaq Merger," *VARBusiness*, 03.06.02.

12. "Hewlett-Packard: The Merger Decision."

13. "Dell Still Tough to Beat in PC Market," CNET News.com, 09.04.01.

14. "Ouster Is an Admission of Error in Buying Compaq," *Houston Chronicle*, 02.10.05.

15. "The Inside Story of Carly's Ouster," *BusinessWeek*, 02.21.05.

16. "Walter Hewlett: The Consequences of the HP-Compaq Merger," *VARBusiness*, 03.06.02.

17. "Northrop Shifts Focus to Cutting-Edge Military Lines—Growth Is Sought in Information Systems and Electronic-Warfare Markets," *Wall Street Journal*, 10.01.99.

18. *Defense Daily*, 202, 42 (05.28.99).

19. Frost & Sullivan Report 5375-16, 1998.

20. Frost & Sullivan, "Analysis of the Northrop Grumman Acquisition of Ryan Aeronautical: A Major Player Is on the Horizon," 06.01.99.

21. Associated Press, 10.26.01.

22. PR Newswire, 04.17.00.

23. Much of this background material is from a National Public Radio interview, 04.18.00. See also the account from the same day in the *Wall Street Journal*.
24. PR Newswire, 04.17.00.
25. National Public Radio interview, 04.18.00.
26. PR Newswire, 04.17.00.
27. America's Second Harvest 2005 annual report.

INDEX

Abbott Laboratory, 171
ABT Electronics, 72
Acquisitions. *See also* Mergers
  of Compaq by Hewlett-Packard, 227–236
  of Cook Pharmaceutical Solutions by Baxter International Inc., 174
  of Dean Foods by Suiza Foods, 203
  of Geek Squad by Best Buy, 178–179, 180–182, 183–184
  of Handspring by Palm Computing, 210–211
  of Kinko's Inc. by Federal Express, 101
  of Mail Boxes Etc. by United Parcel Service, 100–101
  of Quaker by PepsiCo, 226
  of Rover Group PLC by BMW, 46
  of Ryan Aeronautical by Northrop Grumman, 238
  of Snapple Beverage Corporation by Quaker Oats, 219, 222–227
  value of, 217–247
  Wal-Mart and Kmart strategy of, 23
Agassi, Andre, 198
Aggregation, in market segmentation, 81–82
Airlines. *See* America West; Southwest Airlines
Alcoa, 33
American Fitness, 107–109
America's Second Harvest (ASH), 242–245
America West. *See also* Southwest Airlines
  market share, 25–27
  profitability, 24
  Value Map, 73–74
Ametek:
  about, 56–60
  expansion and competition, 71
  Magnetek *vs.*, 70

sales, 68
SMP, 66
Anadarko Petroleum Corporation:
  1996 market share, 95
  strategic market, 96–97
Analyst reports, as information sources, 255
Anheuser-Busch, 82
Arizona Republic, 173
ASH. *See* America's Second Harvest (ASH)
Autodesk, 33
Auto industry, 41

"Bad report card" trap, 126
Baking products Value Map, 149
Bally Total Fitness, 127–128
Bavarian Motor Works. *See* BMW (Bavarian Motor Works)
Baxter International Inc., 177
  Cook Pharmaceutical Solutions and, 173–174
  description of, 169–170
  SMP test, 174–178
  taking pounding on PULSE, 170–173
Baxter Pharmaceutical Solutions (BPS). *See* Baxter International Inc.
BCG. *See* Boston Consulting Group (BCG)
Benchmarking:
  competitive, 196–198
  diagram, 192–195
  at Samsonite, 198–202, 254
Benchmarking-derived knowledge, 197–198
Best Buy Inc.:
  acquisition of Geek Squad, 178–179, 183–184
  applying SMP test to, 182–184
  looking for growth, 180–182
  market share, 183, 184

INDEX

Big Box outlets, 73
Bloomberg, 255, 256
Blue Ocean Strategy (Kim and Mauborgne), 166
BMW (Bavarian Motor Works):
DaimlerChrysler *vs.*, 44, 49
looking to the long run, 45–46
market share and value creation, 49, 51–52
strategy, 52
Boston Consulting Group (BCG), 37–39, 40, 165, 166
Bradley, Todd, 211
British Airways, 187
Business:
goal of, 11
SMP and, 175, 176–177
vs. game of Monopoly, 16–17
Business to business (B2B), 99
Buyer type, in Value Map dimension, 111, 113

C.H. Guenther & Son, Inc.:
description of, 140–142
implementing SMP at, 157–160
market share position, 143
prescription and related challenges, 153–157
sales and marketing organization, 144–148
SMP implications for sales and marketing, 160–161
strategic segments, 148–153
value created by 1 percent improvement, 158
Cadbury Schweppes, 226
Campbell Soup, 4
Capturing value:
introduction to, 79–80
looking ahead, 103
roles and players, 83–84
Car manufacturers. *See* BMW (Bavarian Motor Works); DaimlerChrysler
CarMax, 4
Casella Wines, 166–167, 169
Cast of characters, in SMP, 83–88
Census Bureau, 253
Center for Disease Control, 253
Channels:
Guenther, 149–151
in Value Map dimension, 111, 113
Chrysler Corporation, 47
Circuit City, 4
market share, 183

City market share, 72
Coca-Cola, 220
Cold channel, 221–222, 226
Company data, sources for, 250, 253–256
Compaq Computer, 227–236
Competition, 183, 220–222
Competitive advantage, 60
Competitive and market intelligence:
finding information, 250–256
identifying information, 249–250
primary research and creativity, 257–258
pulling information together, 259
Competitive benchmarking, 196–198
Competitive practices, 196, 197
Competitive Strategy (Porter), 40
Competitors, plotting SMPs for, 122, 124
Computing industry (U.S.) *vs.* Hewlett-Packard, 233, 234
ConAgra, 203
Consumer applications, in end-user industries, 64
Cook Pharmaceuticals Solutions, 173–174
Cost:
in consumer applications, 64
Guenther and analysis of, 144–145
Cost sharing, automotive *vs.* industrial clutches, 117–118
Country-specific government sources, 254
Creativity, 257–258
Crowell, Henry Parsons, 222, 223
Customer-centric services, 180

Daimler, trouble at, 46–48
Daimler-Benz, 41, 46
DaimlerChrysler:
vs. BMW, 44, 49, 51
market share and value creation, 49, 51–52
merger of Daimler-Benz and Chrysler, 47–48
strategy, 51–52
DC/AC/Universal, in Value Map, 63
Dean Foods, 202–207
Demographic segmentation, 83–84
Digital Equipment Corporation, 229
Direct-mail fulfillment company, 119
Disaggregation, in market segmentation, 81
Discounted cash flow, 185–186
Diversification of portfolio, 12
Divestures of Magnetek, 71
Dreyers Ice Cream, 4
Drohan, David F., 174

Drucker, Peter, 40
Dubinsky, Donna, 208
Dun & Bradstreet (D&B), 256

Easy Airlines case, 88–89, 91–92
EBI Foods Limited, 203
E-commerce, 99
Economic benefits of scale or scope, 114
Economics, health club, 134
Economies of scale, 60, 63
Electric motor industry, 56, 57
Electronic games and interactive
    entertainment. *See* Nintendo; Sega
Emerson Electric, 56–59
End-user industries, 64–66, 68–69
Energy industry, 92–98
Engles, Gregg, 203
Eos Airlines, 74–75
Experience-curve model, 37–38, 40

Federal Express (FedEx), 99–103
FHP. *See* Fractional horsepower (FHP)
    motors
50 percent rule, 117–118
Financial metric for investments,
    185–186
Fiorina, Carly, 228, 231, 235, 236
Foodchain, 242–245
Ford, Henry, 37
Fractional horsepower (FHP) motors:
    attributes on Value Map, 60, 116,
      119–120
    industry, 56–60
    strategic market segment, 65, 120
Franke, William, 24
Franklin, 58, 60
Fulfillment companies, 119

Game console systems, Value Map of,
    75
Gatorade, 223, 224–227
Geek Squad:
    acquisition by Best Buy, 180–182
    applying SMP to test, 182–184
    description of, 178–179
General Electric (GE):
    aircraft division, 252
    policy, 53
    PROM model, 37, 41–42
    sales, 57
    share of FHP market, 56, 59
    stepping into adjacent strategic segment,
      186–189
    through SMP lens, 189–190

General management, in corporations,
    84–85
General merchandise retailing Value Map,
    71–72
General Mills, 203
General Motors, 37, 82
Geographic buyer location, in Value Map
    dimension, 111, 113
Geographic scale or scope, 61
Geographic segmentation, 83–84, 183
    of TV and radio stations, 135–136
Global market share, 61, 62, 66, 76, 89
Global scale, 62, 66, 93
Google, 250
Government information sources, 253
Great Retailing Wars, 72
Greenberg, Arnold, 220
Growth. *See also* Growth strategy
    allocating resources for, 92–98
    finding and looking for, 180–182
    and profitability, 6–7, 11–76
    Wal-Mart, 18
Growth-Share Matrix, 38–39, 165
Growth strategy:
    for Easy Airlines, 89
    importance of, 49
Guenther. *See* C.H. Guenther & Son, Inc.
Guenther, Carl H., 140–141

Handspring, Inc., 208, 210
Hawkins, Jeff, 208
Health club:
    cost structures, 129
    economics, 133
    game, uncovering value in, 126–129,
      131–134
Health club industry Value Map, 108–110
Henderson, Bruce, 37, 38
Hewlett, Walter, 231, 234, 236
Hewlett, William, 231
Hewlett-Packard, 227–236
    vs. U.S. computing industry, 233
Home Depot, 180
Home improvement, 180
Hoover's, 256
Horizon Organic, 203–204
Horner, George, III, 214

Incentive structure at Guenther, 147,
    158–159
Industrial markets, 64–65
Industry conditions, SMP and, 192–195
Industry two-dimensional chart, 120–121
Infinity Broadcasting, 136

Information:
  identifying, 249–250
  pulling it together, 259
  searching for, 250–256
Integration, vertical, 94

Kaufman, Wendy, 222
Kelly, Jim, 101
Kim, W. Chan, 166
Kinko's Inc., 101
Kmart, 72, 258. *See also* Wal-Mart
  average profitability, 19–20
  growth, 18
  market segment, 23
  market share, 20–22
  SMP, 21–22
  strategies, 18–19
  value creation, 22
Kraft Foods, 203, 223

L.E.K. Consulting, 5–6, 33
Learning curve, 37
Leff, Deborah, 243
Lowe's, 180
Luggage industry, 199

Magnetek, 122, 124
  about, 56–60
  vs. Ametek, 70
  divestiture of, 71
  market share, 59
  operating margin, 58
  return on sales, 69–70
  sales, 68
  SMP, 66
Mail Boxes Etc., 99, 100–101
Maintenance, repair, and overhaul (MRO),
  187–189
Marginal economies of scale, 109
Marketing management, in corporations,
  84–86
Market(s):
  data, gathering, 250, 252–253
  new, using SMP to find, 165–190
  scale/scope, 61
  served, 42, 43
Market segmentation:
  aggregation in, 81–82
  vs. SMP, 80–83
  Snapple, 221–222
Market share:
  airline industry, 89
  of America West *vs.* Southwest Airlines,
  25–26

benefits of, 38
Best Buy, 183, 184
BMW by platform and class, 50,
  51
C.H. Guenther & Son, Inc., 143
Circuit City, 183
DaimlerChrysler by platform and class,
  50, 51
Dean Foods, 204–205
FHP motors by end-user market,
  59
FHP segments correlated to overall
  returns, 69
General Electric *vs.* Pratt & Whitney,
  188
global, 61, 62, 66, 76, 89
Kmart *vs.* Wal-Mart, 20–22
Mercedes-Benz, 42
national, 61, 62, 74, 76, 89
Northwest Airlines *vs.* profits on select
  routes, 91–92
Palm Computing, Inc., 208, 209
Phillips Petroleum Company *vs.*
  Anadarko Petroleum, 95–96
rate of return and, 15
return on investment and, 40–41
Sega *vs.* Nintendo, 28–30
served market and, 42
U.S. computing industry, 233
U.S. fractional horsepower (FHP)
  motors, 66, 68
weighted average for BMW, 51
Martin, Christina, 243
Matsushita, Konosuke, 56
Matsushita Electric, 56
Mauborgne, Renée, 166
McDonald, Arline, 172
Mercedes-Benz, 42
Mergers. *See also* Acquisitions
  of America's Second Harvest and
    Foodchain, 242–244
  of Daimler-Benz and Chrysler
    Corporation, 47
Microsoft Corporation, 73
Monopoly:
  business *vs.* game of, 16–17
  game of, 11–12
Monopoly neighborhoods, ROI in, 12–15
MRO. *See* Maintenance, repair, and
  overhaul (MRO)

National market share, 61, 62, 74, 76,
  89
Net present value (NPV), 97

Nintendo, 43, 76, 82
  focus of, 28
  market share, 28–30
  SMP, 30, 32
Nonprofit mergers, 241–244
Non-Traditional Research and Innovation
  (NTRI), 170
Northrop, Jack, 237
Northrop Grumman:
  acquisition of Ryan Aeronautical,
    240–241
  description of, 236–237, 238
  SMP test, 239–240
Northwest Airlines, 91–92, 258
Novell, 33
NPV. See Net present value (NPV)
NTRI. See Non-Traditional Research and
  Innovation (NTRI)
NuCor, 33
Nutritional supplements, 170–171
"Nutritional water" market, 170

OECD. See Organization for Economic
  Cooperation and Development
  (OECD)
OEM. See Original equipment
  manufacturer (OEM)
Oil and gas exploration and production,
  93–98
"One sneaker for every person in China"
  trap, 126
Online consumer sales, 99
Operating profit:
  of BMW, 44
  of Daimler-Benz (Mercedes), 44
  of DaimlerChrysler, 49
Organization for Economic Cooperation
  and Development (OECD), 253
Original equipment manufacturer (OEM),
  56, 62

Package-shipping market, 99
Palm Computing, Inc., SMP rebound of,
  207–212
Palm Solutions Group, 211
PC retailers, 183
PDAs. See Personal digital assistants
  (PDAs)
PepsiCo, 220
Performance, 2. See also
  Underperformance
  of companies, differences in, 4–5
  of Hewlett-Packard, 235
Personal digital assistants (PDAs), 208–210

Petty, Scott, 142
Pfizer, 212–214
Phillips Petroleum Company:
  1996 market share, 95
  strategic market, 96–97
PIMS. See Profit Impact of Marketing
  Strategy (PIMS)
Porter, Michael, 39–41, 44
Portfolio analysis, 38
Portfolio diversification, 12
Power ratings, size and, 63–64
Pratt & Whitney, 187–188
PricewaterhouseCoopers (PwC),
  228
Primary research, 257
Private companies, 122, 256
Product retailing and service, 179–180,
  183
Product variety, in Value Map dimension,
  111, 112–113
Profit Impact of Marketing Strategy
  (PIMS), 41–43
Profit Optimization Model (PROM), 37,
  41
Profits/profitability, 12–13, 16–17
  of Guenther by channel and geography,
    145–146
  of Kmart vs. Wal-Mart, 19
  of Southwest Airlines vs. America West,
    24
Public companies, 122
PULSE, 170–173, 174–175

Quaker Mills, acquisition of, 222–223
Quaker Oats Company, 219, 222–227

Rate of return, market share and,
  15
Real-life properties, 12
Regional clustering strategy, 129
Reitz, Bonnie, 74–75
Relevant strategic segment, defining and
  quantifying, 119–122
Reliability, 64
Retailers. See Kmart; Wal-Mart
Return on investment (ROI), 12–15,
  40–41
Revenue:
  BMW, 44, 49
  Daimler-Benz (Mercedes), 44
  DaimlerChrysler, 49
ROI. See Return on investment
  (ROI)
Ross Products, 171

Rover Group PLC, 46
Ryan Aeronautical:
  acquisition by Grumman, 240–241
  description of, 237–238
  SMP test, 239–240

Safeway, 4
Sales and marketing, applying SMP to,
  139–161
Sales management, in corporations,
  83–84
Salespeople, 118
Samsonite, benchmarking at, 198–202,
  254
Scale:
  across end-user industries, 64–65
  within a drilling basin, 93
  economies of, 60, 63, 107
  global, 62, 66, 93
  marginal economies, 109
  scores on Value Map, 129
Scale or scope:
  cost elements impacted by, 114
  dimensions of, 60, 62–66, 68–69
  market, 61
Schrempp, Jürgen, 46–48
Sears, 18
Securities and Exchange Commission
  (SEC) filings, 253, 254
Sega, 43, 73, 82
  focus of, 28
  market share, 28–30
  SMP, 30, 32
Segmentation attributes, 112
Segmentation variables, 111
Served market, 42, 43
Services, as part of product-based retail,
  179–180
"Shareholder Scoreboard" (Wall Street
  Journal), 2, 33, 193, 194
Share of city pairs, 74
Shirt industry, 43
Size and power rating, in Value Map, 60,
  63–64
Skyes, Janelle, 148, 152, 156, 157
Sloan, Alfred, 37
Small-share businesses, 41
Smithburg, William, 219, 223, 224, 225,
  226
SMP. See Strategic Market Position
  (SMP)
Snapple Beverage Corporation, 219,
  220–227
Sony, 73

Southwest Airlines, 125. See also America
  West
  growth of, 24
  market share, 25–27
  profitability, 24
  Value Map of airlines, 73–74
Specialty retail, 179–180
Stevenson, Howard, 53
Stokely–Van Camp, 223, 226
Strategic Market Position (SMP), 4, 5. See
  also Strategic Market Position (SMP)
  test
  allocating resources for growth,
    92–98
  of America's Second Harvest merger
    with Foodchain, 244–245
  of Ametek vs. Magnetek, 66, 68–69
  applying to sales and marketing,
    139–161
  approaches in applying, 136–137
  BMW, 51–52
  broader application of, 33–34
  cast of characters in, 83–88
  complementary acquisitions and,
    99–103
  defined, 16
  Easy Airline case, 88–92
  finding new markets by using,
    165–190
  GE through the lens of, 189–190
  of Hewlett-Packard, 234
  implementation at Guenther,
    157–160
  industry conditions and, 192–195
  Kmart vs. Wal-Mart, 21–22, 23
  lessons in, 53
  market segmentation vs., 80–83
  measuring of market share, 51
  Nintendo vs. Sega, 30
  origins of, 5–6
  Phillips Petroleum Company vs.
    Anadarko Petroleum Corporation,
    97
  plotting for yourself and your
    competitors, 122, 124
  Southwest Airlines vs. America West,
    26
  steps for determining, 110–111
  strong, weak performance and,
    195–202
  success in, 102
  use by companies, 16–17
  value of, 245–247
  weak, 202–212

Strategic Market Position (SMP)
  test:
  applying to Best Buy/Geek Squad,
    182–184
  applying to Northrop Ryan acquisition,
    239–240
  Baxter initiatives and, 174–178
Strategic market segment, 15–34,
    41
  FHP motors, 65–66
  50 percent rule and, 117–118
  SMP and, 177
Strategic segmentation. *See also* Strategic
    segmentation dimensions
  benefits of, 121–122
  FHP motors market, 122
  U.S. energy industry, 121
Strategic segmentation dimensions:
  assigning relative values to, 114–119
  defining, 111–113
Strategic segments, 226. *See also* Strategic
    segmentation
  competitive landscape and, 17
  defined, 16
  elements of, 43
  Magnetek and Ametek, 226
  relevant, defining and quantifying,
    119–122
  in testing SMP, 175–176
Strategic thinking, 37
Strategic value, finding and capturing,
    4
Strategy:
  BMW, 52
  DaimlerChrysler, 51–52
  geographic, 107, 109
  notion of, 36–37
Strategy/Business Development Group, in
    corporations, 84–85
Success, contributors to, 93
Suiza Foods, 203
Sun Microsystems, 228
Supermarket channel, 221–222, 226
SWOT analysis, 37

Tandem Computer, 229
Target, 72–73
Technological scale/scope, 61
Thomas H. Lee Company, 222
Toback, Paul, 127
Town Sports International Holdings (TSI),
    106, 128, 134
Travel industry, 199
Triarc Company, 226

TSI. *See* Town Sports International
    Holdings (TSI)
TV and radio stations, geographic
    segmentation of, 135–136

Uncovering value:
  business decision making and, 76
  in the health-club game, 126–129,
    131–134
  introduction to, 55
  motors and, 69–76
  for two motor makers, 56–60
  Value Map, 60–69
Underperformance:
  addressing, 192–193
  reasons for, 125
  strong SMP and, 195–202
United Parcel Service (UPS), 99–103
United States:
  Department of Labor, 253
  energy industry, strategic segmentation
    of, 121
  innovation value, 167
  market share of DaimlerChrysler *vs.*
    BMW, 49
  number of product innovations,
    167
U-Shaped curve, 40, 52
Uzzi, Don, 224

Value, capturing. *See* Capturing value
Value, uncovering. *See* Uncovering
    value
Value creation, 1–2
  BMW, 49, 51–52
  DaimlerChrysler, 49, 51–52
  Dean Foods, 206
  Kmart, 22
  Nintendo, 30, 32
  Sega, 30, 32
  Southwest Airlines, 27
  Wal-Mart, 22
Value Map, 105
  airlines, 73–74
  baking products, 149
  benefits-of-scale scores on, 129
  DC/AC universal in, 63
  end-user industries in, 64–66, 68–69
  executive organizer/communication
    tools, 209
  FHP motors, 115
  game console systems, 75
  general merchandising retailing, 71–72
  health clubs, 108–109

INDEX

Value Map *(Continued)*
  introduction to, 60–61
  national/global market share in, 62
  of oil and gas exploration and
    production, 94
  size and power rating in, 63–64
Ventura Foods, 204
Vertical integration, 94
Vicuron Pharmaceuticals, 212–214
Vought Aircraft, 237

Wall Street Journal, 2, 33, 39, 193
Wal-Mart, 72, 258. *See also* Kmart
  average profitability, 19–20
  growth, 18
  market segment, 23

market share, 20–22
SMP, 21–22
strategies, 18–19
value creation, 22
Web sites, as information sources, 255
Weighted average market share, 51, 89,
  205, 206
Welch, Jack, 53, 186, 188, 190
White Lilly Foods Company, 159
Whitewave, 203, 255
WHO. *See* World Health Organization
  (WHO)
Whole Foods, 4
World Bank, 253
World Health Organization (WHO),
  253